EVERYBODY
WINS

EVERYBODY WINS

The Story and Lessons Behind RE/MAX

Phil Harkins

Keith Hollihan

WILEY

John Wiley & Sons, Inc.

Published by John Wiley & Sons, Inc., Hoboken, New Jersey.
Published simultaneously in Canada.

For general information about our other products and services, please contact our Customer Care Department within the United States at 800-762-2974, outside the United States at 317-572-3993, or fax 317-572-4002.

Wiley also publishes its books in a variety of electronic formats. Some content that appears in print may not be available in electronic books. For more information about Wiley products, visit our web site at www.wiley.com.

RE/MAX, Above the Crowd, Take a Step Above The Crowd, Out in Front, It's the Experience, The Real Estate Superstars, the red-over-white-over-blue horizontal bar design, and the RE/MAX graphic hot air balloon logo are among the registered service marks of RE/MAX International, Inc.

The "32 Years of Unstoppable Growth" chart is printed with permission of RE/MAX.

Excerpts and data from the National Association of REALTORS® used with permission. For more information, visit www.REALTOR.org/research or call 1-800-874-6500.

Library of Congress Cataloging-in-Publication Data:

Harkins, Philip J.
  Everybody wins : the story and lessons behind RE/MAX / Phil Harkins and Keith Hollihan.
      p.   cm.
  Includes bibliographical references and index.
  ISBN-13: 978-0-471-71024-0 (cloth)
  ISBN-10: 0-471-71024-5 (cloth)
  ISBN-13: 978-0-471-75767-2 (paper)
  ISBN-10: 0-471-75767-5 (paper)
  1. RE/MAX (Firm).   2. Real estate business.   3. Real estate agents.   I. Hollihan, Keith.
II. Title
  HD1375.H345   2005
  333.33'0973—dc22

                                                                          2004021910

Printed in the United States of America.

10 9 8 7 6 5 4 3 2 1

This book is dedicated to Dave and Gail Liniger—and the dream . . .

CONTENTS

FOREWORD

Nothing happens unless first a dream.
—Carl Sandburg

From the beginning, my dream was to grow the best and the largest real estate network in the world, an organization where *everybody wins*— our customers, our agents, our owners, our employees, *everybody*. It took more than 30 years, but that dream has become a reality.

When I was first asked to share our story in this book, I declined. True, the dream had become bigger than me. It was now the dream of the entire RE/MAX family—and it was the family together that made it a reality. But to share it with the general public? We would have to open our personal lives and individual stories to researchers, interviewers, and writers. This had never been about individuals—it has always been about *us*, about the network, about the dream.

A year ago, I changed my mind when someone pointed out: "Sharing this story may help many others create winning formulas for their dreams." It was too hard to resist. After all, RE/MAX has always been about sharing the dream. I now see this book as part of our dream and also as a vehicle for further advancing the *everybody wins* principle beyond the RE/MAX borders. I firmly believe that the RE/MAX formula of *everybody wins* is applicable to all, whether starting a company, trying to grow a current business, helping a school or a church, or even perhaps working the corridors of government. If our story helps you create a winning formula for your dream, then I eagerly open my arms and welcome you into the *everybody wins* family.

I have to warn you, though, that creating a dream is hard work. In fact, most people never manage to get out of the starting gate. The reason is that too many people confuse ideas with dreams. An *idea* is a concept. Lots of people have lots of ideas, but few turn ideas into dreams. Imagine me, a young guy, breaking into the real estate industry, a fabulous industry with unlimited opportunity. I had an idea, which I thought was an incredible idea. I worked the idea in my own mind. I crafted it and I scripted it. Then I began to share that idea with anyone who would listen. But I soon learned a valuable lesson: The idea captured people's minds, but it was powerless to touch their hearts. Only a dream goes to the heart. I wanted to capture both minds *and* hearts. The forming of the first RE/MAX dream team was a uniting of hearts and minds fully committed to the effort to make our dream a reality.

In creating our "dream team," I wanted people who had talent, who were willing to work hard, and, most important, who wanted to make work an integral part of their lives. Finding and recruiting those champions and soldiers who can and will fight for your dream alongside you is no easy task. As you'll read in our story, you have to kiss a lot of frogs to find a prince or a princess. If you look long and hard enough, you can find your princes and princesses. We did, and they ended up comprising the team that developed the core of our organization. Just as important, that team went on to spawn other great teams. Today, RE/MAX consists of thousands of high-performing teams around the world. I eagerly anticipate the creation of the countless future teams that will help continue to change the world of real estate.

One might say that the RE/MAX success story was just good fortune. I do not dismiss that we at RE/MAX have been blessed with many great turns of fate. But picking the right team and our ongoing ability to pick great people to be our associates around the world have not been just luck. It has been all about insight, analysis, effort, and hard work.

In building the RE/MAX family, we believe that as we are selling the dream to potential members, they must in turn convince us that they can become part of that dream. They must really, truly, and genuinely buy in. That, too, has been a guiding principle since Day One. I wanted then— and still want today—to be surrounded by those who believe in the dream as I do, who want it as much as I do, and who are willing to work as hard as all of us did from the very beginning. Even now, I strive to give it my all every single day so that at the end of the day, day after day, *everybody wins*. Everyone inside RE/MAX knows that I am committed. I am what I am, and I make no pretense about being anything else. I want to work with people who share that same commitment, that same passion, that same focused drive.

In all of this, I have never been alone. There is no question that the original team that birthed this organization gave their hearts and spirits, which is now the model for how RE/MAX offices are born around the world. That original team also set the standard for team play and mutual support—principles that are now the prototype in our global network, where more than 100,000 associates in more than 50 countries work together to ensure that *everybody wins*. To that original dream team, I can never express enough admiration or thanks. I wish to thank all of those who have participated in our growth at every stage of our development. From those fledgling days in the 1970s through the tumultuous 1980s to the explosive 1990s and now into the twenty-first century, it has been a wild and fun ride—and will continue to be so.

Indeed, we are nowhere near the end of the story. This worldwide industry, the real estate profession of which I have been privileged to be a part for more than 30 years, still has room to grow. In North America, where we currently have our largest presence, more than half of the net worth of families in Canada and the United States is wrapped into family homes. We are privileged to be part of an industry that helps protect and preserve the wealth of those families. We can also be proud to be part of an industry that has led the way in the removal of so many barriers. RE/MAX, for one, is proud of our legacy as one of the first organizations that specifically targeted women for positions on our teams and in our family. Going forward, we will continue to break down the barriers of race, culture, religion, gender, and age by uniting people from all groups under the RE/MAX balloon.

As I think back, it was the struggle that made RE/MAX strong. We faced every calamity. Together we became a team and were determined to always stay a team, even through the times when we questioned whether we would make it. Those were the times when RE/MAX people pulled together and pushed each other up. I don't believe that truly great companies can exist without an *everybody wins* philosophy. It's the glue that keeps the team together in bad times, the heart of any successful enterprise.

Someone asked me recently, "What is it about your management style that has helped to make RE/MAX what it is today?" I must say that I was stumped because I've never looked at myself as being a great manager. For that reason, I have always surrounded myself with great managers. Together, we have lived for more than 30 years driven by the principle that *everybody wins* as RE/MAX continues to grow, and this truth has extended beyond the walls of the RE/MAX offices and homes. Our growth enabled us to build the Wildlife Experience Museum. We support cancer research, hospitals, and foundations; and as we grow, our contributions increase. That is our legacy; that is what we would like to pass on to the next generation so that they, too, can catch the dream and truly understand what is meant by *everybody wins*.

DAVE LINIGER
RE/MAX
CHAIRMAN AND COFOUNDER

Denver, Colorado
October 2004

PREFACE

Make it a practice to keep on the lookout for novel and interesting ideas that others have used successfully. Your idea has to be original only in its adaptation to the problem you are working on.

—Albert Einstein

Visit the hot air balloon fiesta in Albuquerque, New Mexico, in early October, and you will see something amazing. Hundreds of giant colorful balloons float gently in the air like tropical jellyfish rising above the ocean floor. Adults who bring their children to watch turn into children themselves. Everyone loves a balloon.

The RE/MAX balloon got its start at the Albuquerque International Balloon Fiesta in 1978—the brain child of regional owners Bill Echols and Darrel Stilwell, who wanted to make a big impression on their local customers. Adopted worldwide, the RE/MAX balloon with its red, white, and blue colors and its "Above the Crowd!" slogan is one of the most recognized corporate brands in the world today.

In the history of business success stories, RE/MAX International is an astonishing organization. It was born more than 30 years ago in Denver,

Colorado, from nothing more than a revolutionary idea for a new system of selling real estate and a compelling dream for a company that would have unstoppable growth. It survived all of the challenges faced by any start-up company and then some, including ferocious industry resistance, crushing financial debt, a critical period of staggeringly high interest rates, and personal victories and tragedies that read more like scenes from blockbuster movies than stories from real life. Along the way, in good times and bad, RE/MAX grew and grew. To date, RE/MAX has experienced over 380 straight months of explosive growth and still counting. The more than 100,000 RE/MAX associates can be found in over 50 countries. Together, these people handle more real estate transactions than any other company in the world.

We want to tell the RE/MAX story for a number of significant reasons. At a time in which companies have found steady, consistent growth to be a serious challenge, RE/MAX presents a model of bold innovation, constant improvement, hard-driving persistence, boundless energy, and genuine passion. Indeed, the RE/MAX growth story is an affirmative demonstration that organizational success can improve the lives of many. It is rare to have the opportunity to learn from an organization that stuck to a core strategy and a set of principles without wavering for over 30 years and in the process shared the benefits of its success with so many people. It is rarer still, these days, to turn over every rock and to open every closet door and find nothing but validation, confirmation, and proof of that consistency again and again—colorful stories, thrilling escapades, and comic misadventures aside.

Readers will meet many extraordinary people in this book, perhaps none more fascinating than our "main character," Dave Liniger, chairman and cofounder of RE/MAX. In an age of CEOs polished at Ivy League business schools, Liniger is a throwback to a simpler, wilder, more heroic leadership era—as much John Wayne as Jack Welch. He is highly intelligent yet down-to-earth and hard working; driven by measurable results yet motivated by ideas and people development; tough and prickly on the surface yet deeply caring and compassionate. He served in Vietnam, attempted to lead the first balloon team ever to circle the globe, races NASCAR, and scuba dives in shark-infested waters yet spends free time enriching the lives of children at the Wildlife Experience Museum he built in Colorado and supporting cancer research. He built RE/MAX up from an idea and with his own willpower, convincing others to believe in his dream, too, foregoing his salary when there wasn't enough money to go around. Persistently, deliberately, and relentlessly, he showed his people the way forward, pushed them when they needed pushing, carried them when they needed carrying. And the organization he created embodies that drive and spirit today.

As Dave Liniger's first employee and the cofounder and First Lady of RE/MAX, Gail Liniger somehow managed to hold the back office together while he battled the world outside the door. Her belief in the dream was equal to Dave's own. When we asked her if, in those trying early days, she could ever have imagined how successful RE/MAX would eventually become, she answered, "Yes. In fact, I always thought it should have happened sooner."

We saw many of those same qualities in the senior leadership team. Many companies have war stories of close relationships and powerful friendships from their early days; few of those companies see relationships and friendships last over 30 years. It is amazing that the original leadership team at RE/MAX is largely intact; and the latest generation of leaders, who were selected, groomed, and developed through the ranks, seem more like younger siblings than a new vanguard. While significant business success often divides and distances top people over time, this organization's culture has remained tight.

Even more important, we discovered at RE/MAX a philosophy of doing business that is worth sharing with the world. It is a philosophy based in hard financial terms, organizational strategy, operations, and people practices. It is an attitude of camaraderie that pervades the organization's culture. It is a belief in sharing the responsibilities for success as well as the benefits of success. It is a view of life that values independence and personal growth, yet still somehow manages to invoke a tremendous pride in belonging to a cause greater than oneself. When we thought about what made the organization special, it was this philosophy that we kept coming back to. We began to describe it as the *everybody wins* principle at the heart of the RE/MAX dream. The deeper we looked and the more we learned about RE/MAX, the more convinced we became that it was this value that fundamentally made it successful. We want to teach it to others through the RE/MAX story because we believe that its lessons can be applied widely in work and in life to great benefit.

The Growth Companies Study

Our interest in RE/MAX began on December 12, 2002, in Palm Desert, California, when we first met Dave Liniger. Dave was one of the senior leaders participating in Linkage's annual "Global Institute for Leadership Development," cochaired by me (Phil Harkins) and Warren Bennis, the father of modern leadership development practice. When I spoke to Dave about his organization, I realized that we had come upon a crown jewel. Of course, I knew about RE/MAX in broad strokes. Its balloon logo was a tremendously successful brand. And I even knew enough about the real estate industry to understand that RE/MAX was a major force within it and a leading innovator. But I didn't know the degree to which RE/MAX, a privately held organization, had grown from a dream in one man's mind through a passionate group of high-achieving believers to a global powerhouse.

Our discussion turned to an important and relevant subject and question: How do companies generate steady, sustainable, strong growth over many years? Dave was not reluctant to speak with pride about his own organization's achievement. He pulled out a chart (shown on opposite page) and said, "See for yourself. This is our story." As I looked at the 32 years of growth displayed on the page, a feeling of amazement came over me. *If this were a ski slope, it would be impossible to ski down it!*

I got to know Dave and several members of his top team over the next few days. As a group, they were proud and talked about quality in everything they did. They all also talked openly and often about their dream to be the biggest and best real estate network in the world. I liked them as individuals and could see that Dave had collected a strong family-like group of leaders around him. I could also see that Dave was the driving force in the organization. His senior leaders both reflected and balanced his own leadership style. This was a team that believed in each other and believed in what they were doing together.

Over breakfast one morning, after Dave had returned from his power walk, it finally dawned on me that I was meeting a remarkable, high-

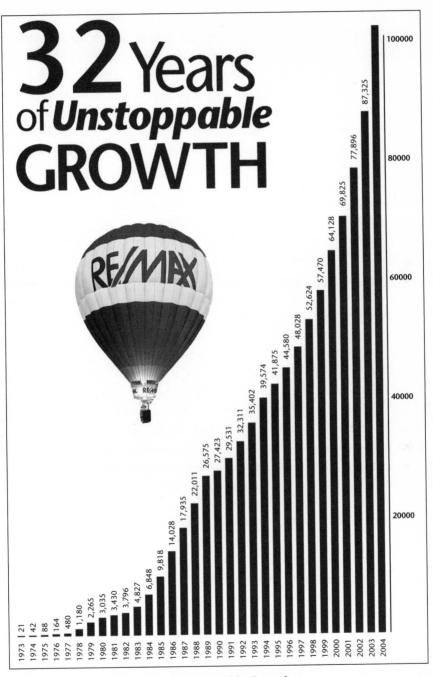

32 Years of Unstoppable Growth

impact leader, like Ray Kroc at McDonald's, Howard Schultz at Starbucks, or Sam Walton at Wal-Mart. I knew, intuitively, that if we could delve more deeply into what made RE/MAX click, a great story would emerge, one with valuable lessons for leaders driving growth in their own firms. My organization was in the middle of developing a major study on high-growth/high-impact (HG/HI) companies at the time, and I asked Dave to consider allowing RE/MAX to participate in that study. As a privately held firm, RE/MAX did not have public data on which we could draw; but in so many ways it seemed to fit, and even exceed, the strict parameters of our study. We were looking for HG/HI companies that were truly global; had demonstrated continuous growth, year after year, for at least 20 years; had created a global brand that others recognized as top-shelf; had a mission to be number one in their space; and had grown primarily through internally generated expansion of products, programs, or services, not by acquisition. RE/MAX, out of the blue, fell into this elite category, despite barriers so stringent that high-growth favorites like GE, Johnson & Johnson, Nestlé, Procter & Gamble, and ExxonMobil had already been weeded out.

Dave turned me down. He thought about it for a moment, and then his answer was gracious but firm. The RE/MAX way was to build the organization out of the spotlight. What value would anyone gain from talking about it? Moreover, the success of RE/MAX was not Dave's personal story; it was the story of many different individuals over many years. It was a very humble view, consistent with what I had already learned about these people. I thanked Dave for considering my suggestion and let it go.

Our research team continued with the growth study, narrowing the field down to six international companies—two from the United States, two from Europe, and two from Asia—that fit our criteria: Wal-Mart, McDonald's, Nokia, BMW, Canon, and Toyota. In parallel, however, we kept in touch with Dave and tried to learn more about the RE/MAX culture. My admiration and respect for the accomplishments of the senior team continued unabated. I talked to Dave about why I believed the RE/MAX story would be of great benefit to other leaders in other organizations, whether for-profit, not-for-profit, or governmental, as well as to young entrepreneurial dreamers just beginning to glimpse the difference they wanted to make in the world. It was that idea of sharing valuable lessons that had the most influence on Dave's thinking. I began to conceive of a book that would be written to explain the lessons of HG/HI companies. I could see RE/MAX serving as a cultural and leadership case study that would illustrate the lessons we were obtaining in the financial and employment data of our six comparison companies. "We'll tell the RE/MAX story," I suggested to Dave, "uncover specific leadership lessons, and expand from there to show the parallels that we found in our growth study." This time, my reasoning had its desired effect. One day, I received an e-mail written in typical Dave Liniger fashion: "Okay, our leadership has agreed. What's next? What's the plan?"

We were off and running.

Studying RE/MAX

Our research team conducted more than 50 focused, multihour interviews with key people inside RE/MAX International and throughout its network. We studied the real estate industry and talked to experts. We spent weeks with Dave and Gail Liniger and got to know the members of the senior team well. We were allowed to poke about, ask questions, and look into whatever we wanted, without restrictions. Everything was on the record. We became big fans of this group of people, personally and from the standpoint of business observers, and make no bones about our overwhelmingly *positive* outlook. If you are looking for criticism, skepticism, or negativity, you will not find it in this book. We liked what we learned about this organization, saw huge positives in what it accomplished, and uncovered valuable lessons about how it did it.

Here are some of the big-picture elements of the RE/MAX story and the fascinating real estate industry:

- In North America alone, real estate is big business; and increasingly around the world, more families own their own homes than ever before—75 percent of an average family's net worth is locked into that investment. In North America, 1 in every 138 working adults (an astonishing 1.2 million people) is a real estate agent. RE/MAX associates currently include more than 7 percent of all real estate agents in the United States and 18 percent of all real estate agents in Canada.

- If RE/MAX were a public company, measured as revenue paid to the firm through its associates, it would be a Fortune 200 company.

- In 2004, RE/MAX generated $360 billion to $400 billion in financial transactions handled by its offices around the world. This number measures how much "product" in terms of house purchases was brokered by RE/MAX. But consider that our comparison benchmark company, Wal-Mart, is the biggest retail business in the world, selling products that are produced by others, and generated less than $300 billion in revenue in 2004. Despite the fact that these products merely passed through Wal-Mart's stores, Wal-Mart is recognized as the number-one company in the world based on retail sales by a public company.

- Total advertising dollars spent across the RE/MAX network of associates is approaching $1 billion in 2004.

- RE/MAX will have approximately 100,000 associates in its network by the end of 2004.

- RE/MAX is the largest global real estate brand in the world, with more than 5,000 offices in 52 countries—and yet it is a privately held firm that grew agent by agent over 30 years.

So, how did RE/MAX do it?

I believe that RE/MAX is organized around a dream. The outward goal of that dream is to become the largest and best real estate network in the world. The participants in that dream believe that it can only be achieved if *everybody wins*. As cofounder and top leader, Dave Liniger created the dream and gave it life by sharing it with like-minded others who brought their own skills and leadership styles to the equation. The dynamic balance of that equation is key to the formula that RE/MAX used to achieve its remarkable growth.

The most simple and helpful way to describe that dynamic balance is through the image of a child's seesaw. The seesaw is supported by "the dream." On one side of the seesaw is the energy devoted to "growing the dream." On the other side of the seesaw is the energy devoted to "managing the dream."

The three critical success factors on the "growing the dream" side of the equation are:

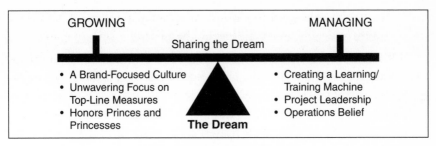

The RE/MAX Growth Model

1. **People.** Find people who say "Yes" to the dream; identify the "Princes and Princesses" among them; and enlist their help while helping them grow.

2. **Brand.** Relentlessly focus on the brand; use it to grow the organization while enabling people to benefit from it. You will learn, "One log makes a lousy fire."

3. **Project Leadership.** Project leadership is different from project management; high-impact leaders are not afraid to "get out in front" on new projects; they utilize the concept of the *pace line* to achieve blistering organizational momentum around turning new ideas into action.

The three critical success factors on the "managing the dream" side of the equation are:

1. **Learning.** Continuous improvement is more than just a numbers game; RE/MAX has a learning/training culture because it knows that people development is critical to both quality and long-term growth; more than a business, it views itself as a "Life Success Company."

2. **Top-Line Measures.** Companies get lost focusing on too many measures; simple and clear top-line measures are more than just numbers to hit—they are "rallying cries" shared by all.

3. **Operations.** Quality, professionalism, and commitment are demonstrated not through large acts but through small ones; at RE/MAX every job description ends with the phrase "and other"; people know that the responsibility to live up to that "other" is more important

than the responsibilities outlined in individual roles; RE/MAX is a culture in which "everyone carries the boxes."

This seesaw represents the RE/MAX growth formula. Children know something very simple but profound about seesaws that leaders and organizations could take to heart. If either side of this equation is out of balance, the efforts will not be successful. Dynamic balance is critical.

As a leader, Dave Liniger's strengths are most oriented toward the "growing the dream" side of the equation. While we found that he is good at "managing the dream" and sets the tone as leader in that regard, he is not as passionate about that side of the equation. Accordingly, he has always surrounded himself with excellent managers to balance his strengths, while seeking that combination in other teams in the field as well. Indeed, each of the incredibly successful RE/MAX regions has shown that balance, too. There is always one leader who is the growth engine and another complementary leader who is the growth manager. Pushing with equal force, they create the momentum that drives the dream.

Reading This Book

In Chapters 1 through 8, you will find the RE/MAX story. At the end of this book, you will find an analysis of key conclusions from our growth companies study and the parallels we discovered with RE/MAX. The six companies that we studied are remarkably consistent in their formulas with that of RE/MAX. They focus on a critical few measures to reach their goals. They have achieved a dynamic balance between driving growth and managing growth. They understand the short- and long-term correlation between brand and growth. They are all strong innovators that understand the importance of honing their products and services without losing the dream. And they all have charismatic leadership. A big "aha" for us in this regard is the nature of that charisma. As Jim Collins in his book *Good to Great* (HarperCollins, 2001) has noted, humility is prevalent among the top leaders of great companies. We found this, too, in high-growth, high-impact companies. We define *charisma* not as a personal characteristic but as a means to an end. A charismatic leader, in that sense, is someone who "believes in delivery on the dream with the team." Charismatic leaders are pace-line leaders, as you will learn in Chapter 7.

We believe that our research will help broaden and amplify the lessons in this book. Chapter 9 contains some mission-critical information, the "how to's," with factual, research-based conclusions on how six HG/HI companies consistently grew through good and bad economies. Nevertheless, you do not need to dig into our growth research to gain a great deal of insight. The RE/MAX story speaks for itself. The lessons that we saw in the real-life struggles that RE/MAX underwent are apparent throughout its history. You will see evidence of the six critical factors that balance the seesaw growth formula over and over. Most important, you will understand why *everybody wins* is such a powerful principle for building a great company.

It is that *everybody wins* principle that is the most profound lesson we take from RE/MAX. In the RE/MAX philosophy, the success of one agent helps drive the success of all others. The network itself grows because other agents see the success of RE/MAX agents and join the team. And the agent's success is ultimately predicated on the home buyer's satisfaction. It only makes sense, therefore, to provide agents with everything they need to perform at the highest level. *Everybody wins* is really about giving people the space and the care to grow. When Liniger took away the barriers and the impediments that were inherent in the traditional real estate system, he gave agents the freedom to become something bigger. His message was simple: *Promote yourself. Advertise as much as you want. Negotiate your own commissions. Decide your own deals. Grow your business the way you know how to grow it.* Without restrictive boundaries, but *with* the support of others dedicated to their success, the agents had the ability to succeed beyond what they had ever thought possible.

Over the years, some other real estate firms have imitated RE/MAX innovations, but none has matched its rate of growth for more than 30 years. We believe that the RE/MAX growth formula and its *everybody wins* principle comprise a defining difference. Indeed, in describing the *everybody wins* idea to many leaders throughout North America, we have seen the power of this simple phrase in how it shifts leaders' views on how business should be done. We would like to see this principle become a formula for our times because we think it can help to create the entrepreneurial conditions fertile for strong economic growth in all organizations.

Ultimately, this book is more than just the story of one company. It is a call for business the way it ought to be played. So much of our lives is spent at work, in the company of our colleagues, at the service of our customers, in the support of larger financial aspirations. RE/MAX provides an ideal of what the pursuit of business aims can do to build up people along the way. Our work life should be fun, driven by a dream, spent with dear companions, growing and learning at the same time. The game should be played fiercely but also generously, making those around us prosperous in the process, building relationships instead of breaking them, soaring to heights we couldn't imagine on our own.

At the end of the day, work—and the organizations to which we commit ourselves—should be an experience that enriches us all. RE/MAX offers an important model for making this happen, an organization that espouses the belief that *everybody wins*.

PHIL HARKINS

Boston, Massachusetts
October 2004

ACKNOWLEDGMENTS

We'd like to recognize the following people for helping to make this book a dream come true. Please forgive us if we didn't mention your name, as there were many hundreds who contributed to this project over the past two years.

This book would not have been possible without Steve Ozonian, who first introduced us to RE/MAX; the core RE/MAX team of Dave Liniger, Gail Liniger, Bill Echols, Daryl "Jes" Jesperson, Joe Reynolds, "Vinnie Tracey, Diane Metz, Bob Fisher, and Margaret Kelly, who generously gave their time and commitment to this project; and Ellen Rosenberg, Karina Wilhelms, and BG Dilworth, who worked tirelessly in pursuit of perfection.

Our deep gratitude to the Linkage Research Team, who dedicated their time, skills, and knowledge in studying growth companies: Stephen Cartelli, Lou Carter, David Giber, Ellen Rosenberg, James Snow, Russell Sullivan, Andrew Wilhelms, and Karina Wilhelms.

Our sincere thanks to the hundreds of people at RE/MAX who graciously gave their time on this project and special thanks to those listed below with whom we spent many hours in meetings: John Alexander, Pam

Alexander, Kelli Amundson, Dennis Anderson, Judy Austin, Bob Baker, Tracy Baker, Nick Bailey, Tom Baron, Jay Belson, Charlie Bengel, Bruce Benham, Jeff Benson, Barry Binder, Bob Blount, Jack Brennan, Lynn Britt, Rob Campbell, Ben Christopher, Joe Clement, Frank Colatosi, Adam Contos, Judy Crowley, Ken Crowley, Leanne Crowley, Peter Crowley, Timothy Crowley, Dennis Curtin, Don Dahlberg, Jim DeCamp, Peter De-Groot, Bill Echols, Bob Fisher, Brian Frantz, Mary Ann Frolick, Emily Moerdmo Fu, Verne Gantz, Peter Gilmour, Ray Glynn, Dave Gravelle, Marilyn Guty, Don Hachenberger, Glenda Hachenberger, Gary Hackney, Gale Haisley, Jason Hall, Steve Haselton, Jim Homolka, Judy Jenson, Daryl Jesperson, Nan Jesperson, Daniel Jiminez, Margaret Kelly, Robert Kline, Gregory Koons, Jack Kreider, Howard Lein, John Lichtenwald, Dave Liniger, Gail Liniger, Ann McAfee, Matthew McAfee, Michael McAfee, Robert McAfee, Norman McClain, Ed McCloud, Ken McLachlan, Richard Mendenhall, Dave Messner, Diane Metz, David Milot, Paul Motzkus, Geoffrey Mountain, James Nelson, Chuck Ocshner, Alice O'Hare, John O'Hare, Bill Owens, Barbara Pearson, Bill Perdue, Alex Pilarski, Richard Pilarski, Frank Polzler, Edwin Quirk, Mike Reagan, Joe Reynolds, Nancy Rieger-Koons, Charles Richard Rose, Ted Rowe, Mike Ryan, Sandra Sanders, Walter Schneider, Kent Sheppard, Heather Skuce, Carolyn Smith, Greg Smith, Bill Soteroff, Stephen Squeri, Jerry Stadtler, Stephanie Stadtler, Gary Stager, Charolette Steed, Kerron Stokes, Sid Syvertson, Gary Thomas, Bob Todd, Vinnie Tracey, Gene Vaughan, Kay Wolfe, Mark Wolfe, Mike Wolfer, Wayne Wyvill, and Graham Young.

Thank you to all of our readers who provided rich feedback, especially those who worked on the many drafts of our manuscript: Cheryl Smith, Lou Carter, Lin Coughlin, Bill Echols, David Giber, Judy Mahaffy, Steve Murray, Richard Rosier, John Stefano, and Judy Timmerman.

We are deeply grateful to the incredible professionals at our study companies who spent time gathering the historical, financial, and employee information necessary for our research: Christa Krieger, BMW; James Cappell, Canon; Will Davis, Nokia; Robert Peterson, McDonald's; and Victor Vanov, Toyota.

PHIL HARKINS
KEITH HOLLIHAN

EVERYBODY
WINS

CHAPTER 1

THE RADICAL REWARD-SHARING IDEA THAT OVERTURNED AN INDUSTRY

Creating the Dream

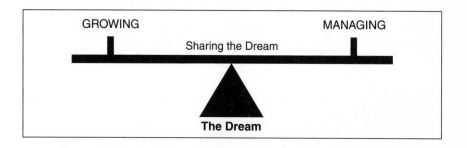

Every improvement or innovation begins with an idea. But an idea is only a possibility—a small beginning that must be nurtured, developed, engineered, tinkered with, championed, tested, implemented, and checked. . . . Ideas have no value until they are implemented.
   —Alan Robinson and Dean Schroeder, *Ideas Are Free*

The man in the office that day couldn't have known it at the time, but the real estate industry was about to change forever. His name was Jack Bradbury and he was a Van Schaack man. On that fall morning in 1972, real estate was still very much a local or regional business. In Denver, Colorado, a city that was wealthy and growing rapidly, being a Van Schaack man meant something. Out of the nearly one thousand small real estate firms with five listings or fewer, the one hundred or so firms of medium size, and the five or ten powerhouses with five hundred listings or more, Van Schaack was number one; and it acted that way.

Being number one meant that Van Schaack had the most market share, represented the best listings, and attracted the top agents—those Van Schaack men. They were college educated, sophisticated, well-dressed, and highly polished. They were all white, in their forties, fifties, or sixties; and they were, of course, all men. They lived in beautiful homes, drove expensive cars, and belonged to country clubs. Their wives played golf or tennis and volunteered in community groups and the local PTA—all the better to meet other wives whose husbands would need a real estate agent someday. Knowing someone personally made a big difference when it came to the sale or the purchase of your largest financial asset. It still does today.

The man in the room with Jack Bradbury also worked for Van Schaack, but he was not a Van Schaack man. His name was Dave Liniger. He was young, in his middle twenties. Although skinny in a boyish way, he was solid and powerful, like a college linebacker who might never make it to the NFL because of his size but would bloody the nose of anyone bigger who got in his way. His crew cut made him look as though he had just gotten out of the military, which was essentially true but off by a couple years. He was married and had three young children; but he did not have any of the sophistication, education, or polish of the other agents. Liniger had dropped out of college and knocked around for a few years, working hard but getting nowhere, before discovering that he was very, very good at selling real estate. In truth, even though he was doing well at Van Schaack, Liniger drove Jack Bradbury a little nuts. On some Sundays, he showed up for work on a motorcycle dressed in jean shorts and a tee shirt. Of course, it was six o'clock in the morning, and Liniger would work at his desk furiously for a few hours before he changed into a suit and went out to sell homes. But still, a Van Schaack man didn't behave that way. Dave Liniger had a drive and a hunger and an energy that the mature, settled, sophisticated Van Schaack men of the world weren't ready for; and he also had an idea that was about to pull down the curtain on their comfortable, country club lives forever.

In many ways, Jack Bradbury was the man Liniger wanted to become. Bradbury was smart, smooth, and at the top of the mountain. He treated his agents well and earned everyone's respect. Even though Liniger did not fit in with Van Schaack, he admired Bradbury immensely. Sitting in Bradbury's office, Liniger could barely contain his enthusiasm for his big idea. His brain was whirling with the possibilities, overflowing with an energy to get started. He was certain that Bradbury would understand the vision and grab onto it the moment Liniger explained it to him. The logic was that compelling. Not only did it have to work, it couldn't fail. The real estate business was local and always would be; but in Liniger's view there was nothing to stop a real estate company from expanding globally and becoming the biggest real estate network in the world. It just needed the right system, the right focus, the right dream. And Liniger, in a blast of insight that had come to him only days before, had finally figured out what that system, focus, and dream should be.

Despite the suddenness of the idea, Liniger's insight hadn't come completely out of the blue. For the past few years, while Liniger was learning how to sell, then selling at top levels, and working for several different real estate firms, he had also been watching the industry closely. Gradually, he had seen its fatal flaw and had begun to question, like any visionary, why no one did anything about it. Almost every firm operated under the same model—they only varied by size, reputation, and, of course, the quality of their agents. Nevertheless, on average, an agent at the mighty Van Schaack made the same commission as an agent at the least imposing real estate firm in the city—50 percent. For most agents, this seemed fine until you realized you were handing over half of your income—income produced by your leads, your hard work, and your sales ability—to a firm that really wasn't giving you that much in return. Liniger knew that real estate agents, like all people with entrepreneurial inclinations, did indeed want to earn as much money as possible; nevertheless, they weren't motivated only by money. As a breed, real estate agents were primarily success- and growth-driven. They wanted to build up their lives and become something better. If they couldn't get there on their own, they wanted help to learn how. They needed teachers, coaches, and motivational speakers to champion them. Essentially, they wanted the tools to succeed and the independence and freedom to make the most of the opportunities available to them. The traditional real estate firm didn't care about a real estate agent's need for growth and success. It only worried about that 50 percent cut and did as little as possible to earn it.

The Vicious Cycle

The agents' dissatisfaction with that approach created something that could only be described as the real estate industry's vicious cycle. Real estate was a low-entry business. In the early 1970s, for about $1,000 a month, a broker could rent a nice office with 500 or 600 square feet, get an answering service and a couple of telephone lines, and hire a secretary part time. Agents were not a significant expense because they worked on a commission split. Most brokers took anyone who came their way—friends, neighbors, people who'd left one career and were looking for another—on the principle that if you threw enough against a wall, something was bound to stick. Few brokers had any desire to spend money providing the training that might help an agent succeed. So new agents were faced with the prospect of having to learn the business—the property values; the complexities of mortgages, financing, and title insurance; and how to deal with appraisers and lenders—all on their own and without a supporting salary. There was also the art of selling. An agent had to learn how to find customers and how to talk to them. An agent had to learn what made a community tick. An agent even had to learn how to get around physically, know a street from an avenue and whether a house on one block was near a school, a reservoir, or an overpass. During that 6-to-12-month learning phase, most agents didn't have the financial wherewithal to survive. That was why the industry at the time was dominated by older white males who had retired from civil service or the military or had sold a business of their own; they had enough money in the bank to float them while they learned how to make money in real estate.

Once an agent had worked for awhile, the job became much simpler. Past customers, if they'd received any level of service at all, were remarkably loyal. When an agent started to build up the repeat-and-referral side of the business, his reliance on advertising and cold-calling went down. Buyers would start coming to the agent on their own, money in hand, looking for help in finding a new home. That's when an agent started to question the system he was operating under. If he was the one generating his leads through reputation and repeat business, why was he then handing half of his commissions over to the firm? If he had become successful all on his own, what loyalty or commitment should he feel to the company whose name he worked under? What was to stop him from breaking away to another firm or forming his own group with a couple of buddies whose commissions he could then scoop up for himself?

Fear mostly. Not all agents had what it took to survive. In fact, 8 out of

10 agents failed in their first year and never renewed their licenses. Liniger knew that to the 2 agents who thrived, a company like Van Schaack was very appealing. Van Schaack put a tremendous emphasis on training and was very modern in its approach to business. Its blue-chip reputation, market share, and brand name awareness also attracted the best listings. A potential customer was much more likely to list with Van Schaack than with some firm they'd never heard of before. But despite all those advantages, Van Schaack was missing the most important piece of the puzzle. Like every other firm, it did not fully realize how much it would benefit by giving its own agents the freedom to grow and succeed. With the best agents, the top brand, and the right system, a firm like Van Schaack could be unstoppable.

Liniger could see that dream so clearly because his experience had been very different from most Van Schaack men. He had learned salesmanship the hard way—by failing time and time again. He wasn't one of those 2 out of 10 who succeeded at every level and kept rising in the ranks. He was one of the 8 out of 10 who by any rational measure should have given up. But he kept working at it, seeing each new failure as an inspirational challenge, until he finally figured out how to do it right. Along the way, he realized something critical: It was true that the money thrilled him when he made a sale; but there were other, deeper things going on. He liked understanding people and figuring out how to meet their needs. He liked growing more confident and skilled. Money wasn't an end in itself; it was the carrot that led to that kind of self-development. Liniger realized that people pushed themselves harder and harder when they knew that they would receive a greater benefit for their efforts. By taking 50 percent of that reward from the agent's own hand, it was almost as though a real estate firm was taking away half of the agent's motivation and will.

How much more motivating would it be for a firm to offer its agents 100 percent commission in return for a monthly fee? Leaning forward in his chair, he explained the concept to Jack Bradbury. The premise was something that Liniger had first encountered in Arizona when he worked for a real estate firm called Realty Executives. Realty Execs was a chop shop, a rent-a-desk concept, in which freelance agents operated under the banner of a firm that provided some support services and a brokerage license. Of course, Liniger readily admitted, the 100 percent idea wasn't going to revolutionize the world on its own. But consider the unlimited potential in the idea *behind* that idea, especially when it was wedded to another idea, one that a firm like Van Schaack represented. Bradbury nodded, as though he had caught a glimpse of the picture Liniger was trying to convey; and Liniger continued, trying not to talk too fast.

Realty Execs was essentially a co-op without any heft. Van Schaack was a blue-chip firm with panache, reputation, training, and quality control. On top of that, a firm like Van Schaack had market share and group advertising. It bought things like signs at big discounts. It had major accounts with the newspapers and tremendous brand presence. It was a very sophisticated company. In fact, Liniger admitted to Bradbury, it was for all those reasons that he had been attracted to Van Schaack in the first place. As Bradbury knew, Liniger was doing very well for himself as a top freelance salesman, but he wanted more. He wanted to be part of something big and exciting. He liked being thought of as the best, and he enjoyed the feeling of belonging to the club. Inside, Liniger knew that he didn't really belong to the club and never would; but that didn't stop him from seeing the opportunities that the club presented—especially when the idea of the club was wedded to a concept that could reinvent the industry.

"Can't you see it?" he asked Bradbury. "What agent, working for the best and most prestigious firm, wouldn't work his tail off if he got 100 percent of the commission from his sales? Why wouldn't every top agent in the world want to work for such a firm? Why couldn't such a firm grow large enough to gobble up the majority of market share not just in Denver, not just in the United States, but around the world?"

Jack Bradbury listened closely. He must have sensed some of the power of Liniger's dream, even if he didn't fully grasp the possibilities. Liniger pitched him hard, but Bradbury took a pass on the radical vision. He couldn't see it, and Liniger left his office, frustrated at his own inability to articulate effectively what he had in mind but still convinced that his idea was right.

Liniger didn't give up trying to push the idea on others in the firm. Whenever he had a chance, he let key people know that the rent-a-desk concept did work and that if Van Schaack were to combine that idea with the Van Schaack model, it would have the biggest real estate company in the world. Even those who gave him a listen laughed at his naiveté. So, after getting nowhere with his idea, Liniger quit that most prestigious and comfortable of firms and went off to build his own organization with little more than his dream and his determination.

Those Van Schaack men didn't understand his dream for a number of reasons. They were all in their forties, fifties, and sixties and extremely successful, disinclined to any kind of new idea, entrepreneurial or otherwise. They had no reason to doubt the system under which they were currently winning. Like other dinosaurs in the history of new eras, they were complacent and unaware of the changes about to come. Liniger was just a kid, sort of naive, certainly enthusiastic, but not polished and sophisticated like them. They had no inkling of how radical his idea really was, perhaps because Liniger hadn't fully grasped how radical it was either. When it came to the way the real estate industry thought of itself, how it operated, how it succeeded, and who its customer actually was, Liniger's idea turned that entire model completely on its head.

It was a Copernican revolution; and Liniger, the determined, unsophisticated kid with no college education but plenty of smarts and 100 percent faith in himself, was a very unlikely Copernicus.

Origins of an Idea

To understand how such an idea came to Liniger, it helps to know where he came from. Liniger's lack of polish and sophistication was deceptive; he was actually a diamond in the rough, not unlike one of his own heroes in some Louis L'Amour cowboy book. If you've ever read a Louis L'Amour book from cover to cover, you've probably noticed that something happens to the writing along the way. So many of the stories start out in fourth- or fifth-grade language, the gunman or sheriff talking to himself as a 12-year-old. You get drawn in by the simplicity of that story; but by the end, you realize that the narrator—the same person, just older, wiser, and successful—is now a sophisticated, articulate individual, who has seen and done a lot and learned some very significant life lessons the hard way. In a very real sense, that's the arc of Dave Liniger's life and the RE/MAX story.

Liniger grew up on a family farm in Marion, Indiana. His parents had a small business in town, so they leased their land for others to work but retained 10 acres surrounded by woods. In the summer, twice a week, it was Liniger's job to mow those 10 acres with a gas lawnmower he pushed for hours. Physical labor and the importance of hard work was part of the family's ethic. Like any Midwestern boy, he belonged to Cub Scouts and 4-H, and he spent a good deal of his time staring at the corn and soy fields and thinking that there had to be something in the world better than this. His heroes were Tarzan and John Wayne. He liked cowboys, soldiers, and fighter pilots; and he told his parents, "The day I'm eighteen, I'm out of here."

As a child, he was highly intelligent and scored well on tests, but he was immature. His parents should have held him back, but they put him into grade school when he was five. Lacking interest, he got Cs by default and picked up As only when something was appealing enough for him to give a damn. His parents were always down on him for his study habits, but he lacked the discipline to stick with anything that didn't keep his attention. He did show an unusual resourcefulness, however. From an early age, he worked every part-time job he could find—mowing lawns, cutting sheet metal, delivering newspapers, even babysitting—because the one thing he knew that he wanted in life was to get rich.

Somewhere along the line, probably when he was 16, he'd read Napoleon Hill's *Think and Grow Rich*. Throughout his life Liniger would be largely self-taught, the kind of voracious reader who finds one or two brilliant and applicable ideas in anything he encounters. Napoleon Hill's book was the first of many to have a strong impression on him. Hill's idea that whatever the mind of man can conceive and believe it can also achieve hit the young Liniger hard. But he lacked anything solid to hitch his considerable attention and drive onto. Because he started grade school early, he started college early, too, entering as a very young 17-year-old. Free from the kind of oversight he'd gotten in high school from his parents and teachers, he showed no self-discipline whatsoever and quickly fell behind. After one semester, he was put on probation. It was a major wake-up call, and he went back the next semester, vowing to put his nose to the grindstone. It worked for a bit, and then Liniger lost interest again. He didn't have the discipline, he realized, because he didn't have a goal. Some kids have a driving force behind them to become a doctor or a lawyer, but Liniger didn't know what he wanted to become. He just knew that he wanted to go into some kind of business.

Lacking any better alternatives, he started up at his father's company. It was union-type work—sprinkler fitting, plumbing, sheet metal—and very quickly Liniger decided it was not for him. He wanted to be a businessman, by which he meant that he wanted to wear a suit. He had the idea at the time—one that he would completely reverse within a few years—that physical work was dirty, humiliating, and low class. But even though he despised the work, he envied the interest that some of the men at his father's company had for their jobs. These sheet metal workers and laborers had found their careers. Liniger, who was into hunting, fishing, and girls (in that order), was just lost.

People who've graduated from the school of hard knocks say that you need to learn from the mistakes of others because you can't live long enough to make them all yourself. Liniger was on pace to making them all himself. He lived hard and played hard. He met a beautiful young woman at a gun range and ended up marrying her. They were both small-town kids, about the same age, and they both loved adventure. When she became pregnant, Liniger joined the military, hoping for glamorous work as a paramedic. But it was 1968, and the military needed fighters to send to Vietnam more than it needed paramedics. Liniger went into basic training and was then posted overseas. He wrote his parents a letter, joking that no matter how bad things looked from afar, Vietnam was definitely better than Indiana. Dark humor aside, to Liniger it really was better. There were helicopters, tanks, and guns—it was the adventure he'd been looking for his whole life.

Still, having a wife and a child all of a sudden changed everything. Liniger had a family to support, and the responsibility was heavy. He made $99 a month base pay and got an additional $33 for separate rations because he ate off base, for a grand total of $132 a month. Even in 1966 that was poverty wages. Liniger had gone from making $4.50 an hour at union work to less than half that and had added a family. There was no extra allowance given to those who had families; in the military, they said that if Uncle Sam wanted you to have a wife, he would have issued you one. Liniger was bound and determined that he wouldn't take welfare and would somehow see his family get by.

He made a major life mistake in not letting his wife get a job. His own mother never worked, and his father had always provided for his family; so there was no way Liniger would see his wife go out of the house to help support them. To compensate, he worked three part-time jobs. He delivered newspapers to newspaper boys at 2 A.M. every morning, worked at a gasoline filling station in the evenings, and put in more time at the filling station or at a movie theater on the weekends. Between those three additional sources of income and the base pay he got from the U.S. Air Force, he was making over $400 a month. It wasn't a fantastic living, but it was a living. Other families in the Linigers' situation did it differently. In those households, the wives worked, the children went into daycare, and the families got by with less strain. Liniger was sleeping only three to four hours a night and was exhausted all the time. He had no life and his family was under strain, but he did manage to buy a house for $10,450. He put only $150 down; but a year later, after it was fixed up, Liniger sold it and made a $4,000 profit. In other words, he made nearly as much money on that house as he had made by working four jobs in the course of the year. The die was cast. Liniger was in the military, but he knew he would get out when his enlistment was up; and when he did, he decided he was going to get into the real estate business and become an investor. That was the kind of man who wore a suit, looked after his family, and got rich.

Those thoughts meshed with another book Liniger read around that time. It was written by a postman who had bought a property in disrepair at a distressed price, fixed it up, made a profit, bought a duplex next, and did the same thing with that. Eventually, the postman became a millionaire and had written his book to explain how. In addition to the strategy of growing wealth, the book included helpful information on property management, writing leases, collecting rents, and things like that. Liniger read every word and imagined himself doing something similar.

When Liniger got back from a stint in Southeast Asia in the summer of 1969, he and his family were transferred to Arizona State University, which was an Air Force ROTC detachment. It was an easy job, so Liniger decided to go ahead with his new plan and start buying some houses. He was so passionate and convincing about the possibilities that 10 officers came together in an investment group to join him and chipped in $1,000 apiece. Liniger got his own one-eleventh stake in the deal for free and made commissions on both the buying and the selling sides. Liniger knew exactly what he was doing, and he steered the group to a 200 percent profit. Everybody made money, so everybody was happy.

In order to handle those sales, Liniger got himself a real estate license, but he had no desire to be a real estate agent. Once again, Liniger had a mistaken impression of a profession because of the hard, physical, and supposedly demeaning work it involved. Being a real estate agent, in Liniger's mind, was low class—a lot of digging for leads and door-to-door canvassing—whereas being an investor meant dealing with wealthy people as their confidante and equal, someone who made them money, someone who belonged in their club. Liniger's view of hard work would change dramatically in the coming years as he actually made something of himself and his company. But in those youthful days, his impression of real estate agents was based on his observation of the sleepy, part-time, unprofessional nature of the industry itself.

In the 1960s, the general quality of real estate agents was very low. Some states didn't even have a license examination requirement, and agents just paid a fee in order to designate themselves as professionals. Today, in Colorado, for instance, you need almost 300 hours of classroom instruction before you can test to get a license; and there are heavy requirements annually for ongoing training, accreditation, and education. There was no technology back then, just paperwork. Agents started with a one-page listing and a one-page sales form. All listing information that came from the Multiple Listing Service showed up on 5-by-7-inch sheets that agents kept in their own three-ring binder, removing and adding them as needed. There was no creative financing; 20 percent down was so conventional that it was practically the norm. There was not much competition between agents in terms of pricing. The listing form actually stated that an agent was required by the Board of Realtors to charge a 6 percent or 7 percent commission fee. Today, any open discussion of what agents should charge in commission would be considered price fixing.

Interest rates were 5 percent or 6 percent in those boom years, so there was a lot of buying and selling going on and plenty of opportunity for an agent willing to do the leg work. Most of the agents Liniger ran across seemed tired and old. Of course, they were only in their mid-fifties; but to a 20-year-old, that was ancient. Given how easy it was to get commissions in the market then, Liniger figured he could run circles around everyone else and sales would be a piece of cake. So he decided to give it a try.

He joined a company called Ed Thirkhill Realty. Ed was a nice, older guy who had several branch offices typical of most real estate businesses at the time. Liniger was a skinny, ex-military kid in his mid-twenties who drove a beat-up old Volkswagen with a cracked windshield and no air conditioning in the desert heat of Phoenix, Arizona. He had a cheap suit and an eager way about him. With his military crew cut and his scrawny frame, he looked like he was 16 years old; and everyone he tried to sell to treated him that way. Agents were a dime a dozen, of course, and someone as enthusiastic and naive as Liniger was perfect for one purpose: He was healthy and energetic enough to go door to door canvassing for leads. Since Liniger was working for commission, his efforts cost the real estate company nothing up front; and there was the off chance that at some point in his travels, after knocking on enough doors, he might stumble across someone who actually had a home to sell and could be convinced to list it with Liniger. In his first six months of trying, he didn't get a single listing, and he didn't get a single sale.

It was an inauspicious beginning, and it caused Liniger to do something he'd never done before: He gave up.

The Power of Selling a Dream

If not for the price of a $20 ticket, that might have been the end of the story. But in the telling of any fairy tale or epic adventure, there are always those key moments when the naive hero stumbles across a piece of good luck. Jack, of Jack and the Beanstalk fame, for instance, came home with three magic beans for which he had traded the family's last asset, a cow. His mother, crushed and beaten by Jack's foolishness, tossed the three beans into the garden, and that should have been the end of it. But the beans were actually magic, and a giant beanstalk grew. Jack climbed the beanstalk, discovered a kingdom filled with riches, killed the giant who ruled the kingdom, and came home to a hero's welcome, making his poor old mom proud of him after all.

In Dave Liniger's case, a $20 ticket to see a real estate motivational speaker amounted to his handful of magic beans.

He went to the talk because he had already paid and, well, . . . what the hell. The magic speaker was a man by the name of Dave Stone. Hearing him talk at the Mountain Shadow Country Club in Phoenix was the turning point in Dave Liniger's life. He sat in the first row, mesmerized. Stone was a brilliant real estate man who loved to teach, the predecessor of all great real estate instructors; and his words penetrated Liniger's brain like none he had ever heard before. At the break, Liniger ran up to Stone and introduced himself. They talked until the speech started up again. Liniger watched Stone from the front row and felt the power of ideas burning in his mind.

At the next break and every break that followed, Liniger jumped up to talk to Stone some more. No doubt, Stone must have been puzzled by the young man's enthusiasm and zeal, but he gave Liniger his full attention. Liniger told Stone that if only he could talk like Stone, explain things the way he did, he would be able to get a listing, too. This admission puzzled Stone, and he asked Liniger how many listings he'd gotten so far in his career. Liniger answered none. So Stone asked Liniger how long he had been trying. Liniger said that he'd been working at it for six months. Stone was probably shocked; but he kept a straight face and gave Liniger a reasonable, sound, and helpful suggestion: Quit.

Coming from a motivational speaker, this might have been a tough piece of advice to ignore. But Liniger took it as a kind of reverse psychology, a test to see how up he was for a challenge. In truth, it was the most motivating thing Liniger had ever heard, and he felt as though he had been knocked out by a hammer and woken up a changed man. On his way home that night, he stopped at the grocery store to buy a carton of milk for his family. A Hispanic girl was in front of him in line. She was about 18 years old, and she was talking to her father, an older man standing next to her. Liniger could understand enough Spanish to know that they were probably talking about real estate, and it inspired him to do something out of character: He spoke up and asked them if they were trying to sell a house. The girl told Liniger that her father was going to be moving from Tempe, Arizona, to Albuquerque, New Mexico, and he had to get rid of his home. Liniger looked at the old man and said, "Señor, do you understand how much a real estate commission is?" The old man shook his head, and the girl said that he didn't speak any English, which was why the whole ordeal was so confusing.

In that instant, Liniger realized that the customer needed him more than he needed the customer. Liniger knew more about the real estate business than the old man did. Liniger could speak English, and the old man could not. He had never felt so capable and confident in his life. "I can help you," he said to the old man. The old man nodded, as though he understood; and Liniger felt deeply touched by the trust and vulnerability in his gaze.

Liniger went with them to see the house the next day. It was a fixer-upper, one that would have easily fit into the book about buying a distressed property and turning it over for a profit. Liniger knew all about fixer-uppers from his own investment projects, so he felt even more confident. He knew he could sell the house. In fact, he knew that people would pay more for a fixer-upper than they probably should. He listed the property, and it sold that very night for full price. When he woke up the next morning in bed with his wife, he said, "Honey, you're sleeping with one hell of a fine real estate agent." She asked him what he meant, and he said, "Do you realize that 100 percent of my listings have sold for 100 percent of the price in one hour or less?" They both laughed because they knew that somehow, overnight, everything had changed for them.

It didn't stop there. The young Hispanic girl and her fiancé were going to get married. Liniger took them out that day, chatting with them like old friends by that point, and sold them a nice house before the afternoon was over. Then they referred him to another Hispanic couple, and Liniger sold them a house, too. At the end of 48 hours, Liniger had four sales and a solid listing. Two days earlier, he had been at the end of a six-month dry spell. The only difference in him from one day to the next was a remarkable change in confidence, a feeling of certainty, and some reinforcing success. He felt suddenly as though there was nothing to this whole real estate business except one huge beanstalk that led straight up to the kingdom of riches. If there was a giant waiting for him up at the top, well, that sounded like fun, too.

Connecting Ideas

Liniger's early real estate experience probably rings a familiar note to many who have ever tried to stand before a potential customer and sell a house. Selling real estate is not like selling anything else; there's too much at stake. A home buyer is putting his or her life, financially speaking, in the hands of a real estate agent. To that customer, anxious enough already, there's a night-and-day difference between a rookie agent, desperate for a sale, and one who knows what he's doing. In the hands of someone who has the capability to figure out what the customer really needs, a home buyer relaxes and the sale becomes that much easier. Dave Liniger discovered just how big a difference his state of mind made. He knew that he had just begun to tap into his full potential.

He threw himself into the business, read voraciously, and took every kind of course he could find. He became a Dave Stone groupie, following him from lecture to lecture, getting to know him better, and carefully fostering him as a personal mentor. (See Figure 1.1.) Life, not surprisingly, began to improve dramatically. With his newfound ability to sell came plenty of money and the respect of the people around him. He got himself a nicer car, with air conditioning. Before he knew it, he got a salesman-of-the-month plaque.

For a restless, growing person like Liniger, that plaque was the sign that

How Dave Liniger Grew the RE/MAX
Idea into the RE/MAX Dream

Figure 1.1   The RE/MAX Learning Model

it was time to move on. Although Ed Thirkhill Realty provided Liniger with an education in what it took to sell and how a business operated, it was a small operation, without much ambition, and would always be that way. So Liniger decided to strike out for new territory and see what would come of it. Twenty years later, giving a speech to a convention hall full of RE/MAX agents, Liniger reflected on how much he had learned from Ed Thirkhill and that first job and how grateful he was for the experience. At the end of the speech, a young man came up to Liniger and handed him his RE/MAX business card. The name on the card was Ed Thirkhill Jr.

After Ed Thirkhill Realty, Liniger joined another company not much bigger in size, called Realty Executives. The owner was a nice man whose philosophy was different from "business as usual." Instead of pocketing 50 percent of agent commissions, he made agents pay a fee to work for him; and in return they got to keep 100 percent of the commissions they earned. Disparagingly, it was described by others in the industry as a rent-a-desk operation. But to Liniger it was no different from a doctor or a lawyer sharing expenses for office space and administrative support with other colleagues and drumming up business on his own. The appeal to Liniger was simple. He just wanted to be left alone. All he needed was a desk, a phone, and a business card, and he was off and running. In return for that, he would rather pay a flat fee than half his commission. The upside was all gravy. It was a deal he couldn't have managed during that six-month period when he hadn't been able to even get a listing. But now that he was a thriving, salesman-of-the-month kind of agent, that was exactly the risk-reward scenario he wanted.

He was making money. He was independent. His family was more secure than ever. He was climbing that giant beanstalk a little higher each day. Everything was perfect except for one thing: Dave Liniger hated the desert. In the winter, it was great; but in August, showing houses in 110 degree heat was a miserable way to make a living. He'd been hearing about Colorado, a hunting, fishing, and skiing paradise, and it sounded like God's country. He knew he wanted more out of life, so he and his wife decided to move.

They liked the idea of a fresh start in a new land. Liniger had accumulated an amazing sales record in a year and a half with Ed Thirkhill Realty and then Realty Executives. It would be very easy to go to the biggest and best companies in Denver and say, "Here's my sales record. I'm moving to town. What can you do for me?" The gamble of uprooting and finding work didn't seem like much of a risk when balanced against the opportunities of a better quality of life.

Liniger interviewed with the top seven firms in Denver and chose Van Schaack and Company. What appealed to him about Van Schaack was how sophisticated it was as a business. Coming from the likes of Ed Thirkhill Realty, Van Schaack had a decidedly corporate way of doing things. It had good training programs, tremendous market share, and great brand name awareness. It owned its own corporate relocation company. It had a huge network of offices, including one experimental location across the street that was built so agents could have their own private office space rather than working out of the typical industry bullpen.

At 26 years old, Dave Liniger drove his family up to Denver on Halloween night in 1971. They rented a house, and Liniger took a few months off for training in order to prepare for the test he needed to take to get his Colorado real estate broker's license. During that time, he took each and every one of the top sales leaders at Van Schaack out for dinner. Liniger was eager to learn everything he could to figure out how Van Schaack became such a premier company. Even as he courted his dinner guests as colleagues, he drilled them for information. What made you successful? What would you do to get a flying start here if you were new to the area? It was all part of his voracious hunger for the best advice and teaching. He wanted to be the best agent in the world.

He got started in early 1972. After only a few months of sales and success, the vicious cycle of the real estate industry kicked in for him again. Van Schaack had provided him with a home and a brand name when he needed one to get up on his feet; but now that he had a network of contacts, a solid set of listings, and a burgeoning repeat business, he didn't really need the company anymore, and it was getting half his money without providing him with much in return.

Because he was now at the top of the food chain in the real estate business, Liniger realized that the source of his disgruntlement wasn't the company he worked for but the nature of the system itself. Van Schaack valued its agents; but like any real estate firm, it didn't really appreciate them, and it didn't really care if they grew or developed. Firms and agents had an adversarial relationship at best, and money was the root source of that friction. The 50 percent commission system was good for firms in the short run but was a long-term detriment. Because agents got so little in return, they were always halfway out the door. Only various threats, ruses, and manipulations could keep the agents in place. Again, it was all focused around the money. Top agents got a bonus in February, for instance, that equaled 5 percent of their commission from the previous year. Why February? Because by that time, an agent already had a stake in the next year's payout and was less likely to jump ship. The agents who showed no sign of decamping were usually those an agency really didn't want. They were coasting along, making a sale here and there, while relying on the brand name of their firm to get enough business to live on. If they lacked an incentive to leave, they also lacked much incentive to grow their own business and profit the firm. Overall, for agents and firms, it was a lose/lose situation.

Liniger knew that his customers were buying houses *from him*, not from Van Schaack. He still liked the sophistication and image of Van Schaack; and he sure understood the value of its training, support systems, brand name, and market presence. But he couldn't help looking back on his days at Realty Executives with a kind of nostalgic longing. Sitting in a diner over coffee, thinking about what made the rent-a-desk concept appealing, he suddenly glimpsed the larger picture.

The answer was not one idea over another; it was a hybrid of the two. If a company could combine the blue-chip reputation, professionalism, and sophistication of a Van Schaack with the entrepreneurial empowerment of a Realty Executives' rent-a-desk operation, it would be unstoppable. The agents would be motivated financially, supported by great training, and free to thrive and grow. The home buyer would benefit tremendously from the more professional service and the longer-term sense of commitment. And the broker's business would grow exponentially as well, as agents flocked to his winning operation. As systems go, it had a beautiful, elegant logic built into its very DNA. The resulting company, if it stuck to those reward-sharing principles, would grow and grow and grow until it became the biggest real estate firm in the world. The question was not how could it work but why not? The appeal was across the board, embracing and including everyone involved. It was an idea in which *everybody wins*.

The fact that no one at Van Schaack saw it that way didn't bother Liniger in the slightest. He knew the people in that company had many built-in reasons to be happy with the status quo. But now that he had finally glimpsed the system that would overturn the industry, his confidence was such that he had no doubts about taking a leap into the unknown and creating that vision on his own. So that's what he did. After only a year at Van Schaack, he quit—and RE/MAX was born. As in many revolutions, hardly anyone knew that a shot had been fired at the time. Looking back, you could see that the real estate industry was never the same again. Dave Liniger had recreated it with a dream.

Strategic Moves

RE/MAX had a dream and a formula, not just an idea.

When we investigated the genesis of the RE/MAX dream, we didn't expect to discover how much time, patience, and preparation went into its formulation. Despite Liniger's young age, the idea had actually been taking shape for years. The moment of inspiration was a gathering of many different strands and a sense of how they fit together in a tapestry of whole cloth. It's clear in our study that big ideas like RE/MAX become implementable dreams through a process. We believe this is a critical success factor for building and growing organizations.

- Ideas are not as powerful as dreams. Dreams are ideas with passion. (throughout chapter)
- Make the dream bigger by connecting it to other ideas. (pp. 5–6)
- Once you figure out the dream, test it, and share it with anyone who will listen! (pp. 6–7)
- People who have talent but lack self-discipline can be engaged by a dream. If you connect them to a dream, they will work toward it. (p. 8)
- Liniger's turn-around moment in the beginning of his career came when he realized that a customer needed him more than he needed the customer. It was at this point that he felt capable and confident. (pp. 13–14)

- In the hands of someone who has the capability to figure out what the customer really needs, a customer relaxes and the sale becomes that much easier. Like all good salespeople, Dave Liniger discovered just how big a difference his state of mind made. Doing so made him realize that he had just begun to tap into his full potential. Working on your personal state of mind helps you to share your dream with others. (p. 15)

- Find a prospective mentor in your field, and pursue a mentor relationship with him or her—at any age and any stage in your career. (p. 15)

- Find the best in your industry and learn from them. Take them to dinner and find out what they did to become successful. Ask them for advice on what they would do if they were in your specific situation. In order to become the best, you have to be intentional about learning from the best. (p. 17)

- Spend the necessary time *going to school* around the idea. Learn everything you can. Be the best by learning from the experts, and then become the expert around your dream. (throughout chapter)

- Once your idea turns into a dream with a focused system, act on it! (p. 19)

Lesson

Unharvested ideas are worthless.

Turning great ideas into workable dreams is hard work. A well-thought-through dream becomes a possibility only after the idea has been crystallized. Harvesting ideas requires diligence and a process. The five-step process is what Dave Liniger followed when he had the big idea and converted it into a dream from which one of the most successful growth companies in the world emerged. (Note that other companies in our study have used similar processes for creating dreams: McDonald's—Ray Kroc, Wal-Mart—Sam Walton,

Microsoft—Bill Gates.) We think it is a terrific template for harvesting ideas and turning ideas into dreams that can come true. The action steps for the RE/MAX conversion of idea to dream are simple:

Step 1. Write the idea down and get the words right.

Step 2. Connect the idea to other ideas to expand it to full capacity.

Step 3. Test the idea to ensure it is sellable.

Step 4. Incubate the idea.

Step 5. Call it a dream and share it.

Modify the idea at each step as depicted in Figure 1.2. What this defines is a learning model for how Dave Liniger turned the RE/MAX idea into a believable dream

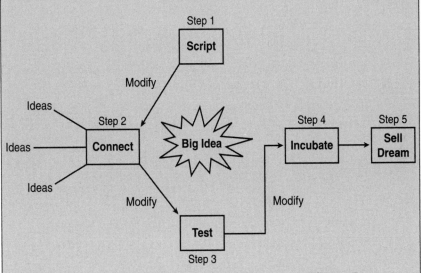

Figure 1.2 The Dream Maker Model: Connecting Ideas to Dreams

CHAPTER 2

ANYBODY WHO SAID "YES"

Drawing the Right People to a Dream

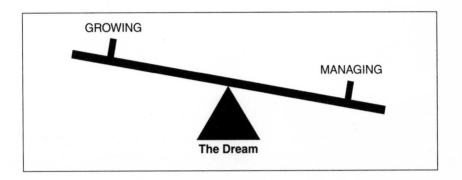

If you want to build a ship, don't drum up people together to collect wood and don't assign them tasks and work, but rather teach them to long for the sea.

—Antoine de Saint-Exupery

When we first began our study of RE/MAX International, it was already the largest real estate network in the world in terms of sales and one of the most successful privately held companies in the history of the United States and Canada. We could see that Dave Liniger, cofounder and chairman, had the dynamism and the persona of an impressive leader. But he also had the track record and the success of a multi-billion-dollar real estate network behind him. In other words, we met a Dave Liniger who was already at the top, someone with firepower and heft, someone who drew plenty of adulation, respect, and notoriety by sheer gravitational force. We wondered, *What was Liniger like before the track record and the success?* Was his potential apparent to those who met him in the early days when RE/MAX was little more than an idea in one man's mind? More important, how did he begin to draw people to him in support of that idea?

What strategy and foresight (if any) went into determining who would be the right person to sign on to the dream?

Once Liniger had been rebuffed by Jack Bradbury and others at Van Schaack, it didn't take him long to get started. And that lack of buy-in did not deter him or dampen his enthusiasm. Fortunately, he was in a good position by that point to take a chance on his new idea. He had some money saved up, owned a few houses, and knew that he could always work as a freelance real estate agent to look after his family. Leaving Van Schaack and launching his own company felt like a relatively minor risk in the larger scheme of things.

Setting Out

It was January 1973 when the new journey began. Liniger woke up early that morning and sat at the kitchen table with his wife to figure out exactly how he was going to get started. Two cups of coffee and a half pad of notepaper later, the phone rang. It would turn out to be one of those out-of-the-blue calls that confirms that you are on the right path.

The caller's name was Jim Collins, a man who worked for a land development firm called Weydert. Collins had heard of Liniger's departure from Van Schaack and saw an opportunity. Liniger was a young star with a great reputation who was well-connected in the real estate community and had built up an amazing sales record in little over a year. Weydert, meanwhile, was on a mission to bring a new kind of development to Denver. It owned the Marble Ski Area outside Denver and believed that a beautiful suburb that gave people ready access to wonderful recreational activities would be the next great thing in housing development. Denver was expanding rapidly and growing more and more wealthy. It only made sense that people would start looking for ways to trade up and take advantage of the tremendous natural resources that Colorado had to offer. To launch its new dream, Weydert planned to start a residential sales department and wanted to interview Dave Liniger to see if he would become its new sales manager.

Liniger listened politely to Collins, but he was already thinking about how to pitch his new venture to him. When the opening came, Liniger fired away. "That all sounds good, Jim, it really does but I'm starting my own company." He explained that his firm would combine the Van

Schaack concept of high-quality formal training and brand name awareness with a multioffice network and a rent-a-desk financial structure. "I believe it's going to be the biggest real estate network in the world someday."

It was Liniger's first opportunity to see how the pitch would go over with an outsider. For his part, Collins recognized a breakthrough idea when he heard one. He invited Liniger to meet the rest of the Weydert team to discuss his new venture in more detail.

Things moved very fast from there, a sign of the energy that Liniger created wherever he went. Liniger met with Weydert—a group of four investors. They were all ex-military men with an established track record of business and land development success and big plans for the future. What's more, they wanted Liniger to bring his dream inside what they considered their larger tent. It was easy to understand why. Liniger was certain that his concept for an international real estate network would attract hundreds of agents. "In fact," he said, "an agent would have to be stupid not to work for me." The Weydert investors could see how well that fit with their own ambitions. Having a national network of real estate agents would enable them to sell land, undeveloped lots, time-shares, and mountain condos anywhere in the country.

Bud Weydert looked at Liniger and said, "Dave, I want you to throw in with us. We're like a family. We'll give you one-fifth of everything we've already got, and we'll get four-fifths of the company you're going to create. We'll also hand you a few hundred thousand dollars to get started. What do you say?"

What *could* Liniger say? On the one hand, he had a feeling it was the wrong move to sign on with a company that might get in the way of what he wanted to do. On the other hand, he was very impressed. The Weydert guys drove Mercedes, flew in corporate jets, and had a dozen different land development projects going on at once. They were polished, experienced, and going places. They had a vast network of military and ex-military contacts, all potential customers, that they could tap into whenever they came up with another new investment opportunity. Although Liniger had created a global real estate network in his own mind, he was the only human being in the world currently working for it. A few hundred thousand dollars and some experienced partners would go a long way to launching his dream. What's more, he truly liked the Weydert guys and felt a connection to them as fellow veterans. They were ballsy and had big dreams. Their offer had come out of the blue, but that didn't mean it wasn't an opportunity he shouldn't seize.

"Let's do it," he said, and they shook hands on the deal.

That night, they sat around the hotel room with a bottle of tequila and some salt and limes and talked about names for the new real estate company. A few ideas sprang up right away but got rejected just as fast. A half bottle of tequila later, the name "Real Estate Maximums Incorporated" was tossed around as a possibility. Nobody spoke for a moment because everyone liked it. *Maximums* meant that everyone would get the most out of the relationship—real estate agents and customers alike. The name did a good job of communicating the *everybody wins* principle at the heart of the endeavor. But after a few more minutes, they realized it didn't quite work. It wasn't snappy enough for a good brand name, and it was too long to fit on a real estate sign.

More tequila got poured. No one could come up with another name that felt as on-target as Real Estate Maximums. Someone suggested shortening it to R. E. Max. That made it snappier and appealing in a brand name sense; but when you wrote it out, it looked too much like a real person's name. You could imagine junk mail arriving at the office in care of Mr. and Mrs. R. E. Max. Collins pointed out that Exxon had formed only a few years before, and the X with a slash through it looked very smart. So Liniger took out the dots and tried a slash through the middle of the word and then capitalized all the letters. They looked at the pad of paper and saw: *RE/MAX*. A silence came over them, followed by a few backslaps and cheers. Everything about the word looked exactly right, as though they were talking about an established global company.

Now, what about colors? They were on a roll. Now was no time to stop. A few more shots of tequila went around while they debated the right look for the new RE/MAX. It didn't take long to figure it out: Everyone in the room was a Vietnam vet and patriotic to the core. The colors, of course, had to be red, white, and blue. When they considered the whole package, they knew they had it. And that's how the idea for the distinctive RE/MAX brand was hatched. Considering the time and resources that get poured into brand development today, their methods might seem unorthodox if admirably effective. No money was spent on advertising agencies, market research, or trademark protection. The only investment was a decent bottle of tequila; the only focus group, a bunch of guys sitting around a room having a good laugh.

But despite the light-hearted moment, Liniger knew that something momentous had taken place. The dream had been manifested as RE/MAX, a brand that Liniger could see and feel was right. On top of that, a new partnership had been formed, sealed with a handshake. All in all, it was quite a day; and yet, Liniger went home that night, uncertain about whether hitching his dream to someone else's wagon was the best move. Despite the lift that he felt through his involvement with Weydert and the thrill of coming up with the RE/MAX name and logo, he had the sense, even then, that a little bit of perfection had slipped through his fingers. Something told him he'd have to work very hard to get it back. But at least he had a company, a name, and some great colors. That, in itself, was an incredible step forward.

Finding the Balance

Almost immediately, the wheels came off the Weydert express. No one had lied to Liniger or puffed up their promises; but Weydert was a highly leveraged financial group navigating a tricky patch of the economy, and interest rates had just taken a sharp turn upward. Liniger found out about the reality of Weydert's situation in bits and pieces.

The first blow occurred right away. Once he incorporated RE/MAX at the end of January 1973, he went to his new partners at Weydert for the few hundred thousand dollars in seed money they'd promised. But Weydert, finding itself in a tight spot, needed a bit more time to come up with the money. Weydert gave Liniger an initial $15,000, which it borrowed from the bank, and told him it would make its significant capital contribution in 60 to 90 days. In the end, that big investment would never come; and in its place, Liniger would find himself saddled with massive business debt that his partners had accrued even before he arrived.

Still, $15,000 was enough to get Liniger started in other critical ways. He rented 450 square feet in a fancy office building, giving him two offices and a reception area. That allowed him to start advertising for administrative help. He went through the employment agencies, interviewed 22 people, and found exactly what he was looking for. If any entrepreneur needs a lesson in the critical importance of early hires, this next story should make them look up and take notice. After all, the administrative assistant Dave Liniger hired would end up coleading his organization one day.

Her name was Gail Main. She was young, beautiful, well-educated, and extremely sharp. Recently married, her husband, a business executive, had been transferred to the Denver area from the Midwest. Back in St. Louis, she had graduated from college with a degree in marketing and management and had then gone to work for Ralston Purina. She would have stayed with Ralston if there had been an opportunity for her in Denver, but nothing was available; so she went looking for new work instead.

If Gail's conservative background—a young married woman from the Midwest with experience working for a large traditional company—caused her to hesitate about joining Liniger's still ramshackle operation, she never showed it. The 450-square-foot office space wasn't even available for viewing yet, but Liniger brought her around to meet the investors. He talked her ear off that whole time, working on convincing her to join him. She had something he lacked, a sophisticated style and attitude, which he knew would be essential for growing the dream. She was also a born manager, and Liniger knew in his heart that he wasn't an administrator—he *needed* someone like Gail. As he drove her to their next meeting, he explained everything he had in mind. "This will be perfect," he said. "I'll be the sales manager, out there all the time, recruiting agents. You'll open the offices, hire the secretaries, set up the accounting systems, and off we go." He could already see it, and his enthusiasm was infectious.

It didn't take Gail any time to make up her mind. She agreed to join for two reasons. First, she understood Liniger's *everybody wins* concept and found its logic compelling. Second, she believed, without any doubt, that Liniger would be able to grow the biggest real estate network in the world; and she wanted to be part of that adventure. For Liniger, Gail's unhesitant acceptance of his dream was a sign of things to come. The people who really got the idea weren't always real estate people; in fact, sometimes it worked better if they were not. But those who did get it understood that Liniger was selling a system, not houses. The nuances of that concept would become increasingly obvious in the next few years as the strategy was refined.

With Gail Main running his office—choosing the look, organizing the systems, and later managing the support staff—Liniger concentrated on recruiting new agents. Since RE/MAX was offering a 100 percent commission system, its success was based on its ability to attract new agents and grow their numbers. Bottom line: Agents paid a monthly fee to operate under the RE/MAX brand. RE/MAX had an incentive to recruit the best agents for a simple reason: Their success selling houses and satisfying customers in the marketplace helped promote the RE/MAX system to other prospective agents. Liniger believed that he would not have any trouble recruiting those top agents. To him, it only made sense that agents who were already successful would naturally be attracted to the idea of getting 100 percent of their commissions instead of the traditional 50 percent, whereas new agents and others less sure of their sales ability would be unlikely to take the chance of working under a system that started them in the hole each month. With that in mind, Liniger readied himself to welcome the top-performing real estate agents in the Denver area who were sure to beat a path to his door.

It didn't happen quite the way he expected, but the evolution that did occur was telling—and instructive for anyone looking to grow a business.

First, Liniger put a small advertisement in the *Denver Post* that said: "Why split your commissions when you can keep the whole thing yourself?" It was a shot across the bow of the local real estate firms and was bound to raise some eyebrows. The ad meant that Liniger was actively recruiting other firms' best agents. In the country club world of real estate, this simply wasn't done. Or, more accurately, it wasn't done openly. Every firm tried to recruit every other firm's best agents. The top firms did it by gravitational pull, benefiting from their position at the peak of the food chain. Agents changed firms all the time, and keeping them was far harder than getting them. But Liniger, the brash, unpolished upstart, was digging the old system's grave—and nobody liked the sound of those shovels.

Over the next month, in response to the RE/MAX ad, Gail Main fielded more than a thousand phone calls. Liniger then did 204 face-to-face interviews. At the end of that grueling process, Liniger signed up four people as RE/MAX agents.

We wondered what Liniger saw in those first four agents that perhaps became a model for determining top agents in the future, so we asked him.

He took a moment, as if to understand our question, and then leaned back in his chair and grinned sheepishly. "Well, hell, those four were the only ones that said, 'Yes!'"

In other words, out of more than a thousand inquiries and 204 recruitment attempts, only *four* people signed on to the RE/MAX dream. Being turned down by so many prospects didn't faze Liniger in the slightest. Despite the fact that he took anybody who said "yes" on that first recruitment drive, each of those prospects had an essential quality that made him or her a critical component in the overall success. It wasn't their smarts that Liniger liked, or their track record, sales numbers, or good looks; it was their hunger. Moreover, those four wanted RE/MAX. They believed in the potential of the RE/MAX system to make their lives better, and they wanted to come inside. And Liniger, in turn, wanted that kind of people in his army.

Another thing about those original four agents was telling: *Three of the four were women.* To understand how radical this seemed, consider this: Van Schaack, the top firm in town, had 300 agents, all of whom were men. Moore and Company, the second-ranked firm coming up fast on Van Schaack's heels, didn't have any female agents either. Women experienced the vicious cycle of the real estate industry in the same way that men did. Those who succeeded left their firms and moved up to another, better company, gradually migrating to the top. But the very best firms were sealed off and out of bounds to women. Although this isn't shocking, given the country club world those firms represented and the position of women in society at the time, it did point to a weakness in the real estate culture. Women had significant advantages over men when it came to selling homes. Women understood the importance of a home to families in a way that men couldn't. And if those families were to admit it, quite often it was the wife, not the husband, who cast the deciding vote as to whether a particular house was the right one. The ability of the real estate agent to understand, empathize with, and meet the needs of the "woman of the house" was often key to the sale. It was relational selling at its most basic. On top of that, women with family obligations needed flexible work schedules, which showing houses allowed them. They were a natural fit for the real estate industry.

Nevertheless, the top firms didn't see it that way, and those top women agents needed someplace to go. RE/MAX very quickly became that alternative. Simply put, those women were fundamental to the success of RE/MAX, and one can imagine how motivated they were to help RE/MAX succeed. In an industry dominated by men, RE/MAX in its early growth period was over 75 percent female. In 1977, when RE/MAX recruited its 289th agent and became the number-one real estate firm in the Denver market, it still hadn't recruited a single male agent from the top two firms in the city. Then, the next year, 200 male agents from those firms finally jumped ship together and joined the women of RE/MAX, exploding the organization's growth in that market.

That slow, steady progress in Denver followed by an explosive jump forward would be repeated in other local markets all over the world.

Princes and Princesses

The experience of Gail Main and those first four agents was typical of the way Liniger recruited others to join his dream. Getting the right person was far more important than getting just anybody. But Liniger learned that the right people were the ones who were so driven to become part of his dream that they basically recruited him. Those people heard about the RE/MAX system from others, became curious about it, approached Liniger to find out more, got hooked on what the system could do for them, and became passionate advocates. Essentially, they self-selected. Only the people who were crazy enough, daring enough, creative enough, committed enough, and passionate enough were willing to throw in with Liniger and go for the gold. In a sense, it was better for RE/MAX to be picked than it was for Liniger to do the picking. The one thing Liniger knew, however, was that you had to kiss a lot of frogs before you found a Prince/Princess Charming.

One of those Prince Charmings was a young man named Bob Fisher. Fisher was from the Colorado area. Like Liniger, he had been an immature, unfocused youth and a mediocre student who had a taste for hard living. An only child, he went to Colorado State University because it was expected of him, and he flunked out because he thought partying was a lot more fun than studying. Shaken up, Fisher knew he wanted to go back to college but decided that a big school like Colorado State wasn't for him.

Instead, he went to Alamosa, Colorado, and enrolled at Adams State College. In that quieter atmosphere, Fisher discovered a lifelong love for education. He finished his bachelor's degree in business and thought that he should probably get an MBA to go with it. Since Adams State didn't offer an MBA program, Fisher had a built-in excuse to take a degree that interested him even more: a master's in cultural relations.

Cultural relations was an offshoot of the larger field of cultural anthropology. Alamosa, Colorado, had a large Hispanic population, which brought the department a focus on culture and group dynamics. Fisher supplemented his cultural theory studies with as many business courses as possible, handcrafting himself an Organizational Development degree in the days before that type of study was widely offered.

After getting his master's, he found a job as a market research analyst with the Gates Rubber Company. As low man on the totem pole, he traveled across the country visiting offices and interviewing employees to determine how well each sales team was performing. Like a corporate spy, he tried to get at the true workings of a team, figuring out the dynamics of each contributor and how the team members gelled to produce an overall performance ranking. Once his analysis was complete, Fisher wrote technical assessment reports that strongly influenced the ratings each sales team received. Salespeople quickly came to learn that they lived or died based on Fisher's reports.

By watching those teams go about their daily jobs, Fisher was functioning much like a cultural anthropologist, who observes a community that is aware of his presence but becomes used to it over time and relaxes its barriers. It was an incredible education in team dynamics and sales performance, but Fisher soon got in trouble. Like a lot of young men in those days, he had a mustache, something his staid, conservative manager insisted he get rid of. Fisher, impolitic to the core, replied in so many words that he wasn't going to do that. The manager told him that he'd better find a different job; so Fisher moved on, mustache intact.

Fisher stayed within Gates Rubber Company but switched to its tire division and ran one of the tire centers. He had a talent for managing, it turned out; and the tire center went from worst in the nation, in terms of production, to second-best overall in just two years. He had high hopes, based on that success and his experience as a top analyst, that he might one day become an elite executive at Gates.

In the meantime, one of his old roommates from college, a man named Gordon Schick, had done something unusual with his own career. Schick had been a teacher after graduating from Adams State but did some tax accounting on the side for H&R Block to make ends meet. Still, he and his wife were both working multiple jobs and barely pulling in enough for themselves and their two daughters to get by on. Out of necessity, a new idea was born. As a tax accountant, Schick came into regular contact with family customers. Schick figured that if he had a real estate license, he would be able to tap into the same customer base to sell houses. So, he quit teaching and joined a small real estate firm.

Once Schick got into real estate, he started hearing about RE/MAX. To a guy who had energy, verve, self-discipline, and a desire to make money, it sounded like a very good idea. Bob Fisher became interested in Schick's new desire to "go do this RE/MAX thing" because he had just gotten some disruptive news of his own. Gates Rubber Company was getting out of the tire business, and Fisher figured that he would soon be out of a job. Over beers, Schick bet Fisher that he couldn't pass a real estate exam. Fisher was filled with confidence in his test-taking abilities regardless of the content of that test, so he accepted Schick's challenge. A few weeks later, he registered for the test. Without studying, he managed to fake his way through and pass. Soon enough, he was glad that he had done so. When Gates Rubber dropped its tire division a few months later, Fisher figured to try his hand at selling real estate. He joined the small firm where Gordon Schick worked; and when Schick jumped to RE/MAX shortly thereafter, Fisher went with him.

It was 1973. RE/MAX was six months old, and Bob Fisher was the thirteenth sales associate to join the firm. Unlike most of the people already on board, Fisher was a novice real estate salesman and knew he had a lot to learn. He put his head down and threw himself into the job. Over the next few months, he met Dave Liniger and Gail Main occasionally. Fisher's impressions of Liniger were strong. Liniger was always selling the dream. RE/MAX, Liniger said over and over, was going to revolutionize the real estate industry, or as he put it: "We're going to become statewide, and then we're going nationwide, and after that we're going intergalactic!"

This was music to Fisher's ears. Even at the age of 26, he had big dreams and was filled with enthusiasm for the great possibilities of life. In college, he'd told Schick and others, "There are Lear jets in my future." Although he didn't know exactly what path he would take to get there, he believed that he would become extremely successful someday. If that required selling tires or selling homes, so be it. But now that he had discovered Liniger and RE/MAX, Fisher felt moved by something bigger than just money. Liniger was an extraordinary force, and Fisher was captivated. *If this guy can come through on his vision as well as he can describe it*, he thought, *then I'm his man*.

A few years later, an idea occurred to him. He was completely and totally committed to Liniger's dream, and now he saw it as his own. His mind was always working on how RE/MAX could be pushed harder. He'd gotten to know Dave and Gail fairly well during that time. There had been plenty of memorable social occasions, a lot of late-night drinking, and endless discussion as to how to make the business better. One night, Fisher put his cards on the table. "For three years before I came here," he said, "I worked for Gates Rubber and did nothing but travel all over North America making them better. I know all about how to expand a business nationwide. I want you to let me do the same thing for RE/MAX. Send me out on the road, and I'll bring others on board."

It was brash talk, but Liniger liked what he was hearing. Fisher probably knew less about expanding a business nationwide than he realized; but what he lacked in experience, he more than made up for in enthusiasm and confidence. Dave contemplated the rim of his glass for a moment and then looked Fisher in the eye. "I'll be straight with you, Fish. I don't have any money to pay you. But we're going to license our name; and if you can sell that license to real estate brokers around the country, you can have 50 percent of whatever you earn for us."

In other words, if Fisher could sell a broker a RE/MAX association, as it was called then, for say $5,000, then he'd take home $2,500 for himself. There was no security of a base salary and less commission money for Fisher than if he just concentrated on selling houses; but it fit with what he wanted to do and what he wanted to see the firm become. Now that he was taking a step inside the inner circle and putting some of the burden of building the organization on his own shoulders, he couldn't argue with the terms. Liniger and Gail were both making next to nothing themselves, having reduced their salaries to the bare minimum in order to see the firm succeed. To Fisher, it sounded like a hell of a lot of fun. So he shook hands with Liniger, and they knocked back their drinks. Fisher was going to hit the road.

He was ferociously eager and optimistic and had great big plans. He knew what it was like to be on the road, meet with new people, and observe how they performed. He understood corporate culture, and he had a sharp business mind. What's more, he had self-selected. That was the way it went at RE/MAX. People saw the opportunities, appointed themselves as the ones best suited to make a difference, and drove that aspect of the RE/MAX dream as if it were their very own. Liniger, as a forceful and magnetic leader, was drawing certain people to him and bringing out something in them that they'd never really shown before. And his personality was such that he gave people all the freedom they wanted or needed to take charge independently and make things happen.

That was an attitude that fit Bob Fisher's personality like a glove. The young man who'd left a job rather than shave off his mustache wasn't the type to be held back by someone with an overblown sense of authority. He respected Liniger because Liniger's actions really were backing up his compelling words. In return, the freedom Liniger gave Fisher paid off in spades. Through Fisher's nationwide travels over the next few years, RE/MAX would learn an awful lot about the business it was actually in.

There was a third roommate. The money Schick and Fisher were making and the fun they were having started poking away at their other ex–college roommate, a man by the name of Daryl Jesperson.

Jesperson and Fisher had taken separate paths after college but stayed close despite their different personalities. Fisher was hard living but intellectually curious, highly intelligent and easily bored—a combination that made him quick to leap into new opportunities without hesitation, not even bothering to check whether the parachute was on his back. Like Liniger, Fisher's attitude was, "Let's just go for it. We'll get there somehow." Jesperson was more cautious and deliberate. When he took chances, especially extremely big ones, they were carefully considered, with all the variables and percentages worked out. But like Gail Main's thoughtful, restrained discipline, Jesperson's commitment and passion to the grand endeavor would prove just as mighty a force.

After college, while Fisher went on to do his master's in cultural rela-

tions, Jesperson became an officer in the U.S. Navy. When his tour of
duty was finished, Jesperson debated getting a graduate degree because that
was what everyone he knew seemed to be doing. But in business, a master's
didn't provide much of an advantage and, in fact, could be a disadvantage
when it came to getting hired. So Jesperson went to work for Texaco, the
oil company, instead.

Texaco had retail gas stations all over the country. It needed young men
like Daryl Jesperson to work closely with the managers and owners of those
stations in order to make them profitable and to align them with the Texaco brand. Essentially, this was franchise development work; but Texaco
and the other oil companies didn't classify their stations as franchises—
they had received an exemption from the franchise laws. Nevertheless, Jesperson's experience working with franchise owners, developing their
potential, introducing new concepts to them, and helping them navigate
problems and market challenges would come in very handy for RE/MAX
years later.

Jesperson was doing fine as a corporate man, but he was starting to wonder about the color of the grass on the other side of the fence. Gordon
Schick had just made "salesman of the year" at RE/MAX. This meant that
he and his wife had gone from making a total of about $15,000 a year work-
ing several jobs to an astounding $44,000 in real estate. Schick and Fisher
were both living the high life. They had plenty of money; they were driving new cars; and they each had a boat and a motor home. Meanwhile,
Jesperson and his wife were tagging along on those family vacations, thinking, *Wouldn't it be nice?* To Jesperson, it became apparent that he needed to
either find some new friends or find a new job.

Still, it wasn't easy in those days to change careers or to hop from one
company to another. Loyalty was prized. Long-term commitment was seen
as a sign of maturity and reliability. In the job market, it was difficult to
find anything that didn't resemble if not exactly match the work you had
been doing all along. Even if you found a company worth signing on to and
managed a little bump in pay, there was little chance you could do something as radical as Schick had pulled off by more than doubling your salary.
Jesperson thought, *What do I have to lose? I'll get my real estate license and
give it a try.*

He wasn't even thinking about RE/MAX at first. He knew about it, of course, and he had even met Dave Liniger; but he was initially drawn toward the more conventional companies. Van Schaack, for instance, loved Jesperson. He fit their mold: male, ex–military officer, ex–Fortune 10 company, someone who looked good in a blue suit and a white shirt. They offered him a position at the traditional 50/50 split. In considering the offer, Jesperson talked it over with Schick and Fisher. Together, they did the math. After one transaction, Jesperson couldn't survive at either Van Schaack or RE/MAX. After two transactions, he'd be doing a little better at Van Schaack and would have just gotten himself out of the hole at RE/MAX. But after three transactions at RE/MAX he would be making more money than if he had done four transactions at Van Schaack, and the disparity grew exponentially from that point forward. Fisher figured it was all sewn up. Even an idiot (or a college roommate who'd gone on to work for a big corporation) could see that it was easier to sell three houses than it was to sell four. Having laid the facts out and analyzed the probabilities, Jesperson, who had never sold anything in his life before, decided to go to the bank, borrow the money he needed to get into RE/MAX, and sign on.

His first day on the job was a good one. He was moving into his desk, putting his pencils in a cup, positioning his notepads in the right-hand corner, when the phone rang. No one else was handy, so Jesperson picked it up. The caller announced that he was interested in looking at one of the RE/MAX listings. It was one of Fisher's listings and Jesperson happened to be familiar with it. "This is a foreclosure," he told the caller. "Is it something you think you'd want to close on in less than a week? Because if you hesitate you're going to lose it." The caller wanted to jump right on it. He made his living by buying houses that needed work, then fixed them up and put them back on the market. So Jesperson took the man out to see the property. They closed on it in eight days, and Jeperson pocketed his first commission check less than two weeks after starting his new job.

It was an auspicious beginning, and Jesperson was completely hooked on RE/MAX. He ended up becoming "Rookie of the Year" that year, not just for RE/MAX but also for the Board of Realtors. It was the atmosphere of the office that helped him. Jesperson had no experience, and all a real estate license had taught him was how to fill out the contract. Like every novice, he hadn't known how to find a customer, what to do with that customer once you found him or her, how to close the deal, or how to leave the relationship on a great note to encourage repeat business and referrals. But in the spirit of a new and great enterprise, the people in the RE/MAX office had taken Jesperson under their wing and steered him along.

And, as Dave Liniger constantly promised, it was a hell of a lot of fun.

Selling the Dream

To the pioneers at RE/MAX, it was "Us against the World." All the brokers who came on board had a variation on a common attitude: They hated the way the real estate business was being run, and they wanted to show the world how good it could be. They had a great deal of pride in being able to talk to a potential agent and sell them on the RE/MAX dream. *This is what we can offer you—the best deal in town, hands down. Come join us.*

RE/MAX was in business to break the vicious cycle of the real estate industry. Every successful agent knew what that cycle felt like. Win big at one real estate firm, feel squeezed out of your own success, move on to a bigger firm, go through the same feeling again, start your own firm, stick to the rules you hated as an agent, and create your own future competition. It didn't make any sense, and it needed to stop. Explaining to a potential agent why RE/MAX was different and why that agent would never need (or want) to go anywhere else again was a very satisfying experience.

That core group of early pioneers, about 50 in number, had no limits to their feeling of drive in this mission. They worked 12 hours a day, 7 days a week. If you arrived at 6:30 in the morning, you might find yourself one of the last people to walk in the door. It became a running joke to see how early the first person could get in. Fisher, figuring he finally had the title, showed up at 5:00 A.M. one day, only to scare the heck out of himself when he ran into Liniger crawling around on the floor in his shorts and undershirt. Liniger had been up all night because he had a big mailing he wanted to get out the door by start of business. He'd spread out the envelopes, brochures, and stamps on every available stretch of carpet and was now crawling among the different piles, folding, inserting, licking, and stamping. Fisher took off his own jacket and undid his tie before dropping down onto his hands and knees to assist. Each person who arrived after him did the same thing. Someone walking up to the door and looking in over the desks might have thought the office was empty—everyone was below desk level.

Fisher was on the road much of the time trying to sell RE/MAX licenses. He rented a motor home with his own credit card, loaded it up with information materials, and went from city to city conducting seminars. In Illinois, he sold a license to a married couple, Dick and Betty Hegner. Somehow, the state securities commission found out about the transaction and cried foul. According to the commission, RE/MAX was not really selling licenses at all; it was actually selling franchises, so it needed to cease and desist. When Fisher and Liniger protested, the securities commission told them that they could pay a fine, go to jail, stay out of the state altogether, or register as a franchising organization and go about their business. That last option sounded like the best one. Liniger looked at Fisher and said: "Well, let's be a franchise then." So that's what they did.

It wasn't easy at first. Liniger and Fisher tested the franchise idea by trying to sell in the Colorado Springs area. Every day they drove down and made presentations. Sometimes the door got slammed in their faces. Sometimes people listened to their pitch and just laughed at them. For Fisher, the lack of success was puzzling and disheartening.

Jesperson covered Fisher's real estate business so that Fisher would have an income while he was trying to sell franchises. Most evenings, after a long day's work, Fisher and Jesperson met in a bar to catch up. The talk always turned to the issue of selling franchises and why it was so tough. Neither one of them could understand why others didn't see the power of the dream. Both Jesperson and Fisher were enjoying the benefits of the RE/MAX system, making more money than they'd ever made in their lives, and feeling great about the future possibilities. What did others not see? Jesperson and Fisher, as was their habit, found themselves brainstorming about the issues. What were Fisher and Liniger not doing right? What could they do better next time? How else could the idea be presented or structured to encourage others to buy in?

Fisher had one good prospect, he told Jesperson, a man by the name of Owen Hyde. But Hyde didn't have everything necessary to go forward. There was always a stumbling block.

"So what does he have?" Jesperson asked.

Fisher thought about the pieces of the puzzle. "Well, he has a broker's li-

cense." In Colorado, you needed one of those to run a real estate office.
"And he has a high profile." Hyde was chairman of the local Multiple Listing Service, so he was sufficiently well known among agents to launch his
own office. "But he's light on capital." Hyde had enough money to buy a
franchise or to open an office, but not to do both. "And he doesn't have
the confidence that it will work."

When they thought about the problem systematically, the solution became clear to both of them. "We've got the pieces he's missing," Jesperson
said. "And he's got the pieces we're missing."

Jesperson and Fisher had the confidence—they could recruit agents easily, based on their own successful experiences. What's more, if they found
a couple of partners and Fisher used some of his commission fee from the
franchise sale, they would be able to raise the money that Hyde lacked.

"If we can't sell franchises," Fisher laughed, "we'll figure out how to buy
them."

They talked about the idea with Hyde, Gordon Schick, and another
RE/MAX agent named Ollie Winters. Everyone was on board. With a
great deal of pride, Jesperson, Fisher, and Schick went to Liniger's office
late one afternoon and told him they were ready to buy the Colorado
Springs franchise.

Liniger's eyes widened in surprise, but he took the news in stride. "How
are you going pay for it?" he asked. They told him. Liniger said that it
sounded great, and he put a piece of paper into the typewriter and prepared
to write up an agreement. After a few pecks on the keyboard, he looked
back up.

"You guys both know the Boulder market really well. Would you be interested in buying that, too?"

The idea sounded intriguing to the trio. The afternoon became evening.
They decided to transfer the meeting to the nearby bar and continue the
conversation. Before the night was over, Liniger had sold Jesperson, Fisher,
and Schick franchises from Colorado to New Mexico, along the front
range of the Rocky Mountains, excluding metropolitan Denver. Liniger
knew they were the right people to take the dream to another level. Because a typewriter was not handy, they scribbled their agreement on a
cocktail napkin and signed it.

In the light of day, Fisher was still gung ho, but Jesperson went through a period of doubt. It wasn't that he didn't believe in the dream—he had plenty of proof that it worked. But he worried that he was moving too fast. Was he going overboard? He had been raised in a conservative family, had enlisted in the navy, and had worked for a conservative Fortune 10 company. Now, all of a sudden, he had money, a Cadillac, and a motor home. It barely seemed real. Would his life come off the rails if he rode it too far and too fast?

He talked to his friends and his family. Everyone advised him to slow down. The advice spoke to his fears, but it didn't speak to his heart; so he sought more advice from someone in the business. Terry Weisner was one of the most successful people Jesperson knew. He was a former Van Schaack man and now sold real estate with RE/MAX. He was also a developer and a home builder. He was rock solid, sophisticated, and mature. Jesperson took him out for drinks and talked to him about his concerns.

Weisner twirled a swizzle stick as he listened to Jesperson's fear of taking the risk. Finally, he asked Jesperson a simple question: "How many pieces are they going to cut you into?"

Jesperson didn't understand. "What do you mean?"

Weisner shrugged. "If you fail, how many pieces are they going to cut you into?"

Jesperson got it. If he failed, he wasn't going to die. But he couldn't fail if he didn't take the chance. He realized that his fear of taking the next step forward was all about having the right mindset. The risks were calculated, not crazy. He knew the business. He had a plan. He had good partners. If they didn't make it, no one was going to have their heads. But if they didn't try, they'd never know whether they could pull it off.

He thanked Weisner for the advice and never looked back.

Jesperson and Fisher opened nine offices over the next few years. They brought solid managers in as business partners, and the offices began to perform. Despite their success, they also recognized a challenge that RE/MAX would need to overcome. The RE/MAX system worked best as a network. A RE/MAX office was like a fax machine. The first fax machine was not a very useful or valuable device because it didn't have any other fax machines to communicate with. But when every office in the world has a fax machine, its usefulness and value is immeasurably increased. In other words, RE/MAX franchises were more valuable when there were other RE/MAX franchises in the network. It was all about developing market presence, creating brand awareness, sharing ideas, and building momentum. The combination of those intangible things helped real estate agents sell more real estate. The overall success of the RE/MAX system helped the franchises recruit more agents. The only way the system benefited anyone was when it benefited everyone. This was the core of the *everybody wins* principle.

Understanding that idea, Jesperson and Fisher set out to sell more franchises and regions. They were doing it for RE/MAX, but they were also doing it for themselves. They knew that their own region and offices would be more successful if there were more RE/MAX offices and agents in the world. It didn't matter if those agents were in Colorado or Ohio.

Fisher and Jesperson drove to Fort Collins one day, just north of Denver, to open a new office. The trip was a success: one more step forward. As they drove back home that night, they could see all the lights of Denver clustered below them. "That's all our inventory, down there," Jesperson said, and Fisher laughed, knowing what he meant. Selling real estate was their security blanket. They could always fall back on that in order to feed their families. Being an agent was an exceptional lifestyle that brought with it a great deal of money. But building a company was more than fun; it was something special. They were changing the way people thought. They were changing the world people lived in.

In 1977, with Liniger's help, Fisher and Jepseron sold 110 franchises around the country. Some were individual franchises in small cities. Others were large regional territories like their own in Colorado. The success was wonderful, but one thing had become apparent: They were going to need to increase their level of organization in order to train all of those people. It was not a bad problem to have.

"And Other"

In 1976, Vinnie Tracey was a basketball player at the University of Tennessee. He was tall and physically talented, and he exhibited a lot of leadership on the team; but he wasn't known just for his athletic skills. Tracey was the team huckster. Any time an alumnus wanted to buy or sell tickets for a big game, Tracey was the guy to talk to. He negotiated arrangements, made deals, and organized swaps with the ease of a born networker.

One of those alumni became a mentor to Tracey. His name was Dr. Robert Overholt. Overholt—"Doc" to Vinnie Tracey—had a successful medical practice, but he also had a taste for business. When Tracey graduated, Doc asked him what he wanted to do with his life. Since Tracey didn't know, Doc set him up as a salesman in a company called American Trophy and Award, in which Doc was a part owner. Tracey visited Little Leagues and businesses on sales trips. He got in a lot of doors because he was friends with some of the more famous athletes at the University of Tennessee and could arrange for speaking engagements. The job was a lot of fun.

Glenn Glass was a football player who had been a freshman when Doc was a junior at the University of Tennessee. In 1977, Glass visited Doc and told him about an amazing new business. It was called RE/MAX, and it had come up with something called the 100 percent commission concept. Glass and Doc flew to New York to meet with Dave Liniger and came back convinced that RE/MAX was the way of the future in the real estate industry. Doc agreed to back Glass financially to buy the Kentucky/Tennessee region.

Tracey learned about the new venture from Doc and was curious. "What's RE/MAX?" he asked.

Doc explained the idea of a RE/MAX office in terms that were familiar to him. "The office is run a bit like a medical practice. All of the real estate agents are like the doctors. The agents have to chip in and cover the costs of running the office; but everything they earn, they get to keep. It's a 100 percent commission model."

Tracey was interested. "Well, that sounds great. How is that different from the rest of the real estate industry?"

Doc was a religious man, so his answer startled Tracey. "Vinnie, I don't know how else to put this. But the traditional real estate broker is like a pimp. He puts agents on the street and gets 50 percent of whatever they make when they sell houses."

Tracey laughed and pushed Doc for more information. "All right, you guys bought the region, but you're not going to sell real estate. So what do you do?"

"We're going to sell franchises," Doc answered.

"I can sell those," Tracey said.

"Do you even know what a franchise is, Vinnie?" Doc asked.

"Doesn't matter," Tracey said. "You don't want me to sell real estate, you want me to sell a business system. Based on what you've told me about the traditional real estate model, I know I can sell RE/MAX."

Tracey was 24 years old. What did he know about business systems? Very little, but he knew how to talk his way into an office and make a convincing sales pitch. In his first six months, he got thrown out of most of those offices, but it didn't deter him. He believed the RE/MAX idea was the greatest idea in the world, and it was only a matter of time before others figured that out, too.

He went to RE/MAX in Denver for franchise sales training in 1978. The way the ideas were presented in the classes crystallized his own thinking about how to sell franchises more successfully. At the end of the week, Tracey walked up to the senior team at the front of the room. Dave Liniger, Gail Main, Daryl Jesperson, and Bob Fisher watched the tall skinny ex–basketball player from the University of Tennessee approach them. "That was the best course I've ever taken," Tracey said, "and the teacher you have is the nicest guy in the world. But I can teach that course better than he càn. If you ever have an opening, I'm your man." And he strode off, eager to get back to Tennessee and do some more selling.

Later that year, Liniger and Gail asked Tracey to fly to Lake Tahoe for a job interview. Gail put a plate of sandwiches on the table between them. "You hungry, Vinnie?" Liniger asked. "A little," Tracey admitted. Flying to Tahoe had sucked up the last of Tracey's meager funds; he hadn't eaten a real meal in days. As Liniger and Gail asked him questions, Tracey finished off the entire plate of sandwiches. They'd been meant for a whole group of people who were coming to the room after the interview. Liniger and Gail just laughed.

Despite his appetite, Liniger offered Tracey a job. He could only pay Tracey $1,000 a month in salary, however. "If you're worth a darn in ninety days," Liniger said, "we'll give you a $250-a-month raise. If you're not, you can pack up your stuff and go back to Tennessee."

Tracey took a day to think about it. Denver was the center of the RE/MAX universe. Back in Tennessee, they had 30 or 40 agents. In Colorado, they had nearly 400. Tracey could barely afford to work for RE/MAX on the money Liniger was offering, but he didn't care. He wanted to be in the middle of the action. He told Liniger he wanted to sign on.

The work hard/play hard culture of the Denver office was the most exciting thing he'd ever been around. Every moment of the day was devoted to working hard. After work, most of the key people met at Gail Main's house for dinner—they could barely afford meals on their own, and it gave them a chance to keep honing the dream. Liniger would throw steaks on the grill. Gail served her green bean casserole. Tracey ate everything that came within sight.

Three weeks into his new job, Tracey almost got fired. RE/MAX threw a big party for all the agents in Colorado at the head office. There were more than 200 people in attendance. Tracey relaxed and enjoyed himself. Near the end of the night, Liniger asked Tracey to stick around and clean things up. Tracey promised he would and promptly left with some of the younger people to continue the party elsewhere.

He came back, a few hours later, expecting that he would be able to tidy things up before morning and Liniger would never be the wiser. He pressed the elevator button, the doors opened, and Liniger stood in the middle of the elevator surrounded by garbage bags. "Where the hell were you?" Liniger asked him. Tracey didn't have a good answer. He reached for the bags to help Liniger haul them to the trash. "Don't bother," Liniger said. "I'm doing it myself."

Tracey's weekend was filled with worry. On Monday morning, he showed up at the office. Gail ran a meeting each Monday to ask the key people what was going on in their departments. She stood at the front of the room, her right arm resting on the podium, her coffee mug in her left hand. When it came to Tracey's turn, she asked him what was happening in training. "Well," Tracey answered, "we have a class this week. We've got three people coming from Calgary, two from Atlanta, . . ."

Before he'd finished, Liniger stood up at the back of the room. "Somebody in this room disappointed me recently," he said. "And I'm not sure they're going to have their job at the end of the day."

Tracey's heart beat hard. When the meeting broke, he waited five minutes, then walked to Liniger's office and knocked on the door.

"What do you want?" Liniger asked. Gail stood next to his chair.

"I really screwed up," Tracey said. "I apologize. It will never happen again."

Liniger let the silence go on, and then he nodded. "I accept."

Tracey felt the weight of the world lift off his shoulders. "I will work harder than you will ever believe."

"You already work hard," Liniger said. "I just wanted to see what you were made of."

Liniger stayed cool to Tracey for another month. In May, on a Saturday afternoon, they ran into each other in the office. Tracey worked every day of the week, including weekends, but it was the first time Liniger had approached him since the party. "Come on," Liniger said. "We're going to Gail's for a barbeque."

They walked out into the parking lot together, and Tracey got onto the back of Liniger's motorcycle. Neither of them wore a helmet, but Liniger tore out of the lot and throttled back hard. The bike reached a speed of 80 miles an hour, whipping through the streets. Leaning into Liniger's back, staring over his shoulder, holding on for dear life, Tracey thought, *Please, God, just let me live!* Liniger talked as they rode, although Tracey could barely understand him. "Vinnie, I'm the guy who owns this place. If I'm willing to pick up garbage, if I'm willing to get somebody a cup of coffee, if I'm willing to stick around after everyone else is gone home, than you ought to be willing to do the same thing." It was a speech that fit in with everything else Tracey ever learned about the work ethic at RE/MAX; and it was a lesson he would teach others who followed. Every job description at RE/MAX listed the duties of each role and ended with the description, "and other." In Liniger's world, the "and other" was more important than everything else that preceded it.

When they finally arrived at Gail's house, Tracey walked around like a dead man. Gradually, he came back to life. He ate, he laughed, and he talked. He had a good time. Midway through the evening, he realized that he had been accepted back into the tribe.

By 1978, Liniger and Gail had given up their own salaries to keep things going. Every penny Liniger earned selling real estate went back into the business. But three months after Tracey moved to Denver, Liniger awarded him a raise. Three months later, he got another raise.

"I don't need it," Tracey said. "You just gave me a raise."

"Vinnie, you're doing an extraordinary job. You deserve it."

After that, Tracey would have taken a bullet for Liniger, he admired him so much. He took the raise and got back to work. He lived and breathed RE/MAX. At every opportunity, they talked about what they could do differently or better.

The training classes got bigger. In 1980, Liniger bought a piece of land near the head office and showed Tracey the plans for the facility he wanted to build on it. To Tracey, it looked like a giant ski lodge. "Vinnie, this will be your training room," Liniger told him.

Tracey was excited just looking at it. "Man, how big is that?" he asked.

"You'll be able to train one hundred people in there," Liniger said. Tracey shook his head.

"Dave, the biggest class I've ever done is twenty-five. What are you thinking?"

"Don't worry, Vinnie," Liniger said. "You're going to need the space."

He might have had his doubts if it had come from anybody else. But when Liniger said it, Tracey knew it would happen.

Strategic Moves

Create a culture that honors princes and princesses.

RE/MAX did not hire anyone who walked in the door—RE/MAX hired people who said "yes" to the dream. In technical terms, RE/MAX spread its dream widely, drawing much interest and attention from potential employees; but it only made an offer once it was sure that a person wanted the dream as much as RE/MAX did. The objective of growing the dream is only actualized through dream sharers—passionate champions who will sell the dream and work as hard as the dream makers.

- Be wary when you're sharing your dream. Other leaders may divert your attention or try to hitch your dream to their wagon. Although this may seem safer or less uncertain, it's the wrong path for a dream. (p. 25)
- Take the time to visualize the dream into a picture that has shape and color. It will become your brand, and this visualization will pull you up whenever you stumble. (p. 26)

- Dreams are only as fragile as the dream maker. Many mistakes can be made, and the dream will survive. Advice: Walk on by, don't look back, it's only the beginning. Don't give up on the dream. (p. 27)

- Be aware of your personal weaknesses when building a dream. From the beginning, hire people who complement you, who are strong in the areas in which you are weak. (p. 28)

- Hire people who buy into the dream and who will be as passionate about making the dream become a reality as you are. (p. 30)

- Develop your own unique hiring profile. You may find dream sharers whom others have passed over. RE/MAX was one of the first real estate firms to aggressively hire women agents, thereby creating competitive advantage. (pp. 30–31)

- The right prospective employees self-select. People RE/MAX recruited believed in Liniger's dream and wanted to be part of it. (p. 31)

- Always go after those who can become royalty. Work hard at recruiting the right people. RE/MAX believed from inception, "You have to kiss a lot of frogs before you find princes and princesses." (p. 31)

- Sell the dream constantly, inside and outside your organization. As a leader, always stay focused on the dream and feed your passion to those around you. Once employees commit to that dream, it will become their own and they will work as hard as you do. (pp. 33–34)

- Be open to modifying the dream, expanding it to what the market commands and will accept. RE/MAX discovered that franchising was its successful formula—an idea that wasn't part of the original dream at all. (p. 34)

- At RE/MAX, people saw opportunities for themselves and self-selected their roles. They appointed themselves as the ones best suited to make a difference in the organization and drove that aspect of the RE/MAX dream as if it were their very own. Liniger's personality as a leader and his trust in them gave people freedom to take charge independently and to carry out their part of the dream. (p. 35)

- Once you have a group of employees who have said "yes" to the dream, they will talk to others and bring more on board. (pp. 36–37)
- In the early days with few resources, set the tone by avoiding specific job roles. Get everyone involved and develop a culture where "everyone carries the boxes." (p. 46)

Lesson

Sharing the dream makes dreams come true.

The subtle lesson in Chapter 2 is that dreams become more believable as they are shared with others. Dave Liniger had an enormous capacity to position the RE/MAX dream as though achieving it would be inevitable. This ability to make the dream seem bigger than its current state enabled him to attract great talent.

The big lesson is that selling the dream requires casting a "wide net." (See Figure 2.1.) The picture to keep in mind is that once the net is cast, you only want a few choice fish. In fact, RE/MAX proved that it is most important to have the fish that want to be in the fish bowl.

RE/MAX has a contrarian recruiting process that produces amazing loyalty to the dream, the brand, and each other. The process begins with the big sell. Then finalists must sell themselves as dream sharers before they are hired. It works this way:

Step 1. Cast a wide net (in the beginning) so that there are a lot of fish to consider.

Step 2. Weed out possibles based on both skills—**required**—and the inner stuff—**attitude and cultural fit**.

Step 3. Interview and sell them hard on the dream.

Step 4. Then select only those who sell you on how much they want the dream.

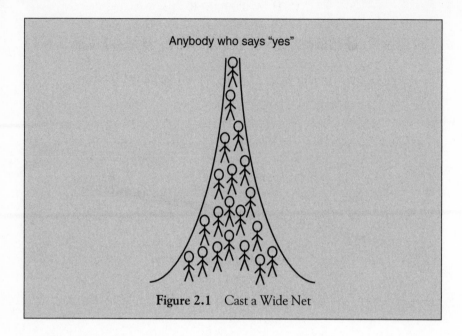

Figure 2.1   Cast a Wide Net

WHAT BUSINESS ARE WE REALLY IN?

Discovering the Niche, Honing the Dream

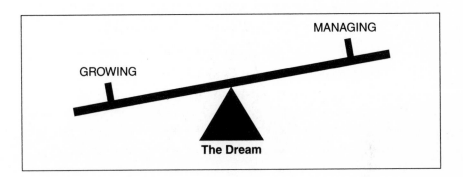

Discovery consists of looking at the same thing as everyone else and thinking something different.

— Albert Szent-Gyrgyi, Nobel prize winner

When Dave Liniger founded RE/MAX in 1973, real estate was still very much a cottage industry. There were perhaps fewer than 12 large brokers nationwide that had more than 200 agents. At the time, Liniger's former employer, Van Schaack, had more than 300 agents and was probably the best-run, most professional, and most successful firm in the country. A number of upstart firms were trying to go national with a franchising approach. These included Red Carpet Realty, founded in 1966 by Andy Yingiss in Walnut Creek, California; ERA, founded by the Jackson family in 1971; and Century 21, founded by Art Bartlett and Marsh Fisher in 1973. Most brokers, however, were small mom-and-pop outfits with only a few real estate agents, many of whom were part-timers or semi-retired.

It had been that way for much of the century. Real estate agents worked on the front lines of the American Dream, assisting families in buying their first home and working with them again as they traded up or moved else-where in search of a better life. It was a highly personal business, the agent and the family sitting across from each other at a kitchen table or a desk band discussing private concerns and hopes. As the country grew and more and more people bought homes, real estate agents could be forgiven for feeling a patriotic sense of pride about their role. It's an emotion captured, albeit grandiloquently, in the *Code of Ethics* adopted by the National As-sociation of Realtors (NAR) in 1913 and still in place today:

> Such interests impose obligations beyond those of ordinary com-merce. They impose grave social responsibility and a patriotic duty to which REALTORS® should dedicate themselves, and for which they should be diligent in preparing themselves. REALTORS®, therefore, are zealous to maintain and improve the standards of their calling and share with their fellow REALTORS® a common responsibility for its integrity and honor.

The NAR *Code of Ethics* emphasizes how radical the RE/MAX business model appeared in that traditional real estate world. The entire basis of the NAR *Code of Ethics* was "The Golden Rule": "Do unto other real estate firms what you would have them do unto you." For those who needed the rule spelled out in legal terms, almost 30 different articles and subarticles detailed the particulars. Article 24, for instance, essentially stated: "Thou shalt not solicit agents from another broker." Real estate franchising was a model that was bound to undermine that rule. But RE/MAX was the first real estate company to break the rule explicitly by asking real estate agents a simple question: "Why split your commissions with your broker? Come work with us and make 100 percent."

As RE/MAX became increasingly successful and agents moved to the red, white, and blue, many local Boards of Realtors reacted defensively and tried to throw Liniger out of their associations with claims that his organ-ization was violating Article 24. It was a harsh threat to the upstart firm, and Liniger took it very personally. He didn't have an attorney, but he sat in on the various board hearings anyway, frustrated and angry, his fuse burning down. When he was finally given the opportunity to speak, he threw down a gauntlet that would force the industry into a reluctant change. "I want you to know," he said, "that what you're doing here today is hindering free commerce. That's antitrust activity, and anybody who violates antitrust goes to jail. I didn't fight in Vietnam to listen to you tell me I can't offer your agent another job at a higher wage. I'm going to file criminal charges against you, and I refuse to participate any further in these meetings because doing so makes me a coconspirator in your price-fixing activities." And he strode out of the room.

His words were not some idle threat. The NAR and several local Boards of Realtors had recently faced antitrust actions by the federal government for price fixing commission rates. The practice had long been standard in the industry, more as a matter of understanding than conspiracy; but the possibility of criminal charges had left the leaders of various prominent real estate firms very nervous. Liniger didn't hesitate for a moment to prey on those fears, and his strategy worked. In response, the NAR eliminated Article 24. Liniger won a major industry battle without spending a dollar on an attorney. In truth, it was a dollar he didn't have.

Identifying the True Customer

As Liniger worked on honing the RE/MAX dream, he studied closely the franchising models used by Red Carpet, ERA, Century 21, and other businesses outside the real estate industry. He saw some limitations and knew he could create a competitive edge. The 100 percent commission system was the basis of that advantage, but it wasn't the critical differentiator. Liniger believed that his organization would ultimately win not because it gave agents more money, but because it gave them a chance for better lives.

Discovering that difference all came down to a simple but powerful idea. Liniger knew that RE/MAX was not in the real estate business; it was in the real estate *agent* business. Its true customer was not the home buyer in the real estate market, but the real estate agent meeting the needs of that home buyer.

The power of that nuance can't be overstated. In every industry, there comes a time when disruptive ideas, technologies, or strategies change the rules, goals, and, sometimes, even the name of the game. Strategy theorists use the term "marketing myopia" to describe a firm's limited understanding of the nature of its own business. What those theorists mean is that

firms that concentrate on what they think they do best are often blind to
the true nature of the service they provide. In the case of the real estate industry, franchising companies and brokers within that franchising system
clung stubbornly to the idea that they were in the business of buying and
selling real estate. Liniger looked beyond this narrow view and saw that
real estate agents sold real estate, but RE/MAX was there to make those
agents as successful as possible by providing them with exceptional service.

That kind of clarity can change an industry and differentiate a firm. In
the 1800s, for instance, railroad companies were among the wealthiest
businesses in the United States. The rapidly growing nation needed the
raw materials and goods that railroad companies hauled over great distances. For a time, there was simply no other alternative. Then came the
motorized vehicle, the truck, the highway system, and the airplane. With
those developments, the great railroad companies entered a long period of
decline. Although their businesses are still critical in today's economy,
they are no longer powerhouses with limitless potential.

Consider what the world might have looked like if railroad companies
had realized that they weren't in the "railroad" business, but in the "trans-
portation" business. Out of that broader yet more nuanced understanding,
a host of different strategies, approaches, and mindsets might have grown.
Imagine the B&O Railroad operating as an overnight express business like
FedEx today or Union Pacific flying a fleet of planes like United Airlines.

Some companies get it right. Those that see beyond their industry's
marketing myopia seem to manage that shift in perspective by focusing on
core competencies. Microsoft realized it was not in the computer business
but in the software business and dominated that market like a colossus.
Disney realized it wasn't in the movie or animation business but in the en-
tertainment business, building theme parks, cruise ships, and brand awareness like none other. Amazon.com realized it wasn't in the book business
but in the online distribution business, broadening beyond books to many
other products. These distinctions do not provide a competitive advantage
forever, since competitors are eventually able to imitate a winning strategy. Nevertheless, during a critical period of time, they can distinguish a
company's sense of mission from that of other firms in its industry, forcing
those firms to play copycat and catch-up, at least until the next disruptive
idea comes along.

Dave Liniger saw the real estate business very differently from the way others around him did. In his first press release, he stated that RE/MAX couldn't be all things to all people. As a result, RE/MAX would specialize in top-producing agents. This did not mean that RE/MAX was ignoring the home buyers whom other firms saw as their true customers. In fact, nothing could have been further from the truth. RE/MAX believed that by serving agents better than any other real estate company did, they would be serving home-buying customers better than any other real estate company did, too.

The idea was simple: An organization that takes care of its employees has a great customer service culture because happy, proud employees treat customers with a sense of personal responsibility. Sears, during its revitalization in the early 1980s, took this idea and made it a measurable objective through the use of employee satisfaction surveys. Basically, employee satisfaction was a leading indicator of corporate financial health because happy employees created happy customers who subsequently did even more business with the firm. Southwest Airlines was one of the first organizations to declare that the customer is not always right. This did not mean that customers were treated with disdain or taken for granted. Rather, Southwest knew that if it hired the right people and provided them with the right training, those employees would do the right thing when faced with difficult customer challenges. Not all customers would be happy with all decisions; but if employees knew that they were critical to the company's success, they would act with the empowerment and responsibility of a CEO or a founder.

Liniger assumed that the end consumer—the home buyer—would be well served if RE/MAX provided its agents with the best training and service. It was in those agents' best interest to take care of those home buyers. After all, these agents kept 100 percent of the commission. For that reason, RE/MAX had better treat those agents right. Top agents had the ability to walk out the door and change their business card as easily as they changed their suit—that was the nature of the vicious cycle of the real estate industry. Without providing that agent with great service, a firm had no way of retaining him or her and building its business.

With that in mind, Liniger did something that no broker had deliberately set out to do before: He created a business driven to figure out, on an ongoing basis, what agents really wanted and needed in order to perform better.

The first major innovation designed for top agents was "Personal Promotion." The rest of the industry taught agents to promote the company. Most companies had the money to do this, but RE/MAX always operated on a pooling system for its advertising. In that regard, Liniger was forced into the innovation of personal promotion partly by philosophy, partly by necessity. In either case, it worked. The RE/MAX message to agents was: "Promote yourself. You are the most important person in the business. Seventy percent of your business is repeat and referral. Take advantage of that and run with it by building yourself up."

To that end, RE/MAX taught agents to use the RE/MAX brand in order to benefit from the RE/MAX network but to put their own name front and center on every promotional piece. This was revolutionary, and the agents loved it. Brokers outside of RE/MAX resisted the idea fiercely because they believed it created competition for themselves from their own agents. In line with personal promotion, Liniger also encouraged agents to have their own private offices. Before then, most agents worked in bullpens. At RE/MAX, because agents were paying their own way and making more money, the attitude was different: *You are a business person. You need to promote yourself. You need a private office, not a cubicle.* A private office went along with helping the agent give customers the feeling that they were dealing with the best.

In addition, Liniger saw the value of having a personal assistant. It was all part of his time management system's approach to being a top agent. Most brokers forced agents to do everything themselves: Write your own ads, put up your own signs, take your own messages, stuff your own envelopes, fill out your own contracts. Liniger did surveys, took copious notes, and built courses on time management to squeeze maximum efficiency out of an agent's day. Why did RE/MAX care whether an agent who earned 100 percent of his or her own commissions made an extra sale every month? Because the more sales an agent made, the more successful he or she was, the better he or she felt about RE/MAX, and the more others saw the benefit of joining, too.

Liniger found, through his study, that top agents spent 20 percent of their time face-to-face with customers. The other 80 percent of their time was spent at Board of Realtor meetings, tours of new listings, sales meetings, and peripheral tasks. In Liniger's view, that other 80 percent could either be done by someone else or skipped altogether. "Why are you having a weekly sales meeting?" he asked brokers. The answer was because every office had always run weekly sales meetings. "Why not spend two hours a week providing teaching or coaching?" Liniger asked. Brokers couldn't imagine what content they could use to fill two hours of teaching or coaching, so Liniger began to supply content, showing brokers how they could serve agents like highly valued customers.

This drive to convince brokers to run a high-performing real estate office was in everyone's best interest. If agents could flip the 20/80 ratio traditional time management to 80/20, they would have four times as many sales. Everything that wasn't directly generating a sale either wasn't worth doing or could be done by an assistant. For $10 an hour, an assistant could be posting signs while the agent spent face-to-face time with the customers—driving with them to the new listing, closing on the deal, or asking them for referrals. Through much persistence, RE/MAX found that one-third of its sales associates began using personal assistants. This approach would evolve naturally into the team concept, whereby top agents mentored and trained new recruits by giving them on-the-job experience while gaining time-saving help for themselves in an ever-more-complex business.

With its focus on improving real estate agents' performance, RE/MAX also led the charge in terms of professional designations. In speeches and meetings, one on one and over drinks, Liniger encouraged RE/MAX agents to take courses, write tests, earn accreditations and to display those certifications prominently in their marketing materials. He had two motives. First, agents with more professional designations earned more money. Second, Liniger knew that professional real estate organizations were anti-RE/MAX, and he wanted to tip the balance by stocking them with his own agents.

The courses were expensive, and Liniger and his staff took all of them to understand their value for others. Quite often, Liniger found himself sitting in a crowded room while the expert teachers took time out from their lessons to mock RE/MAX and the 100 percent concept. What Liniger knew, however, was that agents who obtained professional designations

made more money. Such agents were more curious and more engaged with
the business, a sign of their potential for success. In addition, they gained
a great deal from the networking opportunities at those courses. For instance, if an agent traveled from St. Louis to Chicago to attend a course,
he would also be spending five days with a roomful of people who now
knew someone in St. Louis to whom they could refer a customer for a 20
percent fee. If the agent was smart, he took the attendance list, added it to
his Rolodex, and started building his own directory.

Top agents know that referral sources are critical to success. Most of
their business comes from other agents on their own Boards of Realtors,
because everyone on the board shares listings. But it is just as important to
know people outside of your own state to obtain leads. Doing so dramatically increases an agent's earnings. Of customers buying real estate, 20 percent are moving to another county, and most of those to another state. Top
agents know from experience that the second-best potential customer is
someone who has been referred to the agent by a repeat customer. The
third-best is a "sign call," someone who has stood physically outside the
house and wants to see what it is like inside. But the best kind of potential
customer is a referral from another agent. Why? Because that other agent
knows how much the customer has to spend, knows what the customer is
looking for, and is hand delivering that customer to another recommended
agent for a 20 percent cut of the commission. The customer flies to the
new area and is met by the agent at the plane. The customer has two days
to buy a house. The agent knows what the customer needs, and the customer does not have time to talk to five other agents. It's a can't-miss sale,
closed in a highly expedited time frame.

RE/MAX pushed professional designations for all those political and referral reasons. The agents realized the benefits in terms of increased commission income. Little by little, as RE/MAX grew in number of agents, this
focus on professional designations also helped to shift the balance of power
in various associations and to change the perception of RE/MAX within
the industry. Liniger personally pushed key agents to become presidents of
associations or of their local or state Boards of Realtors. Finally, after many
years, a RE/MAX agent became president of the National Association of
Realtors. It was a long, hard-fought journey for an organization that many
NAR members had discredited publicly and obstructed actively. But today,

RE/MAX has twice the presidential seats on local boards than the firm's per capita rate would indicate it should have. Knowing and understanding how to maneuver in the political world of industry opinion was part of the game for Liniger—one he played like a chess grand master.

One Customer at a Time

When RE/MAX was conceived in 1973, it had four agents. In mid-2004, it had just under 100,000. Almost all of those agents joined RE/MAX through a personal recruitment process. The broker or franchise owner tracks the best agents in the market, gets to know them, tries to figure out what's missing in their lives, and looks for a way to sell them on the RE/MAX dream. In other words, it is an agent-by-agent process.

Imagine building the world's largest company in a given industry one customer at a time. Recruiting top agents was not easy. To hire away the top agents in a market, a new franchise owner usually experienced something that could be best pictured this way: Say there's a brick wall with no doors or windows. You need to get to the other side of the wall, but all you have is a sledgehammer. So you lift the sledgehammer back and swing it heavily toward the wall. The wall trembles but doesn't move. It seems impossible to break through; but you believe you can, so you haul back and swing once more. A few chips fly off. You do it again, and a couple of loose bricks pop through. You keep doing it, and more bricks begin to loosen and fall. You're feeling stronger because you know only a few more whacks will be necessary. Then, with that final swing, the top bricks come tumbling down, and your hard work has paid off.

In a similar way, a new franchise owner faces a wall that can only be brought down swing by swing, agent by agent. In all likelihood, the new RE/MAX broker has a reputation in the market, knows some really good agents, and has perhaps converted his own office or firm to the RE/MAX system. But that is just the first swing of the sledgehammer. Most agents, even top-performing ones, are surprisingly anxious about change. They don't like the uncertainty or the idea of leaving their friends and colleagues. The first few agents who join are like those first few bricks that tumble in. They are probably not the top-performing agents in the region, but they are very good agents who are suffering in frustration at the constraints of the traditional system or who feel pushed out by their broker for personal reasons. Women, minorities, young agents with more ambition and less experience, and others who could be classified as mavericks, early adopters, misfits—these are the types of people who sign on first in a given area, and their success becomes the best advertisement in the world.

As these agents do better under the RE/MAX system and outperform and outearn their peers at other firms, word spreads and better-performing agents become easier to recruit. The RE/MAX franchise grows and gains a reputation in the region. Meanwhile, the RE/MAX franchise owner has been actively tracking and getting to know the top "prize" agents. Through that relationship, the RE/MAX franchise owner learns enough about the top agent to understand what he or she really wants and needs. Recruiting that top performer rocks the confidence of the other firms in the market. When the franchise owner's agents demonstrate how successfully the system works, it becomes easier to recruit more agents. It may take 5, 10, or 15 years; but the franchise owner finally builds a business that is solid and ready for more explosive growth.

A Focus on Top-Line Measures

Other real estate firms in the franchise business worried more about growth than about getting top agents. So why did RE/MAX concentrate on enlisting and growing the best? Partly, this focus was a natural extension of the 100 percent commission system. Only top agents had the confidence to operate without a safety net. But Liniger had other reasons for wanting the best agents: He had studied the incredible difference they really make to the bottom line.

The value proposition that other national franchising companies brought to a bunch of small brokers was simple: Join with us. Together, we will develop a strong regional presence. You will be able to compete with the big boys like Van Schaack. Your agents will get training and a business system, and you will get the same deal on newspaper advertising that those big boys get, and you will look bigger than they do in terms of number of agents, number of listings, and so on. What's more, you will also be part of our larger national firm. You will have access to our giant referral roster. Business will come to you, unbidden, from around the country. You will be independent, but we will be one company, across the nation, with the same stationery, the same sign colors, and the same name badges. All you have to do is wear this jacket.

The jackets were a source of some amusement among those in the industry who didn't have to wear them. At Red Carpet, the jackets were red. At Century 21, they were gold. At ERA, they were blue. When the RE/MAX leadership team, with its strong anti-authority, red-white-and-blue spirit, saw a herd of jackets at industry conventions, one of them would inevitably call out: "The red coats are coming! The red coats are coming!" RE/MAX even ran an ad, more cheeky than usual, showing a male real estate agent in a sharp tailored suit and a female real estate agent in a luxurious fur coat with the suit jacket and the fur coat bearing the slogan: "These are *our* jackets."

The implication was blunt. The other franchise firms saw the distinctive jackets as a way of contributing to a strong visible brand. RE/MAX, with its focus on what top agents really wanted and needed, saw the jackets as a restrictive uniform that didn't convey the proper dignity and respect to people who were very talented and earned a lot of money. Indeed, industry gossip mocked the jackets with claims that they were supplied to those agents because so many were unable to afford professional attire on their own.

The smaller brokers who joined a larger regional franchise like Century 21 or Red Carpet were looking for strength and safety in numbers. But how much were their agents contributing to the overall business? Liniger studied market listings and sales data hoping to find the answers to some key questions: How many listings does the average agent have? How many average agents does a broker need to have as many listings as one of the big players like Van Schaack? His examination of those numbers reinforced the 80/20 rule. At that time, 20 percent of the agents in the real estate industry were making 80 percent of the sales. Would the heft of a national brand improve productivity for the bottom 80 percent? Liniger didn't think so. Over the years, he watched those numbers to see whether his theory would bear out. In his analysis, the bottom 80 percent continued to perform the way it always had even when working for a national franchise; and the top agents continued to outproduce everyone else and to generate the vast majority of sales.

To Liniger, it was a no-brainer. A large franchising network would be unstoppable if, like a Van Schaack, it focused on top agents and gave them the best training and service. From that 20 percent pool, Liniger knew that there were many agents who would not join RE/MAX for a number of reasons. Some were married or related to their broker. Some worked for the best firm in a given market and would be reluctant recruits. Some were arrogant or unethical and would not fit the RE/MAX brand or would do RE/MAX more harm than good. By eliminating those folks, roughly speaking, the overall goal for RE/MAX should be to get half of the top 20 percent to sign on. By reaching that 10 percent mark, Liniger believed that RE/MAX would obtain 30 percent to 40 percent market share because of the higher productivity of those agents. RE/MAX even wrote that objective into its franchising agreements. The battle to become the largest real estate network in the world would be won, city by city, by obtaining half of the top 20 percent of agents and getting 30 percent to 40 percent market share. It was a clear, measurable, top-line objective that everyone in the system could follow. To us, it's evidence that it is not enough to have a dream; an organization also needs a growth formula that is measurable.

Since the mid-1990s, as the professionalization of agents has dramatically improved, RE/MAX has broadened its range to concentrate on recruiting half of the top 30 percent of agents in the belief that doing so will still give it approximately 40 percent market share. In regions where this has occurred, the numbers hold out. In Canada, which has been a powerhouse for RE/MAX, 18 percent of all the Canadian real estate agents are part of RE/MAX, and RE/MAX has 38 percent market share. In the United States, RE/MAX currently has 7.5 percent of all agents and 16 percent market share. In the future, when RE/MAX reaches 15 percent of all U.S.-based agents, it believes that fully 40 percent of the multi-billion-dollar U.S. real estate industry will be brokered by RE/MAX agents. The same idea holds true in all other markets around the world.

If those metrics seem simple and compelling to track, we agree. Following them provides the kind of interest that an avid baseball fan feels watching a pennant race. Dave Liniger's desk is large, empty, and clean. On the twentieth day of every month, a report gets placed on that clean desk. In truth, the report no longer has to arrive on the twentieth—that's just a holdover from the early, noncomputerized days when it took a few weeks to organize and record the data by hand—but Liniger, a person of discipline and habit, still likes to get it on the twentieth. In the report are all the statistics he needs to evaluate how well RE/MAX is doing. The data comes in simple columns: Number of Agents, Percentage of Total, Number Over/Under 15 Percent Objective. A grade school student could walk in, look at the charts, and evaluate accurately how far the business has to go to achieve its goals all over the world. Brokers in every region know the target. This is their battle cry. They have a goal in mind and chase it like a hungry wild-card team, looking for that playoff berth, ticking off the magic number as it draws closer. Each agent who joins knows that he or she is contributing to getting closer to that goal. One agent coming from a top firm means one less agent for that firm and one more for RE/MAX—the sort of double whammy that parallels winning a game against a team in your own division. The battle cry for 15 percent feeds the emotion and the energy of the chase.

Of course, each region is made up of many smaller sales offices, and it is the performance of those offices that makes up the overall region's performance. So RE/MAX breaks things down and tracks each office to watch its agent growth. Over the year, the regional director can monitor whether the number of agents is increasing slowly or rapidly. If for some reason the number is down, one of the Franchise Development Consultants (FDC) at RE/MAX hits the road to see what's going on. Whatever problems the office is experiencing become RE/MAX problems, and the FDC helps solve them.

For its first 20 years, RE/MAX focused only on such top-line measures. Remarkably, no one in the organization cared about financial statements because Liniger believed it was critical to strive for the long-term RE/MAX objective rather than for short-term gains. It's difficult to imagine this mindset being acceptable in a public company today, an indictment, perhaps, of our current system and the way it may actually hamper organic growth. RE/MAX has grown every single month for its 30-odd years of existence, never experiencing a single month of negative growth.

Industry Evolutions and Dead Ends

Despite its gathering momentum, RE/MAX wasn't on many people's radar screens for much of its early existence, at least until 1983. It was simply too radical and too small to be considered a threat to the industry players. In the Colorado area, for instance, where RE/MAX achieved most of its early growth, it was little more than a small fly in the ointment to Van Schaack. Nevertheless, even as RE/MAX was exerting pressure for change from inside the industry, economic circumstances were creating pressure from outside it, too.

In the late 1970s, the U.S. real estate industry was going through hell, and the economics of buying a home were in the midst of radical change. Inflation was out of control. Interest rates, at their peak, had reached an unbelievable 18 percent. Agents who had found it relatively easy to sell a home during good economic times were finding it next to impossible now. Even top agents were having a tough time making ends meet. And RE/MAX was not immune to the crush. As agents at franchises all around the country stopped paying their monthly fees, franchises stopped paying RE/MAX. The business was surviving on dream vapors and a lot of timely help from Canada, which escaped the worst of the stagflation mess. But the tidal wave of difficulty hit all firms hard, and only the best would survive.

The American Dream was changing, too. Once upon a time, families bought a home and dutifully paid off their mortgage over the course of 30 years. In the early 1980s, families began buying homes they couldn't afford in the conventional sense because the cost of the home was becoming less important than its increased value. In other words, inflation was making it more appealing to buy today what you once thought you could not afford to buy until tomorrow. As Joseph Nocera, editor of *Fortune* magazine, noted in his book, *A Piece of the Action: How the Middle Class Joined the Money Class* (Simon & Schuster, 1995):

> That houses went up in price was a direct by-product of inflation. . . . That people began thinking about their homes in this fundamentally new way was a direct by-product of the fact that they were rising in value. People no longer bought a house so much as they "invested" in one; the down payment was their "equity stake." And after four or five years, by which time their investment had doubled in value, they might well be moved to treat it like any other investment—by engaging in some profit taking and plunging the capital gains into a more expensive investment—i.e., another house. (pp. 188–189)

For the first time, real estate prices and interest rates became the hot topic at backyard barbeques, golf courses, and business meetings. Perhaps, for this very reason, it's not surprising that when companies outside the real estate industry finally became interested in owning a piece of the action, the first firms to do so were from the financial services industry.

Merrill Lynch was a different kind of financial services company, aggressively retail, focused on finding other, previously untapped streams of revenue from related services, "bullish on America." Donald Regan, later President Ronald Reagan's chief of staff, had a radical new vision in which Merrill functioned more like a superbank than a brokerage house. Real estate would be just one more doorway for customers to enter that bank. With that in mind, by 1978, Merrill began buying prominent real estate firms all around the country in an attempt to assemble an empire.

Century 21 had gone public by this time. It took the opportunity to sell the company to a larger conglomerate in 1981. Transworld Corp., owner of Trans World Airlines and the Hilton Hotels, among many other diverse holdings, was the buyer. Century 21 was seen by Transworld as one more piece of its giant jigsaw puzzle. While it did not influence Century 21's operating strategy, it did want to tap into its customer base. The idea was simple: Customers would buy their airline tickets, pay for their rental cars and hotel stays, and buy their homes through Transworld.

Sears also entered the game in 1981. As the nation's largest retailer, Sears had a new vision to include financial services among its offerings. Sears stores were already drawing customers to buy garden hoses, carpets, and paint. Why not also provide them a place to shop for their homes, home insurance, and home mortgages? As with Transworld, it was a move toward vertical integration and synergy that made sense on paper but that did not necessarily translate well in the real world. Nevertheless, Sears purchased a regional powerhouse named Coldwell Banker and gave it instant national heft.

Whoever controls the agent controls the customer—that was the thinking. But it didn't work out that way. True, in the lucrative business of corporate relocations, big players like Sears and Merrill had a built-in advantage—they knew and understood large corporate customers very well. But when it came to the retail level, the residential real estate agent was not so easy to influence. It may have been in the corporate parent's best interest for an agent to steer a customer that way for insurance, mortgage, tax accounting, or brokerage needs; but that agent also had a brother-in-law who sold insurance, a personal accountant who gave him NHL hockey tickets, and a banker who referred people his way on a regular basis. Real estate was a local business with a complex web of quid pro quo relationships. Corporate overseers could not divert or channel that network as easily as they had expected.

Transworld sold Century 21 to Metropolitan Life Insurance Company. Met Life had a great idea. Since it already had a strong brand name in insurance, it would give every Century 21 agent an insurance license and help him or her make more money selling both real estate and insurance. But it didn't work out.

Merrill Lynch decided to get out of the real estate business and sold their 450 or so offices to Prudential in 1989, which had been slowly building its own empire on the Merrill model. This was no easy meal to swallow, let alone digest, however. Prudential realized that its exclusive franchise agreements and Merrill's exclusive franchise agreements were often in direct, competitive conflict with one another. It would take years, and hundreds of millions of dollars, to work out the solutions and compromises.

Meanwhile, by 1993, RE/MAX became the number-one real estate network in the country, in terms of amount of real estate sold. Moreover, it achieved that goal not through acquisitions but through an agent-by-agent focus on growth. To RE/MAX, the key to success hinged on the unique way the organization viewed its relationships with agents. At most firms, the agents were employees who worked for the broker. At RE/MAX the broker worked for the agents.

Little by little, the compelling nature of the 100 percent idea started to impact everyone in the industry, and nearly every firm saw its commission split gradually migrate toward the RE/MAX end of the spectrum. RE/MAX, too, began to experiment with variations on 100 percent. Still, this strategy convergence—other firms adopting a 70/30 or 80/20 model, RE/MAX trying 95/5—is typical of maturing industries and illustrates a larger point. Strategies can be mimicked, business plans can be copied, but core competencies are differentiators. The fact that other firms eased toward the RE/MAX side of the spectrum and still saw RE/MAX outpace them in growth was evidence that the RE/MAX focus on the agent as customer really made a difference.

As these economics played out, they hastened the consolidation of the industry. In competing with the big local players at one extreme and the RE/MAX maximum commission system on the other, small firms lost their best agents, disappeared completely, or became scooped up in the nets of larger companies. Insiders had seen this consolidation coming since 1978 and predicted that by 1983, 80 percent of the industry would be dominated by two or three major players. In fact, it would take 20 years longer than expected, and the ratio of agents working for large firms versus those working for small firms would not exceed 50 percent. Real estate stayed stubbornly local despite all the pressures. But the dominance of the national players did indeed increase, little by little, every year. Hospitality Franchise Systems (HFS) emerged as a dominant company by purchasing three brands—Coldwell Banker, Century 21, and ERA—and became Cendant. (See Table 3.1.)

Table 3.1   The Evolution of Real Estate Networks

Year	Chronology of Events
1906	Coldwell Banker founded by Colbert Coldwell.
1971	ERA founded by Jackson family.
1973	RE/MAX founded by Dave Liniger and Gail Main.
1973	Century 21 founded by Art Bartlett and Marsh Fisher.
1977	TICOR Relocation purchased by Merrill Lynch.
1979	Better Homes & Gardens Real Estate Division founded by Meredith Corp. (publisher of *Better Homes and Gardens* magazine).
1979	Merrill Lynch founded real estate division.
1980	ERA sold to Commercial Credit Corp. (subsidiary of Control Data).
1981	Century 21 sold to Transworld Corp. (owner of Trans World Airlines, Canteen Corp., and Hilton Hotels).
1981	Coldwell Banker sold to Sears Financial.
1985	Century 21 sold to Metropolitan Life Insurance.
1986	ERA sold to EMB Capital (Condo Developers controlled by Gouletis family).
1987	Prudential formed real estate division.
1988	Prudential sold first franchise.
1989	Merrill Lynch relocation and real estate division sold to Prudential.
1992	Coldwell Banker sold to Fremont Group (Bechtel family).
1995	Century 21 sold to Hospitality Franchise Systems (HFS).
1995	ERA sold to Richard L.S. (wholly owned by Dick Schlott).
1996	ERA sold to HFS.
1996	Coldwell Banker sold to HFS.
1997	HFS became Cendant.
1998	Better Homes & Gardens sold to GMAC Home Services.

In contrast, the RE/MAX long-term strategy of recruiting and developing top agents paid off. Its productivity per agent far exceeded the industry average and kept it at number one in terms of real estate sold, even as its momentum in agent recruitment continued to build.

After 30 years of agent-by-agent growth, the shakeout in the real estate industry left RE/MAX exactly where it had always planned on being: as the number-one real estate brand. Gail Liniger said, "I always thought it should have happened a lot sooner." But few outsiders could have imagined it happening as rapidly and dramatically as it did. Walk by your neighborhood hardware store or coffee shop, imagine what it would take to become a global corporation like Home Depot or Starbucks one day, and you might get a sense of the journey that RE/MAX managed.

Strategic Moves

Know your customer.

Top-line growth is a mindset. Moreover, it is a strategy and a game plan. RE/MAX focused on growing the business around the dream and kept vigilant efforts aimed at the goal line. RE/MAX adopted its model to the industry and became innovative by changing the rules so that it could have a clear line of sight to unlimited top-line growth. In fact, changing the rules (e.g., putting the agent first) created competitive advantage.

- Growth is neither impossible nor inevitable. It is possible through an unrelenting focus on the dream, a strong leadership team, and a new model constructed without concern for convention or rules. (pp. 52–53)
- Know what business you are really in. Winning businesses are outside of the traditional model. What is your distinct difference? (p. 53)
- Don't allow meaningless tradition or "how it's always been done" to stand in the way of how you know it should be done. (p. 53)
- Firms that concentrate on what they think they do best are often blind to the true nature of the service they provide. (p. 54)

- A company that treats its employees like customers develops a great customer service culture. Such a company must figure out, on an ongoing basis, what its people really want and need in order to perform better. (p. 55)

- RE/MAX focused on getting top people before growth because it knew that it was the people that affected the bottom line. (p. 60)

- In order to grow, RE/MAX set out a clear, measurable, top-line objective that everyone in the organization could follow. (p. 63)

- Consistent growth happens one employee and one customer at a time. (p. 59)

- Give your people personal credit under your brand—they will thank you for it with effort. (p. 56)

- Teach your people how to manage their time and personal resources more effectively, and your company's growth will be amplified as well. (p. 57)

- Training and teaching your people is a slow investment on the front end that pays off many times over in the long run. (pp. 57–58)

- Know and understand how to maneuver in the political world of industry opinion. Industry politics is the first battlefield for the customer's support. (pp. 58–59)

| Lesson |

Leaders dare to ask the hard questions.

Putting leadership sights on growth changes the dynamics of how leaders approach a business. In order to change the rules, it requires serious study and knowing the business that you are in. This is what some experts would refer to as the cycle of innovation. We interpret this as a systems thinking exercise with three steps, an exercise that works for all organizations, regardless of industry. (See Figure 3.1.)

Step 1. Know the dynamics of your business and list the key rules and processes.

Step 2. Identify key assumptions underlying the rules and processes.

Step 3. Come up with better solutions that change the assumptions.

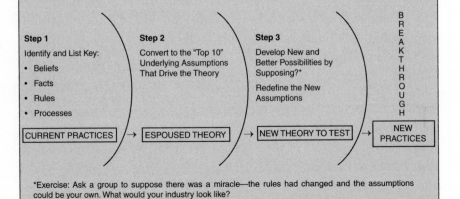

*Exercise: Ask a group to suppose there was a miracle—the rules had changed and the assumptions could be your own. What would your industry look like?

Figure 3.1   Innovation Flow: How to Get to New and Better

CHAPTER 4

ONE LOG MAKES A LOUSY FIRE

Building the Brand, Spreading the Dream

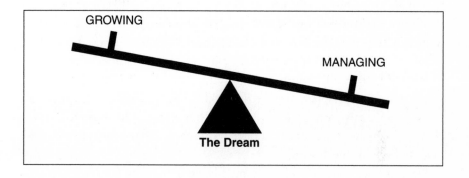

Teamwork is the ability to work together toward a common vision. The ability to direct individual accomplishments toward organizational objectives. It is the fuel that allows common people to attain uncommon results.

—Andrew Carnegie

The proposal was to sell RE/MAX its signs. If things worked out, Don and Glenda Hachenberger's company might become the unofficial supplier for the young real estate firm. Although RE/MAX wasn't much of a factor in the overall industry, it was a good business opportunity, and Hachenberger took it seriously. He visited RE/MAX with some samples, some numbers, and a plan.

Hachenberger was an entrepreneur through and through. He'd been a top salesman in a large company; and although he had a young family, he couldn't control the urge to be in business for himself. He and Glenda got their start when they met a couple looking to sell an advertising company. The business had 130 salespeople in 17 western states and specialized in promotional items—everything from pencils, calendars, and corporate gifts to real estate signs. The Hachenbergers bought the company in the early 1970s, and things went well, with Don and Glenda both managing the company and sharing the load. A few years later, Louis Lowe, a salesman they'd hired in Kansas City, gave them a call. Lowe had been working Dennis Curtin's RE/MAX office in Kansas and a smaller office in Lincoln, Nebraska, providing them with real estate signs. In the process, he had caught the RE/MAX fever, the symptoms of which included a surprisingly strong enthusiasm for a freewheeling idea and a sense that RE/MAX was bound for big things. Lowe knew the real catch would be to make a deal with the corporate headquarters in Denver. "I think you ought to give them a call some time and see if we can get some business from them," Lowe told Don. So Hachenberger started looking into things himself.

Glenda's sister happened to be dating a RE/MAX agent. The firm then had 15 offices in Denver and a few in other states. Although RE/MAX hadn't yet made much of an impact nationwide, that agent assured the Hachenbergers that it would.

Hachenberger knew a fellow named Dave Whitman, who had actually worked with Liniger, and checked in with him. Whitman, using some colorful expressions, described Liniger as a force to be reckoned with. "You'll know what I mean when you meet him," he said to Hachenberger with a laugh, only upping the intrigue.

The office in Denver was small but busy. Hachenberger met Dave Liniger and Gail Main and was impressed by what they had going, if a little bit amused by the level of enthusiasm shared by everyone working for them. Liniger was as confident as Hachenberger had been warned, but in a good way, positive and outgoing, filled with bravado and certainty. He had a vision; and, man, was he selling it. The people around him walked and talked like the followers of some brand-new religion; they were true believers working flat out on a mission to revolutionize the real estate world.

Hachenberger's interest was building, but it was still intellectual more than emotional. To his entrepreneur's brain, the 100 percent commission concept was a revelation. He loved it and wished he could see a way to apply it to his own business. He had the same problem—20 percent of his salespeople were doing 80 percent of the work. But the economics were different for the kinds of products that advertising and promotion sales offered. With an industry like real estate, however, the sky was the limit. There was only one catch: Hachenberger could see why 100 percent commission was good for the agent and good for RE/MAX; but he couldn't see how the broker would make big money, and the broker, to him, was key. Still, this was a formula and a culture that was going places—you could tell.

Hachenberger and Lowe brought their sign samples and business proposal to Liniger and his team. The meeting was friendly, the discussions relaxed. The numbers seemed to work for the RE/MAX people. They didn't argue and push on the edges like some small operations did with vendors. Liniger's only question had to do with payments. "Can we have an open account?" he asked. It wasn't a big deal to Hachenberger, as long as he got paid within 30 days. "Why not?" he said, and they shook hands on the deal.

Hitching On

He didn't know it, but Liniger had been awfully eager to sign that deal. In fact, RE/MAX was at loose ends. All of their other suppliers had just cut them off because RE/MAX couldn't keep up with the bill payments. Liniger's casual manner had been all poker face, nothing in his hands, no money to back up his bet, just a projected confidence that things were going forward anyway and that anyone who signed on was getting in on a good deal. Not all vendors would have taken kindly to learning about those bad accounts, but it didn't matter to Hachenberger by the time he found out. Looking back, his timing couldn't have been better. He had just stepped in as supplier to an organization that was going to grow like crazy. Even though there were some rough edges to the young renegades running the show and they didn't have much of a sense about marketing, Hachenberger felt those entrepreneurial juices flowing as soon as he met them.

The Hachenbergers' lives would never be the same. Glenda went with Don to the first RE/MAX convention in Las Vegas in 1976. They were the only suppliers; no other company had bothered to come. They set up their booth with some samples and a bunch of photocopies of their price list for real estate signs. Don had been telling Glenda about Dave Liniger for some time, what a dynamic guy he was, how much vision he had; and Glenda was eager to meet the great man. She didn't expect to see a short, square-shouldered guy with long hair and a mustache, wearing a brown business suit and—of all things—sandals. Liniger talked a good game, she could see that; but Glenda couldn't get her mind off those sandals. It turned out that Liniger was wearing them because he'd just had foot surgery; he just never thought about how odd it would seem to others.

While Don was attracted to Dave Liniger's inspirational force and drive, Glenda found the solidity of Gail Main and Daryl Jesperson more appealing. With her Southern Baptist upbringing, she was feeling around for a solid foundation. She felt uneasy about Liniger and his hard-charging, hard-living ways. To Glenda, Gail Main and Daryl Jesperson were the rocks who assured her that there was something steady and good behind all the RE/MAX rough energy and bravado. Looking at Gail, she saw a smart, kind, beautiful woman who was well grounded and as capable as any business executive she'd ever met and who believed in RE/MAX with the same intense confidence and certainty as all those riverboat gamblers. Glenda liked and trusted Gail immediately. There was just something about her that made you feel good.

The women's friendship would grow strong over the next few years, and Glenda would need it, as the adventure was about to begin. Liniger liked what he saw in Hachenberger, a smart marketing mind and a mature businessman—someone who understood the retail nature of branding, advertising, and sales and wasn't afraid to take a chance and go for the gold. He was the kind of prince Liniger liked having around. So he started working on him, hoping to get him to loosen his grip on his own business and throw in with RE/MAX. "Hack, you've got to get into this thing now," he said to him after one of their meetings. "We need your talents. One of these days we're going to have ten thousand agents. We're going to be flying in jet planes and hopping and bopping all over the country. Man, you don't want to miss out."

It was a hell of a picture. Ten thousand agents. Hachenberger couldn't stop thinking about that number. That meant an organization 15 times the size of the one Liniger was running now. Out of most people's mouths, Hachenberger would have considered it just talk; but when Liniger said it, you could see the promised land as though he had pulled back a curtain and let you in on the view.

The RE/MAX account became the best part of Hachenberger's business.

Aside from a few other good clients, Hachenberger wouldn't mind letting go of the rest. So Hachenberger cooked up a scheme to sell the bulk of his business and keep the part that dealt with RE/MAX. Liniger was all for it. Glenda would run it. For their first new employee, they hired a graphic artist named Bob Brown, a ponytail-wearing hippie with a gift for words and visuals, who would end up being executive director of corporate image for RE/MAX years down the line. What would they call the new company? Brown did some research and suggested the name "Special Effects." It was 1977, *Star Wars* was the big hit, and everyone liked the idea. Don started in the RE/MAX marketing department as employee number eight, with a desk in the hallway outside Gail Main's office.

It was a big change, and Hachenberger was eager to start a new chapter in his life. He had all kinds of ideas for how to sell this RE/MAX thing. Glenda was just as ready to take over the management of Special Effects. She had a few misgivings, all related to the intensity of the work environment, the hours on the road, the hard-partying ways. But she knew how energized Don was by the opportunities and saw RE/MAX as an organization with balance, more serious and grounded behind the scenes than you might know from its relentless zeal. Maybe that put her in the right frame of mind when Liniger called their house on the Sunday morning before Don was to start, warning them not to believe a word that had been written about him on the front page of the *Rocky Mountain News*. They didn't get the paper yet; so, of course, she had to run out and buy herself a copy. It was not, to put it mildly, a very kind article; and it was a tough welcome to their new life. RE/MAX was going bankrupt, the headlines said, although Liniger swore it wasn't true. She could only laugh. It was a bit like seeing Dave Liniger in long hair, a suit, and sandals—except this time in black-and-white print.

Foot Soldiers

They called it the Crack Marketing Team and hatched a plan of attack that would be repeated over and over in cities all across the country. Hachenberger was the field colonel. There were seven other commandos in the group, and Liniger was the four-star general who flew in from headquarters to survey the battlegrounds and review the troops. The goal was to sell franchises—lots of them—and to spread the RE/MAX revolution. The tactic was guerilla warfare.

The first target was Cincinnati. They flew in on a Sunday and doubled up in rooms at a cheap hotel called "The Carousel." The initial mission would last a week. They met for breakfast on Monday morning, game faces tense, eager to get into the action. Hachenberger took a map, drew lines across it, then cut the map into eight pieces, and gave each commando his territory. Everyone had his own rental car. They left the restaurant and headed off in eight different directions, planning to drive down every street in the city, looking for real estate companies.

The people in those real estate offices had no idea what was going on when a member of the Crack Marketing Team walked through their door. No one had ever walked into a real estate office and solicited agents before. Usually, the only visitors were home buyers, people who thought they might like to become an agent, or bill collectors. These guys were carrying pamphlets as though pushing religion. The pamphlet was titled "Changing Trends in the Real Estate Industry," and the messengers were inviting those who were interested to attend a Thursday-night seminar in order to find out exactly what those changing trends would mean for their business.

Some people were amused. Some were interested. Some threw the Crack Marketing Team member out of their office. On Thursday, Dave Liniger flew into town to give the seminar. That first week, the team had managed to round up about 30 interested, if slightly bewildered, attendees. They'd all registered at the front desk, leaving a business card behind, and had gone in to find a seat. Liniger must have struck a curious figure as he strode to the front, took his position next to the podium, and began his slide show. He talked about how real estate boards were formed and what the Multiple Listing Service did. Then he discussed regional companies and the rise of the national franchises. It was interesting stuff, an eagle's eye view of changes these real estate people could feel occurring all around them. Liniger was an entertaining speaker, charismatic, insightful. While the attendees contemplated the impact of those trends on their own lives, Liniger changed tack. The 100 percent commission concept was the next major force in real estate, he said. He explained how it worked, because hardly anyone had ever heard of it before, and answered some questions. Then he described RE/MAX and how it worked. A national franchise. An *everybody wins* culture. A 100 percent system. At the end of two hours, just before the cocktail party, Liniger announced that he had a bunch of RE/MAX people with him in the room to answer any other questions anyone had. They were here to sell franchises; and if anyone wanted to find out more, he'd be eager to talk.

Friday morning, Liniger flew back to Denver, and the Crack Marketing Team met for breakfast, this time to split up the business cards and go after prospects. They made appointments when possible, in or out of the office, or sometimes just showed up at the door. Some of those prospects had already had enough of the RE/MAX nut cases from Denver and refused to talk further. Others had thought about it overnight and were interested to learn more. In those days, you could buy airline tickets in bulk batches. Each member of Crack had two tickets to Denver in his pocket, ready to hand over to the two best prospects he could find. The only way you could close someone on a deal for a new franchise was to somehow get them to Denver to see how good it really was. You wouldn't believe it if you didn't see it. A half dozen agreed to fly to Denver the following week and do just that.

Three weeks later, the Crack Marketing Team hit Cincinnati again. This time, the city was ready for them. Brokers from competing offices had told each other stories about a strange group from Denver descending on the town. They warned everyone they knew to stay away from some seminar called "Changing Trends in the Real Estate Industry." Only eight people were interested enough to come to the Thursday-night seminar. But those eight were a bit more intrigued than the 30 had been three weeks before. The Crack Marketing Team had a feeling that they were beginning to make inroads. Within five months, they sold 15 franchises in the city.

Pittsburgh was next, then Toledo. The work was door-to-door, day after day. They invented new and better strategies along the way, trying anything that made sense, repeating what worked. They created mass mailings. There was a red brochure. There was a blue brochure. Ten thousand pieces of direct mail would reliably net 20 or 30 leads. They followed up those leads with calls, visits, more meetings, and those free tickets to Denver. And they sold a ton of franchises.

It was retail marketing at its most down and dirty: long weeks on the road, long days back at the office, a constant selling of the RE/MAX dream, signing up anybody who said "yes," explaining to them what business they were really in. Every time Dave Liniger got up before a roomful of people to teach the RE/MAX concept, he came alive and energized the audience. The Crack Marketing Team knew every single word by heart, and they'd heard it a thousand times before. But as Liniger said, "It's a broken record to us, but it's opening night on Broadway to them." The raised eyebrows, the laughs, the eager questions—it was hard and draining, but it was a hell of a lot of fun.

Most important, the team was starting to see something amazing happen. The dream—franchise by franchise, agent by agent, sign by sign—was beginning to spread.

Why Networks Work

It all came down to a simple truth about what it really took to build a great organization. As Sid Syvertson would later put it, "One log makes a lousy fire."

Syvertson was the biggest win RE/MAX had achieved to date. In partnership with Steve Haselton, Syvertson ran a successful, leading-edge firm in California. Named Spring Realty, it was considered one of the best in the country. Its business model was already quite close to a franchise approach in the way it compensated and empowered office managers. But Spring Realty knew that if it wanted to really grow, it would have to take the leap and become a pure franchise network.

Syvertson and Haselton kept close tabs on their best competitors, and they already had a thick file labeled "RE/MAX." When they asked around to find out more about the firm from Denver, they heard some pretty negative comments. The RE/MAX idea was "dangerous," people said. RE/MAX had an incredible ability to capture the more independent, professional, mature sales associate with an established client base, leaving other firms to scramble over entry-level agents. *What's so wrong with that?* Syvertson thought. He and Haselton already prided themselves on the quality and professionalism of their agents. The 100 percent idea made a lot of sense. They decided to look into the RE/MAX possibility more closely.

Syvertson called Liniger in Canada and told him that he wanted to buy the rights to California. Liniger's response was typical. "Who the hell are you?" he asked. Syvertson suggested that Liniger take some time to think about it and get back to him. When Liniger called Syvertson the next day, it was obvious he'd done his homework. "Are you the guy who runs Spring Realty?" "Correct," Syvertson answered. "The Spring Realty Company that is considered one of the Dirty Dozen in Real Estate?" "That's me," Syvertson said. Liniger laughed. "Well, we're having a broker owner meeting in Canada right now. Why don't you and your business partner fly up and come see what we're all about." Syvertson and Haselton flew up to Toronto and were very impressed by the professional group that was gathering there.

Syvertson and Haselton bought California shortly thereafter. RE/MAX hadn't done any sizable conversions before, and suddenly they were faced with transitioning a group of offices with almost a thousand agents. But Syvertson and Haselton were well prepared. Their managers were growth-minded businesspeople. Their agents were high quality. Syvertson and Haselton were eager to turn their attention to building a network, selling more franchises, and providing better services for those franchises. They never looked back.

Syvertson and Haselton understood what Liniger was up to with his strategy of intensifying the presence of the RE/MAX brand in a given market by maximizing the number of agents and franchises. Most brokers and agents were against it. They feared the competition with each other because they couldn't see the bigger picture. Liniger knew that creating overwhelming market presence (OMP) would benefit all agents and franchises together. He just needed a way to explain it.

The term Liniger came up with was Premiere Market Presence (PMP). There were five aspects to PMP: (1) market share, (2) brand name awareness, (3) customer satisfaction, (4) quality associates, and (5) community service (see Figures 4.1 and 4.2). Most agents and franchise owners had trouble with the idea of market share. They didn't like rubbing shoulders with other RE/MAX agents and brokers. In his first few years, Liniger had sold franchises with this sensibility in mind, giving brokers large, exclusive regions that minimized competition from RE/MAX itself. But Liniger could prove that the more RE/MAX agents there were in a given area, the higher were the average earnings of each agent. The benefits were expo-

Note: In a service business, best people create brand through RER (relevance, experience, and recognition), which, combined with consistent, effective advertising, gives you overwhelming market present (OMP).

Figure 4.1   RER: Service Company Branding Strategy

nential. In a new area, where there were few RE/MAX agents, selling real estate and recruiting new agents under the RE/MAX brand was a struggle. In areas where PMP had occurred, RE/MAX agents got 70 percent of their business from referrals and repeats and benefited from extensive brand name awareness. Every RE/MAX listing, "For Sale" sign, promotional brochure, billboard, or sponsored community event was an advertisement for every other RE/MAX agent in that system. The more RE/MAX agents and franchises there were, the more everyone benefited.

Liniger had seen the kind of mistakes that Realty Executives, the original 100 percent concept company, made in creating exclusive franchise territories; and he did not want to fall into the same trap. It all came down to the essence of what made franchising worthwhile. Franchises are at-

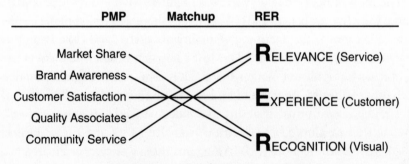

Figure 4.2   PMP Matchup with RER

tractive vehicles for businesspeople because they provide the power of a larger brand, a unique product or service, a higher-level training capability, and group purchasing. Realty Executives had sold exclusive rights to isolated cities out of fear of internal competition, but in the process they had diminished the power of franchising. In the same city where Realty Executives had one franchise and 12 agents, RE/MAX would sell 30 franchises. It didn't matter if those franchises were in the same neighborhood or even on the same block. Starting with no agents at each of those franchises, at the end of the year, each of them could reasonably be expected to have 10 agents in total, providing the RE/MAX brand with 300 agents in the city. Meanwhile, the single Realty Executives franchise had perhaps tripled its agent total to 36. There was no way Realty Executives could compete. RE/MAX would have 10 times the listings, 10 times the brand awareness, and 10 times the market presence. In addition, the RE/MAX group of franchises would have greatly increased its access to bulk purchasing of advertising; it would be offering the same unique products and services (software, computer technology, office space, training facilities) but at a much lower cost per person; and it would be able to afford more and better training, not only within the region but throughout the whole nation. At the end of the year, RE/MAX agents would be better served and better trained at a lower cost per agent; and the RE/MAX brand would have achieved much higher top-of-mind awareness among consumers. That gap would only grow exponentially the following year. By expanding RE/MAX into each new market with the Premiere Market Presence strategy, the network would go through the same experience everywhere in the world—struggle, grow incrementally, create some big wins, feel the momentum forming, tip the balance, grow exponentially.

Nevertheless, Liniger found it difficult to convince people intellectually what he knew in his gut. Naturally enough, every individual franchise owner and agent was worried about his or her own situation first and foremost and had a hard time seeing the direct relevance of Liniger's statistics. Liniger was chewing that problem out loud with a group of brokers and RE/MAX leaders one night during a weekend trip to Lake Apache in Arizona. They had played hard during the day, eaten a good barbecue, and drunk a lot in the evening, enjoying each other's company. Finally, the night was getting late and most had turned in. The few who remained up were sitting around the campfire, roasting empty wine bottles, watching them melt. Out of nowhere, Sid Syvertson looked up at Liniger and said. "Dave, one log makes a lousy fire." Liniger, sensing something there more than just talk, asked him what he meant. "That's the meaning of RE/MAX," Syvertson continued. "You have one log, you try to light it, you can't get it to really burn. It just smolders. You take ten logs, add some kindling, light it with a single match, and you get a terrific bonfire. It does something. You're creating one hundred thousand burning logs, Dave. And that's unstoppable."

Liniger nodded. That was it. That was exactly what he was trying to do. It was easy to understand when it was put that way. One log makes a lousy fire. That was the RE/MAX strategy, and the payoff was a bonfire you could sit back and get warmed by and feel proud about. Liniger contemplated this idea for hours, watching the fire burn, until he finally turned in that night.

Everyone Benefits

Getting to the bonfire point, however, was about finding those logs and kindling and nurturing the flames, building the fire bit by bit. It wasn't easy, starting from nothing. It took incredible diligence, patience, stamina, and a willingness to build slow.

The cornerstone of RE/MAX was—and still is—this slow, steady buildup. From the beginning, Liniger knew he couldn't compete with the big powerful firms. The money that other firms had was limitless; and there were always other, more powerful companies entering the fray, snatching up competitors, pumping money into their systems, willing to spend whatever it took to establish brand name awareness. The only competitive advantage RE/MAX had was its *everybody wins* principle. By making the broker rich and successful and by giving agents the freedom to promote themselves and to build their own careers like a business, RE/MAX was giving away the credit and gaining more logs for its fire in return.

In comparison, most large companies had a subservient culture, even the franchising companies. The head office wanted the company to be all powerful and wanted the individual sales associates to be thankful. The message was clear: All of your success comes through the power of our brand—you are nothing without the brand. RE/MAX wanted a different kind of culture. Liniger knew that, in reality, a real estate brand was not nearly as important as the individual. The individual drove the customer to six or ten different open houses. The individual had all the personal relationships. If that individual quit, chances are the customer would be loyal to him or her, not the company brand.

Liniger's personal promotion innovation was a radical one, and he taught it again and again. *Promote yourself, put your name on the sign.* No one had heard such a thing in the real estate industry before. It had always been about the company—the individual just a cog in the wheel. But Liniger knew people worked for more than just a paycheck; they wanted a place where they felt good about themselves and where they felt at home.

In large seminars and small, Liniger taught agents how to set up their own advertising budget; how to measure how many calls came in; how to analyze how much was spent on ads and how that broke down in terms of dollars per customer; how to hone and maximize that personal strategy. It was an evolution in his role as a leader, one he understood to be absolutely necessary. He kept himself well fueled and at the cutting edge by attending any course, training session, or seminar he could find that would be relevant. He went to American Management Association meetings and spent many days a year in classrooms learning tips on how to manage a privately owned company; how to understand financial statements when you are a nonfinancial person; how to create a personal direct-mail campaign. Whatever was valuable, he incorporated into his own lectures and coaching sessions, giving agents and brokers everything he knew, all to make them better and in the process to add logs to the bonfire.

Building Brand Awareness

Still, the hardest part was opening the door. RE/MAX regional owners were eager for any traction they could get on public perception. The retail approach to selling the dream was working, no question about it; but the challenge was how to kick-start it, push it faster, achieve some big leaps. That's when Bill Echols, a regional co-owner in New Mexico, had the kind of idea that comes out of nowhere and seems like it has been right in front of you all along.

Echols had been in the real estate business since his late twenties and took genuine pleasure in the work. To him, it was a happy-go-lucky industry, lucrative and satisfying, especially if you loved people. It was the kind of work, as he put it, where "you can be a salesman and still feel good about yourself." He had a firm with his father and brother for a number of years but got burned out by the age of 35; so he sold it, did some consulting, and taught real estate. It was then that he started hearing about the 100 percent concept offered by Realty Executives. He loved the idea—running his own firm, he'd trained many agents only to see them leave for another broker or their own company—and he thought about getting back into the business. But the Realty Executives' fee structure simply didn't work for him.

One day, while teaching a course in Clovis, New Mexico, he got an urgent phone call. He left the room, picked up the phone, and recognized the voice on the other end. It was his best friend and college roommate, Darrel Stilwell. "It's called RE/MAX," Stilwell said, cryptically. "Meet me in Denver tomorrow."

Stilwell had been attending a National Association of Realtors (NAR) Convention in Miami when he saw the RE/MAX booth. It was exactly what he and Echols had been looking for. Together, they flew to Denver in November 1977. They loved what they saw and wound up buying the region of New Mexico/Arizona/Nevada.

It was hard work. Being a regional owner back then meant you had to wear a lot of hats. You were opening offices, recruiting and retraining agents, *and* selling franchises. Recruiting alone was a full-time job, and it was your life blood—without agents you had no revenue. The key to success, if you could find such a key, was somehow getting the agents to come to you. Echols and Stilwell learned a few strategies from Liniger, Fisher, and Jesperson. They set up forums and discussions at Realtor conventions speculating about the future of real estate, asking Realtors to think about where they might be in 8 or 10 years. That sparked a lot of curiosity, and plenty of people came to find out more. *What do you mean, where am I going to be in 10 years? Aren't I going to be here, doing the same thing that I'm doing now?* The answer opened the door to a discussion of RE/MAX, the 100 percent commission system, franchising, and other "changing trends in the real estate industry." Once someone asked about RE/MAX, Article 24 was breached, and the door was open to a very different kind of conversation. Echols tried the same approach at open houses. He went to them all, everywhere in the city, every single weekend, and offered his card to the agent showing the property. *RE/MAX, what's RE/MAX?* "Well," Echols would say, "let me tell you about it."

It wasn't easy, and they were getting nowhere fast. They knew, from the experiences of others, that this was how it went; and they were fully prepared to ride it out. But that doesn't mean they didn't have their moments of nervousness during that long initial dry spell. It took three months for Echols and Stilwell to recruit their first agent; and when they finally did, they got five at one time.

Deanna Dunn was a sweet woman who worked for the biggest broker in town. She had a lot of listings and was always busy with open houses. Echols knew she would be a prize recruitment. So every Sunday, wherever she was showing, he'd manage to swing by, just to say hello and ask her how she was doing. It was a pleasant, easy-going kind of persistence that Echols was showing; but Dunn knew he meant business. "Deanna, what questions about RE/MAX do you have that are unanswered?" he'd ask her with a smile, knowing once she figured out how good RE/MAX was, she'd sell herself on the idea. And Dunn always answered: "Well, Bill, I just don't know." And they'd leave it at that for another week.

People were afraid to make the change to a new system. Mostly, they were afraid that they wouldn't be able to pay the monthly fee. They had this ingrained idea, completely false in Echols's experience, that they got much of their business because of their broker's name. That was the ace card that Echols played after two and a half months of working Dunn gently. "Deanna, this is my last phone call to you," he started. Dunn protested that she really was thinking about it seriously; he shouldn't lose faith in her so soon. But Echols pressed further. "No, I'm serious," he said. "We've been doing this for a while now. Do me a favor. Do yourself a favor. Just go to your file cabinet and pull out every transaction you've had since you've been with your broker, and you can decide where your business came from. Did you generate it, or did your broker? I've seen you in action, and I've got a feeling it was you. But when you figure that out, just call me back and tell me, because I'm interested to know."

About 48 hours later, Dunn called him back. It was 7:30 in the morning, and she had energy in her voice, as though she was still feeling the adrenalin of a surprising discovery. "You're not going to believe this, Bill," she said. "Do you know how many transactions I got from my broker? None." Echols chuckled lightly. "Well, what's your plan now?" he asked. This time, there was no hesitation in Dunn's tone. "Why, I'm coming over to talk with you this afternoon, and I'm bringing four gals with me." In short order, every one of them joined.

That success, and others like it, reinforced Echols and Stilwell's belief in what they were selling; but they knew they had to do something about this fear-of-change thing. Their first major innovation in that regard came right away. They created something that they called the TAP program. TAP stood for Temporary Associate Program, and it was designed to ease the transition to the RE/MAX system. For agents who were hesitant because of the money issue, the plug went something like this:

> Right now, you're on a 60/40 split. You come over to RE/MAX, and we'll give you the same deal for three months. We're going to charge you $100 a month extra for accounting purposes, but we'll track all your deals. You'll get your 60 percent at the end of three months. You can look at that, compare it to what you would have earned, and see whether you want to switch to 100 percent or not.

Smoothing the transition was a huge innovation, and they got a ton of agents soon after. They even helped agents ease away from their old brokers without acrimony, letting the original broker keep the original split on any old listings. That allowed agents to still profit from listings they might have otherwise lost, without burning any bridges in the process. Hey, it's always better when *everybody wins*.

Still, if there was a way to begin that recruitment conversation a little earlier, advance it along faster, and even have people come to you, that would make a huge difference. The problem was, RE/MAX had no brand recognition. Outside of those who *knew*, nobody had heard of it. Agents didn't know about it, so their learning curve was steep. But, just as important, home buyers didn't know about RE/MAX either—and agents were sensitive to the customer's point of view. Every region went through the same steep climb. Until you reached that tipping point, and people started knowing who you were, it was a constant, agent-by-agent battle to build the business and spread the dream.

The regional directors got together every quarter, somewhere in the country, to talk to each other, share ideas and problems, and assess how each of them was doing relative to everyone else. At one of the meetings, it was suggested that they form an advertising committee. To that point, RE/MAX had no group advertising at all—they didn't have the money—but the big brokers/owners were starting to feel the urgent need. Bill Echols had spent 12 years in radio before he'd gotten into real estate, so he was appointed chair. At the next quarterly meeting in Lake Tahoe, the issue of advertising had become even more pressing. Archrival Century 21 had a new commercial in which they were using children in a neighborhood setting. *Damn, but they were good.* Everyone could see how powerfully that message came through. The company's "neighborhood professional" image was having a big impact. That's what real estate was all about—kids; neighborhoods; families; and your friendly, helpful, always-there-when-you-need-him professional real estate representative. The members of the advertising committee chewed it over. They knew they had to come up with some idea for a message that would become a household brand—a word, a slogan, a feeling, . . . something. But what would that be?

Echols was a great believer in letting the brain do its thing rather than forcing it to come up with a solution. He knew that Einstein had slept in a chair with a nail in his hand and a metal bucket below his clenched fist, or so the story went. When Einstein finally drifted off into deep sleep, his hand would unclench, and the nail would fall out, ringing in the bucket. When Einstein opened his eyes with a start, the idea he'd been struggling to discover would be there, right in front of him. As chairman of the advertising committee, Echols decided it was time for a little Einsteinian creativity theory. The committee should break, he declared, and everyone should go home. He was certain that somewhere out there, one of them would come up with the right branding idea, probably when he or she least expected it. And yet, Echols was still surprised when that someone turned out to be himself.

In New Mexico, a week later, he was driving in his car heading back to the office from lunch. He had an agent with him in the passenger seat, a woman from another realty office, whom he was trying to recruit. They were talking about casual stuff, most of the business talk having been handled at the restaurant. In the corner of his windshield, he saw something that took his mind completely away from the conversation. Over there, beyond the field, were four hot air balloons. That wasn't the most unusual sight in the world when you lived in New Mexico. The Hot Air Balloon Fiesta had been running in Albuquerque since the early 1970s; and although it wasn't the giant gala yet that it would later become, still, people were accustomed to it. But this time, seeing those balloons floating gently in the blue sky, Echols felt the nail drop from his hand and ring in the bucket.

The woman in the car with him knew something had happened, but Echols was so absorbed in his thoughts that he couldn't even talk about it. He dropped her off at her office, swung back to his own, parked, and ran inside. He saw Stilwell and grabbed his arm. "We've got to talk," he said. Stilwell was confused. "Bill, we've got a meeting set up. I told Tommy we'd meet with him as soon as you got back." Tommy Thompson was their new manager. Echols knew he couldn't put him off. It was about the only thing he could imagine, short of a walkin by a bus load of new agents eager to sign on, that could have made him delay acting on his new idea. Reluctantly, he agreed to proceed with the meeting.

Sitting there, his heart was jumping, his mind racing. In walked Tommy Thompson. The three of them shook hands and began to talk. Thompson had an idea; it was almost the first thing that came out of his mouth. "My next door neighbor is a Kodak district representative," he said, "and he's a sport balloon pilot. He got rid of his balloon last year, but he wants to buy another one, and he wants me to partner with him on it. I told him it's not my thing, but my bosses might be interested. What do you think? Could be good advertising."

Echols couldn't believe what he was hearing. "We'll do it," he said.

Stilwell looked at him in shock. "What the hell are you talking about?"

"That's what I wanted to tell you about," Echols started, aware that in his enthusiasm he was probably sounding like a madman. "The brand. The image. The thing we've been looking for. That's it. We need to have a RE/MAX hot air balloon. Can't you just see it?" He framed his hands to catch the image, up there on the ceiling tile. "The RE/MAX red, white, and blue colors on a hot air balloon in the sky!"

Thompson and Stilwell looked up. Damn, if they couldn't see it, too.

The RE/MAX Balloon

They didn't tell anyone what they were up to—not anyone on the advertising committee, not anyone in the other regions. They certainly didn't tell Dave Liniger. They wanted to see if it would work. They wanted it to be a surprise. The Kodak guy wanted them to put a RE/MAX banner on the balloon. Echols said, "No way. We're going to make the whole balloon red, white, and blue. The balloon is going to be the RE/MAX sign!" Of course, none of them knew what to do with a balloon, where to put it, how to look after it; so they leased it instead of buying it outright. They ordered the balloon from the Barnes Balloon Company and gave the colors—192 Red and Reflex Blue. It came in, as ordered, without the lettering. Now, this was getting exciting. They brought it to the World Balloon Corporation in Albuquerque to get the logo put on—red letters with a blue sash. "Uh uh," the balloon designer said, "you don't want to do that. Red letters on the white background of the balloon won't show up in the sky." Echols thought about it for 10 seconds and then told him to reverse the colors.

They got the balloon finished only one day before the Balloon Fiesta. Tommy Thompson was a Super 8 movie buff. The Kodak representative was their pilot. Excited as the rest of them, he supplied Team RE/MAX with enough free film to do a remake of *Gone With the Wind*. Thompson got footage of the balloon every which way possible.

They developed it, edited it, canned it, and got on a plane. The Balloon Fiesta was entering its final weekend, but the regional owners were meeting in Chicago at the Marriott O'Hare. Walking into the meeting, Echols pulled Liniger aside and asked him for a little time to show a promotion that they'd put together. Liniger was busy, grumpy, and distracted. "Maybe after the break," he said, "but I might tell you to shut it off if we don't have time." Break over, Echols and Stilwell set up the reel and turned the film projector on. The footage flickered, ran through its numbers, and cleared—a blue sky; a field of hot air balloons; and the RE/MAX red, white, and blue soaring among them.

The regional owners went wild. Anything that had RE/MAX on it was a big deal to them, but this was unbelievable. There was something about that seven-story balloon, floating in the sky, with those RE/MAX colors and that RE/MAX logo. Everyone loved it.

Except for Dave Liniger. He sat there, arms folded, unimpressed, annoyed at the enthusiasm around him. "I don't like it," he said. Echols asked why, and Liniger could only shrug. "It's the wrong damn colors."

Liniger didn't see what balloons had to do with the real estate business. He thought it was distracting from the real mission—all pizzazz and no content. And the color reversal bothered him immensely. He was ferociously protective of the RE/MAX brand, and he saw this flipping of red and blue as totally wrong. He didn't care about the explanation; all he could see flying up there was a misprint.

The other owners could see his point. The motion to reverse the logo colors was unanimously disapproved. Liniger said, "If you want one for your region just for fun, take it out to walkathons and grand openings and charity events, go ahead and buy one. But in Colorado, those colors will be the way they are on everything we do."

The meeting was about to break for lunch. While the owners relaxed and talked among themselves, Liniger and Jesperson went across the hall to the Firehouse Bar to buy some drinks for everyone and bring them back. Waiting for the bartender, Liniger and Jesperson looked up at the television and saw the RE/MAX balloon floating by on the screen. "What the hell? What's this about?" Liniger asked the bartender. "That's the *Dinah Shore Show*," the bartender answered. "She's broadcasting from some balloon festival down in Albuquerque; and every time they go to commercial break, they show that RE/MAX balloon."

Jesperson ran back to get the others. Drinks in hand, they all stood around the television and waited for the next commercial break. Sure enough, there was the RE/MAX balloon, seven stories high. The regional owners gave a loud cheer, clinked glasses, clapped backs, shouted swear words, and had another round.

Spontaneously, another vote was held. Should the RE/MAX balloon become the official logo of RE/MAX, and should the RE/MAX colors be reversed? All in favor?

Once again, the "No" vote was unanimous. Echols and Stilwell went back to New Mexico, without victory, but feeling pretty good. Echols figured the others would come around, little by little; and in the meantime, he was going to use the RE/MAX balloon every chance he had.

Echols knew it was the right thing to do. When you're starting a new business and nobody knows who the hell you are, any kind of question like *"What is that?"* gives you a chance to tell your story. The balloon made for a great story.

They took the president of the Board of Realtors for a balloon ride. She later became a franchisee. They took up agents, dignitaries, and the media. They even had a RE/MAX agent get married in the balloon, and the exposure started to work. The balloon drew a crowd wherever it showed up. It was fun. It gave people a good feeling. For the following year's Hot Air Balloon Fiesta, they enlisted volunteer help from the offices. Every day of the Fiesta, the balloon needed a ground crew to be on-site at 4:30 A.M. for a 5:30 A.M. launch. At the time, Echols's firm had 17 sales associates. He asked how many of them would like to be involved. Every single person put up his or her hand. They decided to get some team jackets made up. But didn't a jacket require some kind of slogan? Tommy Thompson suggested, "Above the Clouds." Echols thought about how the RE/MAX concept meant being "above" the other real estate firms, so he tried, "Above the Crowd!" That worked for everybody. RE/MAX was trying to recruit the top agents by providing above-the-crowd service and maximum commission for the highest producers. "Above the Crowd!" just seemed to fit. The jackets were made up. They'd assigned everybody in the organization a morning to come out and work, knowing they needed four or five people each morning. People brought their whole families, their neighbors, their friends. The balloon had become a community attraction, and RE/MAX was growing closer as a result. The sales associates knew each other as colleagues—most of them had known each other as competitors before joining RE/MAX—but now they were coming to know each other as friends. It helped RE/MAX and it helped with recruiting, as these family members and friends started talking about the RE/MAX story. They told people how much fun they were having, how much they loved the organization, how successful they were becoming. In the eyes of those people, RE/MAX had gone from being a 100 percent commission concept to a fun and growing place where it felt good to belong.

Other regions started building their own balloons once they saw how excited people got when they saw it flying overhead. In Colorado, a year later, they followed suit. By this time, the Colorado region had a few hundred agents and was fast becoming number one in market share, but that didn't necessarily translate to market visibility. In the media, RE/MAX just didn't get any press—any *good* press, anyway. The powers that be would never do a positive article about the company for their industry newspapers. So Liniger figured he'd start his own magazine, call it *Liniger's Real Estate*, and fashion it after *Forbes*. Before he jumped into that venture with both feet, he hired a consultant who had a local weekly business magazine. It was 1978, and RE/MAX was number one in Colorado, Dave bragged. The consultant went off and checked some data. A week later he came back. "Dave, I thought you said you were number one." "We are," Liniger said. The consultant shrugged. "Well, we do an annual survey of customers on everything from ski slopes and health spas to real estate companies; and you're perceived to be the eighth-biggest real estate company in town."

Liniger looked at the data. It was broken down in a hundred different ways. You could sort by any number of demographics, including length of time in the city. Among people who had lived in Denver for more than 20 years, RE/MAX wasn't even close to eighth place. Among new residents, RE/MAX was either first or second. All the cumulative years of advertising for Van Schaack and Moore and those other long-term players had a lot more momentum than he would have realized. *One log makes a lousy fire.*

For Liniger, that was a moment of truth. He went back to his agents and told them that RE/MAX had a problem. "We're number one, but nobody knows we're number one. I think we've got to get on television." They took a vote, and everyone decided to throw $50 a month into the pot and buy some TV advertising. They saved the money for a year and ended up with $180,000.

Liniger called the TV stations and asked them if they made the commercials or did RE/MAX have to go elsewhere. The TV stations recommended an outside firm called Communi-Creations. Gail and Dave went over there to see about making some commercials.

It was going to cost about $150,000 to do a really good spot. But that didn't include the money they would need to buy media time. So he went back to the agents and explained the issues. "A good spot's going to cost us some. If you want, I can stick a sign in the ground and say, 'Hi, my name's Dave Liniger, founder of RE/MAX, and I want to tell you about my company, the number-one firm in real estate.' But I think that idea sucks." Nobody else liked the idea either. It didn't seem right for an organization built on the backs of so many different agents. So someone spoke up and said, "Dave, you're a pilot. And we have this red, white, and blue balloon. Why don't we just launch it, and you fly around in a helicopter and take a picture of it, and we'll have a voice over saying, 'RE/MAX. Above the Crowd!'"

Everyone loved the idea. So they decided to do it. Since RE/MAX was now all over the country, they wanted to get a simple shot, with just blue sky—no mountains or distinctive regional features. It was incredibly tough getting a shot of the balloon from a moving airplane with a gyro-mounted camera on it without the shadow of the airplane falling across the balloon or without the mountains or ground in the background. But finally, after about two hours of hovering around, they had about 25 seconds worth of footage good enough to make a commercial. An eight-week campaign was launched, and they spent every dime in their advertising pool, just in time for the next annual survey of consumers in the Colorado region. The survey results came back and Liniger's consultant couldn't believe the numbers. "It says here, you've got 66 percent of people unaided who say that your corporate symbol is a red, white, and blue balloon. And 36 percent of people unaided say that your slogan is 'Above the Crowd!' In all my studies of advertising, this is the greatest impact for a logo I have ever heard of." Liniger soaked that in, but the consultant wasn't finished. "Now tell me, with the little money you spent on this balloon commercial, why the hell isn't this your corporate logo for real?"

So Liniger flipped the colors on the balloon and gave his blessing. The balloon went onto signs, business cards, and corporate stationery from that moment forward.

The Power of Brand

Liniger's resistance to the balloon and the reversed logo seemed unusually strong, and yet it was characteristic of his leadership approach in one compelling way. It is true that Liniger is more open to new ideas and more open to learning from people around him than most leaders we've met or studied. He manages his firm "open book" and allows the individual to take precedence over the organization. But he is fiercely protective of his brand. He has argued, sued, and gotten into fist fights with anyone who has ever tread on the brand or bled on the colors. Like the great brand leaders of our time—Richard Branson, Philip Knight, Walt Disney, Ray Kroc—he knows that, more than anything else, it is the power of the brand that builds market presence in a global company. Nevertheless, you can't fault Liniger for being unwilling to see the error of his ways. Once he recognized the power of the balloon, he embraced it. But Liniger's thinking about brand was adapted to the needs of his industry. As previously noted, real estate is a profoundly local business. The big firms with backgrounds in other industries don't always understand how poorly a brand can translate to the customer. Real estate is a business built from referrals and an individual agent's personal reputation, over and above the reputation of the firm that that agent represents. It really does take a whole bunch of logs to create a fire that people can see, let alone feel. A high-powered executive and one of the greatest marketers of our time is an expert when it comes to brand awareness, but even he found real estate a strange brew. At an industry conference, he remarked casually, with a touch of deep frustration, "You know, the thing that really drives me nuts about this business is that it's the only one I've ever seen where brand awareness doesn't extend to brand usage. It's completely crazy, but that's the way it is."

Unlike the other national franchises, RE/MAX had a predisposition to letting individual agents do their own advertising. Personal promotion had always been the principle behind the independence a top agent was given to push his or her own business in the way he or she saw fit. As Liniger said to his agents and brokers, "You're the reason why you're successful, not your company. But as we become more successful, we will give you that added advantage which will put you over the top." If agents wanted to put their name in big letters, they had Liniger's blessing. But he cautioned them not to lose the power of the brand. Those who thought they were bigger than the network and walked away often came back. They didn't know how tough it really was to go it alone without the RE/MAX brand behind them.

As the logs on the fire piled up, the power of the brand accelerated the value to all the agents. Today, the average RE/MAX real estate agent in the United States spends close to $10,000 on advertising. With 75,000 agents in the United States, that creates a group budget of around $750 million. Only about $35 million of that gets devoted to national TV and

another $30 million to local or regional TV. In an age when other compa-
nies are decrying the diminishing impact of TV spots, the bulk of the advertising budget spent by RE/MAX agents was invested in "For Sale" signs,
Internet sites, personal brochures, classified ads, and whatever else they
managed to come up with in the field. It cost those agents relatively nothing to have 100,000 other agents worldwide paying their advertising, re-
minding their own customers of their great service and market reputation.
The impact is incalculable. In the end, brand awareness comes down to
the power of selective perception. If you've ever had a golden retriever for
a pet, you'll notice golden retrievers everywhere. Once you're aware of the
RE/MAX balloon, you'll see little RE/MAX balloons on real estate signs in
every neighborhood.

That power of the brand extending to the neighborhood level is critical. People want to do their real estate business with someone who lives in
their local market. One of the early ads that RE/MAX struggled to develop
convinced them of this very point. In 1974, in the second full year of operation, RE/MAX was trying to counter the negative publicity that had
been engendered by press reports that it was going to go bankrupt. Liniger
called the agents and told them that he wanted to put a full-page ad in the
newspaper if each of them could chip in a $100. That first year, they ran an
ad that had the number $33,930,000 across the top and a list of sales asso-
ciate names. The ad read, "In our first full year of business, the men and
women of this company have set a sales record unmatched by any other
real estate company." The next year, the ad ran, and the number was $80
million. The year after that, it was $400 million. The fourth year, it
reached $1 billion, and the list of more than 500 sales associates ran eight
pages long. Everyone was looking forward to the insert, excited and unbe-
lievably proud. But Dean Gattis, one of the first managers to become a broker owner, vetoed the idea.

Liniger was furious. He wanted to celebrate the success, and he needed
unanimous consent to do it. Gattis put his foot down. "You can't run it,"
he said. "If you put this ad in the paper, what are you telling the general
public? They see us driving Mercedes, and they think our commission rate
is too high, and you're telling them we're billionaires." Liniger, seeing his
point but still bitter, said, "Well, what the hell would you run? We worked
for years to reach this number." Gattis thought about it for a short mo-

ment. "I have it," he said. "The five hundred and thirty men and women of RE/MAX featured on these pages would like to thank the 39,000 families who used us to buy and sell their homes this year. We live in the same neighborhoods, our kids go to the same schools, we see each other in the same churches and synagogues. We are your neighbors. We are in love with the real estate business, and we are in love with our customers. Thank you for allowing us to provide for our families by serving you." It was accurate, brilliant, and true.

Premiere Market Presence was also about giving back. It was a combination of factors. When an agent goes in to compete for business, he or she has a quiver full of arrows at his or her disposal. One arrow says, "We provide quality service because RE/MAX agents are the best." One arrow says, "We live in your neighborhoods, and we give back to our communities because that's what makes business meaningful." And one arrow says, "We're the biggest real estate network in the world with one of the most recognized brands." Like the Coca-Cola colors, the golden arches, or the Nike swoosh, the RE/MAX balloon communicates the organization's message in any language.

Strategic Moves

RE/MAX developed a branded, focused culture.

RE/MAX never underestimated the power of branding. Intuitively, it seemed, RE/MAX leaders understood that the brand started with the accumulation of stories that would be told about the organization. Everything, including its colors and symbols, became part of its branding strategy. Although it was iterative (i.e., building in a day-to-day fashion), it was also planful and artful. It was as if the power of branding was part of RE/MAX's strategic application that set in motion a purposeful set of behaviors. This strategy required teaching every associate coming on board how to think like a product-minded manager. From this branding mentality emerged powerful concepts, like overwhelming market presence (OMP) and Premier Market Presence (PMP).

- When you meet a prince or a princess in a different firm or even a different industry, pursue him or her despite the fact that he or she may not be looking for a job. Sell the person on the dream and never let up on filling your company with the right people. (p. 74)

- When pitching the dream, remember, "It's a broken record to us, but it's opening night on Broadway to them." (p. 78)

- RE/MAX used the concept of Premier Market Presence to achieve overwhelming market dominance. This is a proven method of focusing on growth in markets. The five aspects of PMP are (pp. 79–80):
  1. Market share
  2. Brand name awareness
  3. Customer satisfaction
  4. Quality associates
  5. Community service

- One log makes a lousy fire. One log doesn't burn very well on its own. But with 10 logs (and some kindling), you can light it with a single match and get a terrific bonfire. If you get 100,000 burning logs, you get a fire that is unstoppable. Create winning relationships with your associates and customers. (p. 82)

- Building a bonfire of 100,000 logs is a slow process. You have to find the right logs, nurture the flames, and build the fire gradually from nothing. It takes a lot of time, patience, stamina, and diligence; but in the long run, it creates a powerful flame. Through the *everybody wins* principle, RE/MAX was able to build its network by making the broker successful and giving the agents the freedom to promote their own business and build their careers. (p. 82)

- Believe in your employees (or potential employees) more than they believe in themselves. They will rise to your expectations. (p. 85)

- Recognize when people are having a hard time adjusting to a new system or situation, and create a program that will make the transition easier and smoother. (p. 86)

- Make your corporate culture fun, and your employees will enjoy projects, involve others, hone the dream constantly from the perspective of their role, and share the love of their work with others. (p. 91)

- Fiercely protect your brand, and go to extremes to promote it to the public. (pp. 93–94)
- Your brand is only as powerful as your customers' experience of it. As in real estate, "all branding" is local. The power of the brand extending to the "neighborhood" level is critical. In today's global marketplace, people still want to do their business with someone who "lives" in their local market. Your company's advertising needs to pursue that level of brand recognition. (pp. 95–96)

Lesson

Overwhelming Market Presence (OMP) grows dreams.

In growing dreams successfully, it is critical to go after overwhelming market presence (OMP). If the end game is growth on a consistent basis, then grabbing and holding market share in key geographies is mission-specific to winning. All the benchmark high-growth/high-impact companies (HG/HI) in Chapter 9 demonstrate OMP. RE/MAX understood that its associates benefited the more agents were working a specific market. McDonald's is the best example of the value of positioning stores in the backyard of franchise holders. Consider how brand and market dominance (OMP) play against each other. OMP requires a premier market presence (PMP) plan. PMP has a natural role in the *everybody wins* formula for growth as it generates an internal competition circle where the brand appears to compete against itself, yet actually generates more opportunity because of more market awareness. It takes persistent internal selling to pull off a successful PMP program and to overcome internal pressures not to do it. RE/MAX spent significant time internally proving that PMP does increase revenue in a defined market before implementing the concept widely.

OMP strategy with a linked PMP plan is tantamount to building and holding brand awareness and dominance. It is clear in the case of RE/MAX that both of these concepts were necessary for turbo-charged growth. We believe this is a valuable lesson that is transferable as a growth concept and a model for other organizations to follow. (See Figure 4.3.)

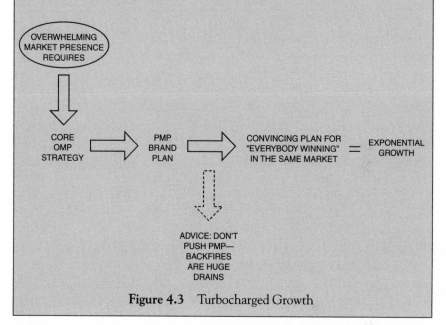

Figure 4.3   Turbocharged Growth

CHAPTER 5

SHACKLETON LEADERSHIP

By Endurance, We Conquer

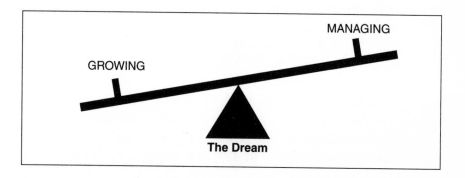

You wait. Everyone has an Antarctic.

—Thomas Pynchon, *V*

There are many stories of leaders who accomplish great objectives, but there are few that describe how they lead through adversity. Surviving adversity may not always be the traditional stuff of Hollywood legend, but we think that its role in the shaping of any great organization is underexplored. Certainly, in the case of RE/MAX, adversity, survival, stamina, persistence, and great camaraderie became critical elements in the organization's culture and contributed to its ultimate success.

For many such reasons, the story of Ernest Shackleton and his quest to cross Antarctica on foot resonated deeply with Dave Liniger and the core RE/MAX leadership team. They encountered Shackleton's story in 1999 and immediately felt that it reflected their own hard-earned understanding about what it takes to persevere through great odds. They saw the lessons of the story as a great learning tool and began to teach those lessons to RE/MAX associates and leaders around the world. Comparing what happened to Shackleton and his crew with what RE/MAX experienced in its first 10 years helps to emphasize how much determination is really behind any great venture.

Shackleton's Story

Ernest Shackleton was a British citizen of Irish descent who had explored many of the world's far reaches. Twice, he had been part of expeditions attempting to be the first to reach the South Pole, only to be beaten in that quest by Roald Amundsen of Norway. His obsession with Antarctica didn't wane, however. His dream evolved, and he wanted to be the first explorer to cross Antarctica on foot. A team of men attempting such an adventure would need to cross an icy 1,500-mile wasteland, face winds of up to 100 miles per hour, and brave temperatures that might reach –70 degrees Fahrenheit. Shackleton knew that only a rare group with the right qualities could make it. In 1915, he posted a notice that read: "Men wanted for hazardous journey. Small wages. Bitter cold. Chance of return doubtful."

Whether it was Shackleton's wry honesty about the stark challenges, some projected sense of his leadership, or the adventurous spirit of the times, about 5,000 men applied to be part of the expedition. Shackleton handpicked 28. His ship, The Endurance, drew its name from his family motto: "By Endurance, We Conquer." The men set off from England for the distant Antarctic, cheerful and eager, unsure if they would ever return.

What unfolded is one of the great leadership stories of all time. By all accounts, Shackleton inspired his men deeply. He had their unshakeable confidence through unimaginable trials. When The Endurance got stuck in the ice a thousand miles from land, Shackleton did not show any disappointment but told the men, in a clear assessment of the facts, that they would have to set up camp and wait out the winter. To sustain morale during the long months to come, Shackleton kept everyone busy and in good spirits, playing games, singing songs, exercising, and rationing meager supplies with a sense of camaraderie and friendship. When spring finally arrived, however, The Endurance was not freed from the ice, as Shackleton had hoped, but was crushed by it. The odds of achieving a safe return had been reduced to almost nothing.

Shackleton scrapped his original plans; his expedition no longer had any chance of crossing the Antarctic. But in its place, he put forward a new objective—to bring everyone back alive. To the men, Shackleton's resolve provided the certainty they would need to go on. He did not lament or dwell on past failures. His vision was always forward looking. What had happened was over, only the future was worth their attention and energy. They would survive together, in good cheer, with a sense of the historic greatness of what they were attempting to accomplish, and would look after one another when the body or the spirit was weak.

The expedition spent the next five months on an ice flow. They called their new home Patience Camp. Everyone made an effort to stay active and in good spirits as they waited for the ice to drift closer to land. All of Shackleton's energies as leader were focused on holding his men together, beyond their weariness and despair. When the ice finally shifted, Shackleton made the decision to abandon camp and enter the lifeboats they had rescued from *The Endurance* to row the rest of the way. Their destination, an island where supplies had been left behind, was 800 miles off. The risks were enormous. A storm could overturn their small boats or wedge them into the ice. Weather conditions were so bad that after four days of unceasing effort, the currents had actually forced them 30 miles farther away. Shackleton mocked the impossible odds and his crew kept going, heading to a different island instead.

When they finally reached Elephant Island, it was the first time their feet had been on dry land in over a year. Shackleton realized they would never be rescued on this remote island, so he tried another daring gamble. Stripping materials from the boats, he rebuilt one small sailing vessel—the *James Caird*—and with four other men set out in a desperate attempt to reach South Georgia Island, where there was a whaling station and the promise of help. In what would be considered one of the greatest open-boat journeys ever accomplished, they successfully crossed one of the roughest seas on earth. However, they lost their rudder and landed on South Georgia on the side of the island opposite the whaling station. Two of the crew were critically ill and couldn't go on. Shackleton and two others were healthy, and they were faced with crossing an unchartered mountain range in order to reach help. Without pausing to rest, they accomplished this in 36 hours with a rope, a carpenter's ax, and nails they fastened to the bottom of their shoes for traction. It was another six months before Shackleton was able to return to Elephant Island where he successfully rescued all of his men—and met his goal of not losing a single one.

Shackleton's men made it through more than two years of impossible conditions with only the slimmest of hopes, thanks to Shackleton's remarkable leadership. He had shown unwavering strength and stamina, a relentless focus on a single-minded objective, and creative ingenuity in meeting and overcoming each new challenge. Just as critical, Shackleton had provided his men with a sense of esprit de corps and greater mission that lifted their spirits long after they might reasonably have expected to give up. Although they traveled halfway around the world and failed in their original objective, together they accomplished something greater than what they had set out to do: They survived.

Perseverance

It's easy to see why Liniger identified with Shackleton's story. Almost from the beginning of his odyssey aboard RE/MAX, all hell broke loose. In those first few months, when Liniger secured financial backing from the land developers at the Weydert Group, he believed that he was providing his young organization with a much-needed boost. But then came the OPEC oil embargo.

Like any group of highly leveraged speculators, Weydert fell off a cliff when the economy took a hard turn. The Weydert strategy had been to build a resortlike suburb far out of the city, in the mountains, for high-income families—an idea that was decades ahead of its time. The recession curbed the strong growth on which Weydert had been counting. The high price of fuel and the long lines to buy gas changed everyone's vision of the future. No one thought that living 30 miles outside the city, commuting back and forth each day, was a good idea anymore. Weydert's development projects went bankrupt. Because Liniger had signed on as a partner, he not only lost their financial backing, but he also assumed his share of Weydert debt.

In some ways, that was to be the least of Liniger's worries. The real estate industry backlash to the fledgling organization with the 100 percent commission concept would prove even more challenging. Anti–RE/MAX talk became rampant with gossip about unethical practices. An anonymous letter-writing campaign was started, and the letters found their way into the hands of governmental agencies. Liniger could not afford a lawyer. He fielded all legal attacks personally, rebutting them with a sharp understanding of the industry; but the assault was relentless. The FBI stepped in to investigate anonymous claims that RE/MAX had made fraudulent FHA (Federal Housing Authority) and VA (Veterans Administration) loans. RE/MAX wasn't even a mortgage company, and the FBI quickly backed off; but the announcement of an investigation made the papers, and the damage was done. The SEC (Securities and Exchange Commission) was next. It investigated RE/MAX for fraudulent stock offerings, even though RE/MAX had never issued any stock. The Colorado state real estate commission followed with its own shot, issuing RE/MAX a letter of reprimand for inappropriate accounting. They had found an extra dollar in a RE/MAX trust account, left over when the bank did not issue a stop-payment fee for a lost cashier's check. While the notice of reprimand was made public, the amount of the discrepancy was never mentioned.

At every step, as RE/MAX pursued its growth goals, obstacles, challenges, and threats were repeatedly thrown in its way. Perhaps this shouldn't have been too surprising. RE/MAX was doing the unthinkable in the real estate industry—actively recruiting other brokers' agents—and it was doing so with an attitude that struck many as arrogant and disrespectful. All revolutions bring hostile reactions from those who are threatened by the change. But Dave Liniger's rough, bold, nothing-held-back persona intensified the extremes of loyalty and hostility that he engendered. He was arrogant, quick-witted, and hyperintelligent; and he was not afraid to lash back at those who resisted him, threw up road blocks, or slighted his organization. He was fundamentally shy and surrounded himself with people he could trust totally, almost as a form of self-defense; but he was not afraid of attention or public glare when it came to defending whatever or whomever he believed in. He seemed to have been born to lead in foxhole conditions, and he had an under-siege mentality, which made him tremendously loyal to and compassionate for those fighting with him and inspired equally powerful hostility from those he saw as a threat.

Liniger was conscious of the need for balance in his top team; however, the people around him did not take his battles quite as personally. Instead, they acted to counter his intensity with more measured, diplomatic, and reasonable demeanors. They saw when RE/MAX was being treated unfairly, and that angered them; but they focused on doing what needed to be done to smooth the way. They were just as committed as Liniger was and just as willing to cross lines in service of the cause; but they seemed less angry and emotional somehow, almost as if they recognized that all those passions—even Liniger's own—were arising in the context of a great (and fun) game. Nevertheless, despite their comparative calm, that inner group of people showed love and admiration for Liniger with a genuineness of emotion that seems rare in a corporate setting.

Like Shackleton's adventurers, they knew that Liniger had a vision and a sharp understanding of human nature, which they experienced enough times to figure that it bordered on a kind of genius. He showed a willingness to admit mistakes, vulnerabilities, or lack of knowledge, which inclined others to extend forgiveness or a helping hand. He seemed to understand individuals in a deep, personal way that they did not always recognize at first, until they realized that Liniger had given them exactly the opportunity, break, reward, or challenge that they needed to feel as though life was a great and wonderful thing. He took care of people when they needed it, for whatever physical, emotional, or financial reason. He was the type to take nothing for himself and to give the shirt off his back to others. The dream of RE/MAX was everything to him, and he poured all his own financial resources into it while taking nothing out, even as he made sure that others around him received not only what they needed but also what they deserved. He helped boost morale with his limitless optimism and his "mock the odds" approach to troubleshooting. He was the kind of leader who could face a devastating payroll shortage on a Friday, fly down to Las Vegas for the weekend, and come back on Monday morning with enough money in his fist to keep the ship afloat for another couple of weeks. He worked hard, played hard, and shared his thoughts and dreams intensely, sweeping others up in his interests. He was constantly growing, learning, and evolving; and by example, he helped others go through similar journeys of their own.

It is no wonder that when he told them they would not only survive but ultimately win, they believed him.

Many of the problems RE/MAX faced in the early years were external ones; but Liniger was creating his own difficulties just as fast. Very quickly, because of financial debts and mistakes, Liniger found that he could not make payroll. He went off salary. Then Gail Main went off salary. And when it was necessary, Bob Fisher and Daryl Jesperson went off salary for long stretches, too. For two years, Liniger lived on credit cards, without a paycheck, while his credit spiraled downhill. Bills went unpaid. Creditors began filing notices. The phones got cut off. And in a crushing blow, the Internal Revenue Service (IRS) threatened to padlock the RE/MAX office doors. In his business naiveté, Liniger had assumed that the IRS was like any other creditor. He didn't know that withholding payment could get you shut down on a moment's notice.

The feeling of being overwhelmed was almost too much; but like Shackleton, Liniger had set himself up with a new objective—*he would not file for bankruptcy*. Still, he had to admit to himself that he didn't know how RE/MAX was going to survive. That was when Gail Main took him into her office, closed the door, and told him what they were going to do. They were both selling real estate themselves by that point, but they were pouring their commissions back into the business. They were stretched thin, straining beyond physical and emotional limits. But Gail had a presence of mind and a sense of calm about what needed to be done.

"The only way we are going to save this company is for you to concentrate on making sales and recruiting agents," she said, gently but insistently. "Let me take over the rest. I'll handle the creditors. You don't need to talk to them anymore. I'll work us through those problems. You concentrate on making us grow."

For Liniger, this simple division of labor was a relief and a release that gave him a renewed boost of stamina and belief. For Gail Main, it was the chance to take on a level of challenge that few executives ever face.

She brought a sense of grace, integrity, and openness to her dealings with the creditors and somehow won them over. Whereas Liniger might have blustered at them and forcibly sold them on a plan, Main brought them along as partners and even collaborators. A situation that might have been humiliating and deeply emotional to Liniger, she was able to handle objectively, competently, and maturely—as well as with sensitivity for the feelings and relationships involved. She took every creditor in turn and sat with him or her in private. She opened the RE/MAX books and exposed the vulnerabilities as well as the bright hopes. She worked out payment plans and stuck to them, nibbling debts down, month by month, dollar by dollar. While Liniger sold others on the dream, Gail Main showed creditors how their needs would be satisfied if they continued to believe.

It was a combination that worked, and it brought the sense of possibility and energy back to the team. Liniger regained his forceful single-mindedness. Even when debts did intrude, he was able to handle them with more of his typical aplomb. Once, while recruiting an agent, Liniger was interrupted by his secretary. A man in the reception area was trying to repossess the office's one IBM Selectric typewriter because he was owed $142 on a $200 machine. Liniger asked the agent to wait a moment, went out into the reception area, assessed the situation, and asked the typewriter salesman to hang on for five minutes. Liniger then went back into the office to continue his conversation with the agent. This time, his insistence and encouragement had risen a few notches. "This is where you belong," Liniger told the agent. "This is what's best for your family. You're going to thrive here." And then, in the next breath: "What I need from you now is a five hundred dollar deposit."

The agent didn't even know why he did it; but he had a few hundred dollars in cash in his pocket and wrote out a check for the rest, on the spot. Liniger took the cash; said, "Be back in a minute"; and then went out and paid the typewriter salesman. He was back sitting with the agent, reveling in the dream, within the next eye blink, even as the agent tried to sort out what had just happened. Walking out of the office a half hour later, ready to embark on a new career, he had the sense that he had just been picked up by a tornado and placed somewhere else, hair mussed but otherwise unharmed, with a bright new outlook on life.

The Agents Never Left

Even with all the turbulence, the successful agents never left. That was the real reason RE/MAX was able to survive and grow. Liniger had focused on the agents, from day one, as the firm's true customers and collaborators. His organization did the same thing; and they made sure that those agents always felt involved and knew they were being looked after, no matter what RE/MAX itself was going through.

They were in it together. No matter how many bill collectors were on his back, no matter how desperately he needed to sell a property in order to keep the venture afloat, Liniger still found immense quantities of time for his agents. At any given break in the day—breakfast, lunch, dinner, drinks—Liniger gave access to whoever needed his attention at the time. While many leaders in his position might have been afraid to show vulnerability, Liniger was open about his problems and the firm's near bankrupt condition. He complemented this openness, however, with his compelling vision for the future and the enthusiasm he brought to their great adventure. Liniger told them, "This is your company. I don't know how to run the damn thing. Look at all the trouble we're in. What would you do?" He asked them what worked best at their old company, what didn't work at all, and what they would do differently if the world were a perfect place. It wasn't an act or a facade of false modesty; he truly meant it. All the best ideas came from the good and loyal people in the ranks. "How would you run it?" Knowing that he needed input from all levels, Liniger attended advisory councils and committees, insisting that a representative from each office be part of the various gatherings. In this way, he could stay in touch with every group, keeping informed of their concerns, networking their best ideas.

One such idea had to do with how agents got paid. The traditional, top real estate firms played games with agents' money, holding on to commission checks for as long as possible, up to a month in many cases, forcing agents to go to managers, hat in hand, to ask for an "advance" if they couldn't make it. It was humiliating. "All right," Liniger said. "We'll pay you the day you close." RE/MAX created a separate account for agent commissions, structured it so that creditors could not touch it, and made sure agents had their commission checks within hours of handing over the check for the home. It didn't matter that the officers were living off their credit cards and living hand to mouth. The agents had earned that money themselves, and they deserved to have it in their pockets right away. At a time when many agents in even the most established companies were feeling the pinch of a very tough recession, that gesture meant a tremendous amount to the agents and allowed RE/MAX to continue to grow month over month.

Liniger focused on whatever the agents needed to do or learn in order to improve their performance and make more money for themselves. He was eager for those agents to succeed because he knew that that was the key to the organization's survival. In public, he spoke about those agents as though they were the best. *They were top performers, the cream of the crop, the very highest quality producers.* In reality, RE/MAX was taking average performers with incredible potential and turning them into the best. He coaxed them and shaped them. He gave them tips, tools, and advice. He went with them on sales calls and coached them. And he spread that attentive "learning organization" approach through other teachers and coaches as RE/MAX got larger.

Liniger's concern for the agents was critical to the organization's success. One make-or-break moment occurred in June 1975. Things had started to smooth out in terms of the financial difficulties; but one evening, Liniger got a call from one of his branch managers. He had eight such managers running branch offices in Colorado, and his relationship with them was not always good. Now one of them wanted to buy him a couple of drinks.

Before Liniger left for the bar, he got a second phone call. On the other end of the line was the voice of the first agent Liniger had ever recruited, calling from a payphone, sounding panicked and anxious. "Dave, your managers are calling a special meeting with all the agents," she said. "They want to bankrupt RE/MAX and start a new company. They're saying you can't possibly save it any longer. What should I do?"

Ah, hell, Liniger thought, utterly deflated the instant he understood what was really going on. He didn't even blame the managers. He knew he had lost contact with them over the tough year. Under tremendous pressure, he had pushed them hard, without any sense of diplomacy or sensitivity, and they were sick and tired of him. What really got him down, however, was the fact that RE/MAX had truly turned a corner. He had shown the managers proof that they were nearly at breakeven and would be debt free in two years because of Gail's careful and realistic strategy. That was the shame of it all; and now he had to go have drinks with one of them, pretending nothing was wrong, while the others conspired against him.

"You go ahead," he told his agent on the phone. "See what they have to say, and let me know what's going on. And thanks for telling me."

He went out with his branch manager. They both kept getting interrupted by phone calls at the bar. Finally, at 10 o'clock, Liniger was too tired and sick of the whole charade to go on any longer. "Let me ask you something," he said, looking at him straight in the eye for the first time that night. "If I promise not to go to the special private meeting, can I go home now and go to bed instead of sitting here drinking with somebody I don't want to drink with?"

The branch manager was surprised. "What do you mean?" he asked.

Liniger felt his anger rising up. "I know where the meeting is. Half my agents have already called me. They're going to tell me what's being said anyway. So I don't see much point in you and I pretending anymore."

That finished it. He went home and got himself ready for bed. The phone rang. It was one of his loyal agents. All the agents wanted to have a breakfast meeting with him first thing tomorrow. They wanted to see him alone, without his officers.

Liniger did not go alone. He brought Gail Main and Bob Fisher. They were confronted at the door. He was supposed to come by himself. Liniger snapped back, "You seem to forget something: Your real estate license is with me. I own this company. You don't tell me how to run it. You can quit, if you want to; but until you do, I am the broker here, and we will conduct this meeting properly with everyone who ought to be involved." It was the first open expression of his anger since he'd learned of the revolt, and it righted the strange power dynamic that had been tangible in the room. Feeling the ground more stable beneath his feet again, Liniger sat down at one of the tables and opened his hands. "All right, now tell me what you want to meet about."

The agents recounted what had happened in the meeting the night before. The branch managers had told them that RE/MAX was finally going bankrupt and that the only way to save the firm was for all the agents to leave at once and re-form with the managers. That kind of talk had rattled them severely and brought many bad feelings and lingering anxieties to the surface. They were sick of the infighting between Liniger and the branch managers, tired of the negative press and the rumors about bankruptcy, and weary from the constant crisis management. They wanted to clear all matters up, once and for all.

When they had finished speaking, Liniger lifted a cardboard file box and put it on the table. "This is our debt," he said. "All the records, every scrap of paper, right in this box. Let's go through it, and I'll show you our payment plan and how we're going to do it."

The mood in the room changed as the debts got discussed openly. The agents could see the bills and the payment plans attached to them, as well as the itemized numbers on sheets of a yellow notepad. When he had finished answering all their questions, Liniger spoke for the first time about how he viewed what had happened the night before.

"We're going to make it," he said. "The managers saw this stuff two days ago. That's what really bothers me. They're not trying to bankrupt me to save your jobs, they're trying to bankrupt me to start a new company and have you work for them. I don't hold that against them. I tried to take you away from the companies you worked for, except I didn't have any fiduciary responsibility to those companies. They were my competitors. These guys are trying to destroy my company, and I pay them for a living."

It didn't sit right with any of them. Liniger knew this was a chance to start fresh with them all, to give everyone the freedom to be with him or to not be with him. "You do what you want to do," he said to them, filling the empty silence. "RE/MAX is going to make it. If you decide to leave, pay me your final bill, and I will release your listings to you."

The agents didn't want that. Liniger had been brave enough to give voice to their biggest fears, and now those worries did not seem so large anymore.

"We're staying with you," one of them said. "We worked hard to build this company. We're not quitting."

"All right then," Liniger said. "Thanks for saying that. Now let's get back to work."

An hour later, the eight branch managers showed up at Liniger's office. They were downcast and sheepish. "You beat us," one said. "Here are our resignations."

Liniger had been through one of the toughest, most draining 24-hour periods of his life. He looked up at his eight managers and saw their vulnerability. "Listen," he said, emotion in his voice. "This isn't about somebody beating somebody else. I don't blame you for what you did. I really don't. For the last two years, you guys have taken more crap than anybody. And I know I'm not the best guy in the world to work with. Come on, we saved the company today. I can't run it without you. Now's not the time for you to walk out. Better days are ahead, and it's a shame to give up when we're this close to getting there."

They were all near tears. What was left for them to do but have a drink? They broke open a bottle of the hard stuff and started to talk. Some cried. Some laughed. The feelings poured out, anger became diffused with laughter, and their intense worry dissipated. The revolt started to take on its rightful context almost immediately, one more colorful event in the history of big, crazy battles they'd fought in the service of a common cause. There had been fights before. Screaming matches. Threats and anger. Even power plays. But the hard feelings were usually over pretty quickly. This was up there with the worst, way up there; but in context, it was all part of what it took to survive. By the time they'd finished their drinks and clapped backs and parted, they were bonded once more. It was time to go back to work and fight the competition. They were one team against the world again.

The Spiritual Revival Meeting

Dennis Curtin couldn't have known what he was walking into, but he found out pretty quickly and stayed anyway. As the first person to ever buy a RE/MAX franchise, Curtin showed up in October 1975, six months after the branch manager revolt, just in time to give RE/MAX the nudge it needed to survive its next great crisis.

Curtin was from Kansas City and had gotten into real estate by default. After college, he'd wanted to be a stockbroker; but the company he signed on with looked like it was going to go out of business in the tough recession of 1973, so he joined a small father-son real estate firm instead. He was 24 years old and eager to succeed. He got promoted to branch manager at one of the offices and took on a leadership role. Kansas City was a competitive market for real estate. Though small, the firm was ambitious and wanted to make a mark. They worked hard on training agents but got tired of seeing those agents jump ship to more established firms once performance numbers had improved.

Curtin and his partners started looking around for a better model. An article in the *Kansas City Star* caught their eye. It was about a Realtor in town who had embraced the 100 percent concept and started a firm called Real Estate 100. The article gave backhanded credit to RE/MAX of Denver for initiating the idea. Curtin gave Liniger a call and said that he and

Jim Donaldson, his boss's son, were interested in visiting him and sharing some thoughts. Liniger had no idea who they were or why they wanted to speak with him, but he agreed to see them anyway. So the team from Kansas City flew up.

They were eager to meet Liniger and to talk to him about his ideas, but their eagerness dwindled when Liniger was late picking them up at the Marriott in South Denver. Finally, a beat-up car with a cracked windshield rolled up to the curb, and Liniger got out, wearing a bomber jacket. *Holy cow*, Curtin thought to himself. *Is this the guy we've wasted our money coming up to see?* Gail Main sat in the front seat, and Curtin and Donaldson piled into the back for the short drive to RE/MAX headquarters. In the 15 minutes it took to get there, Curtin and Donaldson went from thinking that they had made a big mistake to realizing that Dave Liniger was an original visionary. His insights into where the real estate industry was headed and how RE/MAX was positioning itself to get there were startling.

Curtin and Donaldson wanted in, and the negotiations started that evening in Curtin's hotel room. Liniger, Gail Main, and Bob Fisher were driving a hard bargain. Their buy-in numbers started off the scale, at $250,000. Donaldson's father, participating in the meeting by phone, wanted the Kansas City area for free. Many high balls were downed, and the talks continued. Curtin fell asleep on the bed. When he woke up in the middle of the night, Donaldson and Liniger were still hammering away at a deal. In the morning, Donaldson's father called off the negotiations. He was an old-time developer, steeped in his ways, and he could not see beyond the idea of changing his firm's name to RE/MAX. Disappointed, Curtin and Donaldson flew home, empty-handed.

Six months went by. The recession was dragging everyone down. Things were brutal not only for RE/MAX but for the real estate industry in general. Yet RE/MAX continued to grow due to its unwavering focus on top-line growth and its passion for sharing the dream. Curtin's firm had stopped paying commissions. As a newly married man with a young baby, he looked around again, searching for better options. The RE/MAX vision had stuck with him all that time, so he gave Dave Liniger another call.

"I don't know if you remember me," Curtin said over the phone, "but

I'm no longer with my firm. Would you be interested in selling me a RE/MAX franchise?"

Liniger said, "Sure," then cupped his hand over the phone, and yelled out, "Hey, does anybody here know what a franchise is?"

Curtin flew back to Denver. He brought his checkbook. By noon that day, he bought the first RE/MAX franchise. For the rest of the afternoon, he went through training with Liniger and a couple of other new people. That evening, Liniger invited Curtin to Gail Main's house for dinner. It was a nice meal. Curtin felt at home with the easygoing group. But before he went back to his hotel, Liniger pulled him aside in the driveway.

"Here's your check back," he said to Curtin. "I'm not going to be able to take it."

Curtin was shocked. "What are you talking about?" he asked, certain that something about him had failed to meet Liniger's standards.

"No, it's nothing like that," Liniger said. "I've had some bad news today. The creditors are all over us. They're going to put us into Chapter 11 tomorrow. It's going to hit the front page of the *Denver Business Journal*."

Curtin couldn't believe it. "What are you going to do?" he asked.

Liniger shrugged. "I've got a sales meeting for all my people tomorrow, and I'm basically going to tell them it's over. I'm going to do what I can to protect their commissions, but even that's going to be tough. You're welcome to come if you want."

Curtin, who just didn't feel right about giving up on this enterprise when he'd come so close to it, insisted that he wanted to attend. Liniger told him he'd pick him up the next morning at six o'clock.

Liniger, worn out and beat, figured the jig was finally up. Curtin drove with him in the morning. Sure enough, when they arrived at the restaurant where the meeting was to take place, they saw the devastating headlines on the front of the *Denver Business Journal*, the words "RE/MAX" and "Bankruptcy" blaring from the page. Liniger put a quarter in the newspaper box and hauled all the papers out so those who hadn't seen the edition yet wouldn't. Curtin followed Liniger into the meeting where almost 50 agents soon showed up. What happened next, Curtin would never forget.

Liniger stood up before the people in the room and told them what had happened. His story was outrageous and crazy—the strangest thing any of them had ever heard. The newspapers, Liniger said, are trying to put us out of business. "Folks, we made a gallant run," he declared. "I'm just sorry it didn't work."

Everyone was stunned. Despite all that had happened, nobody expected RE/MAX to fail. And now Liniger was telling them it was over. All the sacrifice, risk, and high hopes wasted. The hostility came forward in shouted questions.

Grant Goodson, an insurance man, had been one of Liniger's earliest backers. Well dressed, dapper, and smooth, he stood up as the emotions began to overheat and spoke out. "I've known Dave Liniger for the past couple of years," Goodson said, as the agents stopped to listen. "He's a good man," Goodson continued, choking up. "I have to tell you that I believe in RE/MAX. I believe that this concept will work. I believe in Dave and Gail. And I'm going to stay with it."

The next man to speak was over six and a half feet tall with a drawl, sounding to others like a Southern Baptist preacher. "You know something, I've been in the real estate business for over twenty-five years," he said. "And I've been with six different real estate companies over that time. This RE/MAX is the damnedest one of them all. There's a major crisis every quarter. I haven't been to a sales meeting yet where we weren't fighting and laughing, sometimes at the same time. Well, I don't know about the rest of you, but I'm going to stick around. I wouldn't miss seeing how this is going to turn out for the world."

Everyone laughed, even as there were tears in many eyes. Curtin couldn't quite believe the level of emotion he was witnessing. It was like a revival meeting in an old church or a baptism for born-again sinners. Before he knew it, he was standing up, speaking to the rest of the group himself, overwhelmed by the feeling that he needed to be heard.

"Guys, you don't know me. I'm Dennis Curtin from Kansas City, and I just bought the first RE/MAX franchise. Dave Liniger gave me my check back last night. He told me I would need the money because they're going to come after me, too, now that I'm connected to RE/MAX. Well, I have no idea what kind of organization you've built, but I can tell you've really got something good going here." He handed the check back to Liniger. "Here. You need this money for legal fees more than I do. I'm your first franchisee."

Curtin's declaration seemed to put them over the top. It was one thing for the insiders to pledge loyalty; it was quite another for a complete stranger to give his vote of confidence. Almost at once, a unanimous and positive feeling rose in the air. "Ah, screw it," one of them yelled out. "You go save the business; we're going to sell real estate. We're not leaving you now. Let's beat the bastards."

Bolstered by that surge in feeling and the sense of leadership responsibility that went with it, Liniger, Gail Main, and Bob Fisher left the room that day to work to rescue RE/MAX. The emotion and energy from the revival meeting were channeled directly into their voices; and over the next 48 hours, they were able to convince each creditor, and anyone else who mattered, that RE/MAX was not only going to make it, but it was going to thrive.

For Dennis Curtin, it was one of the most important and deeply affecting days of his life. He felt as though he'd gotten the full sense of RE/MAX, all the tough times and raw emotions, in a single wallop; and he left Denver that week a different man. There were lessons there, about leadership and business and what it meant to join with other human beings in common cause, that he would never forget. The meeting had been a healing process and a galvanizing event all at the same time. Three hours of complaints and questions, answers and testimonials, promises and commitments. More than half of the agents were women—still unusual in a male dominated business—and their presence in the room let even the men be more open and raw about their feelings.

Liniger had admitted failure and defeat, and his vulnerability dissolved the anger and hurt. Curtin watched how something about Liniger changed over the hour. He went from being the son of a bitch at the front of the room to "our son of a bitch"—nobody outside the organization had better try to take him down. The man who had seemed so overwhelmed the night before when he'd tried to hand the check back to Curtin now seemed as strong as anyone Curtin had ever known. "I made you change your careers," Liniger said at the end. "You bet on me, and you bet on this company. Some of you came from top firms. I promise you, as long as you support me, I'll support you. And if we do that, there's nothing that can put us out of business. We're going to make it."

Curtin knew that he had witnessed a moment when RE/MAX could have fallen and died. But instead, it kept going out of sheer tenacity, the will to do something unheard of and great, and the spirit of camaraderie in the face of overwhelming odds. More than anything else he understood: *By endurance, you conquer.*

General to General

The personal transformation that took place that October night in 1975 didn't mean that Liniger had suddenly lost his rough edges or his mode of constant battle. But the success of RE/MAX was rooted in that meeting. From that day forward, it seemed, a different level of energy was present in the organization.

The Crack Marketing Team went on the road, while Gail, Fisher, and Jesperson held down the fort in Denver. As time went on, the boundary between work life and home life continued to blur. They went through marriage problems together (and divorces), slept on each other's couches when things were bad, and looked after each other whenever health or family issues knocked any of them down. Every night, they worked late, then drank together even later, and got back at it early the next morning. They were inseparable in and out of work, bought motor homes and boats, and took family trips together. No matter how bad things got, they managed to have fun; and inevitably they became best friends.

The Colorado operation was growing rapidly. RE/MAX added its first franchise in Kansas City through Dennis Curtin in 1976. Offices opened in Calgary, Alberta, and in Washington, D.C. Within two years, RE/MAX grew to 100 franchises. In early 1977, it divided the country into regions and sold master franchises. Every region that opened went through the same pattern of struggle: the letter writing campaigns, the anonymous accusations, the rumors about bad ethics. Its almost laughable predictability gave other regional owners the courage and the tenacity to see themselves through. As RE/MAX grew, it became more sophisticated to run. The franchise agreements that had once been scribbled on cocktail napkins or pads of yellow paper grew in length. Every time RE/MAX ran into a problem, a new contract provision got added or an existing one amended. RE/MAX was a madhouse, barely under control; and it continued to transform the lives of those inside and to make believers of them along the way.

One such believer was Frank Polzler, an Austrian who emigrated to

Canada when he was 20 years old, barely able to speak English, with only $30 in his pocket. He worked odd jobs in the Toronto area for five years until he ended up in real estate. After a year of selling, he picked up his real estate broker's license in 1959 and learned every aspect of the business.

In 1967, he founded his own company, Polzler Real Estate, which grew to 160 people in six offices. But in the late 1970s, Polzler began to realize that no matter what he did or how he managed to survive, his company would always be a local real estate firm. Unlike the United States, Canada was dominated by large national companies. He knew he needed to affiliate himself with a brand name in order to grow.

Polzler had a young manager working for him by the name of Walter Schneider. Schneider was only 24 at the time, barely out of college; but Polzler had already promoted him to development manager and head of training. Schneider had a corporate sensibility, an inclination to see the real estate business become more sophisticated; and he joined Polzler's hunt for a leading-edge product, some way to break through the hold that the large multinationals had on the Canadian real estate market.

In 1979, Polzler and Schneider drove across the border to Detroit to attend a real estate symposium. Polzler had lunch with a colleague, one of the major brokers with more than a thousand agents in the Michigan area, and asked him what he saw that seemed new in the real estate industry. Technology was playing an increasing role. Firms were becoming more corporate. Franchises were going to become bigger and bigger because the little no-name companies needed a brand, better training, and some organization. This last comment hit Polzler to the quick, and he dug further. "Is there anything specific you see out there?" His friend nodded. "There's a little franchise out in Denver called RE/MAX. They'll only hire established, good people, and they're making major inroads all over the place."

At the time, RE/MAX had only a few thousand associates. Polzler and Schneider continued at the symposium, neither of them making any further mention of the company. Then, during the five-hour car ride back to Toronto, Polzler brought it up again. "Do you remember that franchise's name?" he asked. Schneider knew exactly what he was talking about. "RE/MAX," Schneider answered. Polzler nodded. "You've been thinking about them, too, huh. Why don't you look into them when we get back."

Schneider found information about RE/MAX in a magazine and wrote a letter. The address was wrong and the letter got returned. In the meantime, he flew to Calgary to visit the RE/MAX establishment there. The Calgary people had opened a few offices, and they were growing. Their enthusiasm and positive outlook intrigued Schneider and Polzler even more. Schneider decided to contact the RE/MAX people in Denver directly, and he and Polzler made arrangements with Greg Gilmore, their top salesman, to fly out and see things for themselves.

Everything about RE/MAX was wonderful except for one thing: Liniger was nowhere to be found. Polzler and Schneider thought they had an appointment; Liniger thought different. He was too busy, traveling too much, taking care of too many issues to guarantee an appointment with someone who just wanted to find out more about RE/MAX. Polzler wrote a brief note. "I came here to meet you, General to General, and you weren't good enough to see me." The team from Toronto went home, disappointed and frustrated.

Liniger felt bad that he'd missed them, but he felt angry, too. There was something about that note that got under his skin, an implication or an insinuation, and he couldn't shake it. He flew to Toronto and took a cab to the Polzler Real Estate office. Mr. Polzler was in a meeting. Liniger walked by the secretary anyway. He saw three men in a room. "Which one of you is Frank Polzler?" he demanded. Polzler nodded. "I am." "Well, my name is Dave Liniger, and I flew from Denver to Toronto to see you face-to-face because that's the kind of general I am. Now I'm going home." He turned, walked out of the room as abruptly as he had entered it, and was gone.

Polzler and Schneider were stunned. What had just happened? They'd never met anyone like this before. Could it have been a misunderstanding? They jumped up and raced after him, catching him getting into a cab. Liniger was still fuming, and it took a pantomime of explanations and counterexplanations to calm everyone down. Finally, they agreed on one thing: Liniger would stay over night to discuss the possibility that Frank Polzler Real Estate would buy a RE/MAX franchise.

They went to the Harbor Castle Hilton to continue their talks in an empty conference room. Everything about Polzler was wrong for RE/MAX, Liniger felt. Polzler had European manners; he was incredibly polite, highly distinguished, and older. His own firm wasn't going to make it. He didn't have what it took to make RE/MAX work. He couldn't commit any financial numbers. And the young guys were *too* young. They didn't have any franchising experience. But if Polzler was nothing else, Liniger discovered, he was insistent. In the obstinacy department, Liniger had finally met his match. Polzler wanted all of Eastern Canada, and Liniger finally relented and agreed to take their check for $20,000.

"So how do we sell franchises?" Polzler asked.

Liniger needed a pen but didn't have one. Because the hotel was being refurbished, there was dust on the glass table tops. So he drew a rough map of Toronto with his finger in the dust, then divided the city into grids and gave them their first and best lesson on how to sell franchises. Then Liniger headed back to Denver.

He called Gail from the airport, already filled with regret. "I screwed up," he said. "I should never have sold to these guys. They don't have a chance." It was, he declared, the biggest mistake he'd ever made. In a long history of some notable doozies, that sort of claim was cause for concern. In truth, Liniger couldn't have been more wrong. Out of all the gut decisions he had ever made for RE/MAX, the decision to sell to Frank Polzler and Walter Schneider would turn out to be his best. In fact, Liniger would later tell everyone who listened that, "RE/MAX was saved by Canada."

Changing Strategy to Stay True to the Goal

Meanwhile, Polzler and his team went to work. What do you do with half a country? Polzler focused on building his own RE/MAX franchise while Schneider hit the road and began selling franchises to others within their new territory, which stretched from Ontario in central Canada to Newfoundland out in the harsh North Atlantic. Polzler had tremendous confidence in Schneider. He had a rare ability to see solutions where others only saw problems, and he was driven and committed, if a little underconfident. Schneider felt like he was in over his head, but he didn't have time to be scared. He was 25, traveling widely for a "real company" for the first time in his life and holding things together on a shoestring budget. He was also becoming a hell of a salesman.

It took a struggle to even begin to sell, however. The Ontario real estate commissioner wouldn't allow Polzler to try the 100 percent concept. It was illegal in the provincial system, and the registrar told Polzler to get the entire scheme out of his head and leave him alone. Polzler, angry but always polite, told the registrar that he'd be speaking to his lawyer. "If it's illegal, you won't hear from me. But if the concept only needs some slight adaptations to be legal here, we'll be back." He believed he could make it work. He knew it would change the real estate industry. After a lot of legal discussions and negotiations, Polzler finally got his way. In the final compromise, Polzler agreed to include a 5 percent service fee for the broker. The RE/MAX 100 percent system became known as the 95/5 in Canada, jokes about exchange rates aside.

Polzler was well-known and respected in the Canadian real estate industry, so his conversion to RE/MAX turned more than a few heads. Competitors and colleagues wanted to know why a broker would do this, what was so different about the RE/MAX system, and how it would work. People were desperate for a better way.

The real estate industry was experiencing a terrible squeeze in the early 1980s. Things were particularly bad in the United States, where interest rates were hitting highs of 18 percent. Many businesses that had been around for years were now going under. RE/MAX had a radical new approach with the potential to be recession-proof, since the system was built on top agents more fit for survival.

Incredibly, Schneider and Polzler sold more than 30 franchises that first year. In the beginning, they didn't even realize the extent of their own success. But when they checked in with other regional owners in the United States, they understood that their rate of growth was off the charts. Half way through their second year, Polzler called Liniger with a new crisis. The contract he'd signed with Liniger stipulated that he couldn't sell more than 45 franchises. "Dave, I think we're going to sell more than sixty." Liniger laughed. "Forget about the stupid contract; just keep selling." He had gained a trust for Polzler and Schneider that overruled anything legal or contractual. It wasn't just their success. He had seen them in action and realized that he had completely misjudged them in the beginning. They were not only going to make it, they were going to break the mold.

For the rest of RE/MAX, Polzler's success was still under the radar. Canada was an outpost, a Fort Apache in the Wild West. Nobody knew them. Polzler attended a convention in Kansas City in the summer of 1983. A group of regional directors was seated around a bar speculating about when Liniger was going to go broke. Polzler was surprised by the negative talk. He'd been isolated from the power plays and politics south of the border; and frankly, he'd been too busy growing his business. The comments got under his skin. "We just got into this thing," he said, when the other owners asked him about his own experience, "but it's going great for us. I don't want to participate in this kind of conversation. You guys are all going to go broke if you don't change your attitudes. Instead of talking negatively, why don't you get out there and sell something?" It was the last talk he had with them—each and every one would end up leaving RE/MAX; and as far as Polzler was concerned, it couldn't be soon enough.

RE/MAX was hurting badly in the United States. Historic high interest rates were discouraging consumers from buying houses. Agents weren't making commissions and couldn't pay their brokers. Brokers couldn't pay their regional directors. Regional directors couldn't pay RE/MAX corporate. If not for the money that was pouring in from Canada, RE/MAX might well have gone broke. Even so, it barely survived.

Getting Out of the Boat

By early 1983, things got so bad in Denver that Vinnie Tracey, the head of training, left RE/MAX. He told Liniger that he wanted to go into another kind of business. He couldn't tell him the real reason. In truth, Tracey didn't feel that RE/MAX could afford to keep him on. Gail and Liniger kept giving him steady raises and kept praising his hard work, but there wasn't enough of that hard work for Tracey to do. The training classes had gone way down. They'd been running one every two weeks, with five or six trainers on staff. But now they were down to one every three weeks, and there was hardly any need for more than three trainers. If someone was sick in accounting or sales, Tracey would hustle over to help out and do that person's job for the day—sending mailouts, organizing materials, anything. But he wasn't doing the level of work he was being paid to do, and it was eating him up. Rather than take the organization's money any longer, he lied to them. He told them he needed to seize a new opportunity and move on, even as leaving broke his heart.

At the same time, Glenda and Don Hachenberger were feeling the strain, too. They knew RE/MAX was turning the corner, but the road was still rough. Don traveled constantly. Life was a juggling act. As an officer, there were weeks when Don was asked not to deposit his paycheck because the funds simply weren't there. Like the other officers, Don had picked up some franchises around the country in the belief that he could look after them while he traveled for the Crack Marketing Team, but that kind of part-time management simply wasn't viable when the real estate industry was in such trouble. Glenda, running Special Effects, spent much of her time visiting RE/MAX offices that couldn't pay their overdue bills, all while trying to manage her business. Even the kids and her father-in-law helped. She believed in RE/MAX and, most of all, the people. But she was having more and more difficulty with the hard-working, hard-partying, hard-living approach that seemed like fuel to everyone else. When the opportunity arose to sell Special Effects, she seized it. She'd built the firm up and made it a huge success within the RE/MAX marketing world, but it was a relief to let it go.

One of the RE/MAX franchise owners in Denver encouraged her to join him, and she agreed. Despite her RE/MAX life, she didn't know a thing about selling real estate; so she put a big bowl of candy on her desk and asked questions of any new colleague who came by to grab some. It was fun to be on the other side of the fence for a change and to feel like one more member in a larger team. Still, she and Don just weren't as happy as they wanted to be. Don was feeling the strain of all that travel, and he was growing tired of the corporate life. He was an entrepreneur at heart. While RE/MAX was in its most entrepreneurial phase, he'd felt juiced up every day; but now that RE/MAX was getting bigger and more complicated to run, things weren't quite as exciting. By the fall of 1983, the Hachenbergers decided that it was time to start thinking about making a major change.

Then, in October of 1983, Glenda got a call from Bob Fisher. His voice was hoarse. She could tell it was difficult for him to speak. She felt a chill run through her limbs.

"There's been a terrible plane crash," Fisher said. "Gail's hurt."

Oh, God, she thought. *Not Gail.* Fisher voiced her worst fears next.

"Glenda, we don't know if she's going to live."

Never Giving Up

No one knew it, but Dave Liniger and Gail Main were going to get married. Their first marriages had fallen apart during the tough early RE/MAX years, and they had fallen deeply in love with each other. It was going to be a surprise wedding, a fun event with their friends, disguised as an invitation to a celebratory dinner at the Chateau Pyrenees. Liniger had booked the restaurant, made the arrangements, and set it all up. It was to take place right after a trip to Canada for a RE/MAX convention.

They stayed at a resort in northern Ontario called Deer Hearst. Frank Polzler invited Liniger and Gail for a quick side trip by seaplane to visit his new cabin located on a nearby lake. Gail had never been on a seaplane before and was eager to check it out. Liniger took a pass; there were some people he wanted to talk to that afternoon. He watched from the dock as the plane took off. It reacted as though it were heavy, to his trained eye, skimming across the water. Even as he went back inside for a drink with some colleagues, he couldn't shake the feeling that something bad was going to happen.

It was only a 15-mile journey. The plane landed safely on Polzler's lake. It was not a sunny afternoon, and there was no reason to linger. They got back in for the return flight. As they accelerated for take off and started to rise, Polzler couldn't believe what he was seeing—they weren't climbing fast enough. The pilot had misjudged the distance he needed to safely clear the lake's edge. There was no way they were going to make it.

Polzler had time to slip the life jacket over his head before the plane hit the trees. The propeller sounded like a lawn mower going through the branches, chewing and spinning. The impact threw him forward and lurched him back, flipped the plane over and then slammed them down hard. He blacked out. When he opened his eyes, he thought he must be waking up from a bad dream. But when he tried to move, the pain in his side and hip was excruciating.

Back at the resort, Liniger knew that too much time had gone by. He called the local hospital and asked if they had heard anything about a plane crash, fearing the worst, already knowing what he would learn. Yes, they told him. The ambulances were on the way. Some of the passengers were dead.

People on the lake had seen the crash and rushed over to look for survivors. The wings had snapped off when the plane sliced through the forest, and there was an overpowering smell of gasoline from all the fuel that escaped. The plane had actually cut a power line—it was a miracle that a fire hadn't started. The body of the plane was bent in half and crumpled like a sardine can. The pilot was dead. But they managed to pull Polzler and Gail out. Polzler was in bad shape but not critical. Gail looked much worse. Instead of taking her to the local hospital, the ambulances rushed her to Sunnybrook, in Toronto, which specialized in severe trauma cases. When Liniger finally reached her, he found her in a coma.

Liniger wouldn't leave her side. For him, RE/MAX had come to a stop. The doctors told him that Gail might never wake, might never walk again, might never be the same. But Liniger wouldn't believe them and wouldn't even permit that kind of talk around her. He read to her. He brought their golden retriever in to see her. He played her motivational tapes. He talked to her constantly. He told her over and over that she was going to be all right. "We'll beat this," he said to her. "You're stronger than this. You're going to make it."

Polzler got a visit from Liniger. Despite the horror of what he had been through, the only thing on Polzler's mind was Gail. He had insurance, and he knew Liniger would need all the money he could get to help Gail survive, let alone recover. "It's yours," he told Liniger. "I don't need it. I'm going to be fine. I'll be walking again soon." He had a crushed hip and a bruised kidney, but it was nothing compared to what Gail had suffered: head injury, partial paralysis, shattered bones. It was awful, but Liniger didn't lose faith. As a combat veteran, his attitude was rock certain: He'd never left anyone behind before—Gail was going to make it.

Back in Denver, the other officers knew that they had to keep RE/MAX going. In a sense, they needed to take over for Liniger, as though he had been in that plane crash, too. Fisher called Liniger every day. He wanted to come up to see Gail. Everyone did. Her room was filled with flowers, sent from all over RE/MAX. Liniger told Fisher he wasn't welcome. He was needed back in Denver. Fisher ignored him and flew up anyway. "She's my friend, too." When he got into the room, he was shocked. Patients with severe head injuries don't sleep in a regular hospital bed. Instead, they are placed in a floor bed, resembling a child's wading pool, and are allowed to thrash about while the swelling is most severe and the brain struggles to reroute its motor connections. Standing before Gail, he spoke quietly with Liniger, who was as defiant as Fisher had ever seen him. She was going to make it. She was getting better. You went through the bad stuff first, then the recovery could start. Once she stabilized, Liniger would somehow get her into the Craig Hospital back in Denver. It had the best head trauma unit in the country.

Gail must have sensed that they were there. Her words were badly slurred, but clear as day.

"Hey, Fish," she said. "Where's my beer?"

Fisher and Liniger stood next to her and cried.

Gail was flown to Craig Hospital in Denver on a special plane. A new routine took shape as the long months of rehabilitation and recovery began. The doctors told Gail she should get used to life in a wheelchair. Gail told them again and again, struggling to get the words out, that they were wrong—when she left the hospital, she was going to walk.

Although Liniger was with her every day, he never let go of RE/MAX. In fact, he had negotiated the sale of the New England region to Frank Polzler in the hospital in Toronto and kept up on every decision and important meeting. But he focused his formidable willpower on helping Gail. She needed him. RE/MAX needed her. He was going to see her through. Others came to visit every day. Seeing Liniger through this was just as important to them. They made sure he ate. They took him out for drinks, anything to get him out of the hospital for even a short time. They replenished his supply of books. Fisher was amazed at the ferocity with which he read. Liniger got the equivalent of an MBA in the next few months, reading every business book he could get his hands on, obtaining some critical idea or kernel of understanding from each one.

Leading the day-to-day operations, Fisher and Jesperson tag-teamed. Formal titles had never mattered anyway, and they just did what was necessary and gave whatever it took. It was easier, in some ways, to stay focused during this dark period. The tragedy and the high stakes concentrated the mind—one foot in front of the other, never looking up. RE/MAX had been barely hanging on financially because of the recession and the high interest rates. Other real estate franchising companies were losing numbers fast and terminating franchises left and right for not paying their fees. But RE/MAX didn't want to do that; it had worked hard to build its network. It believed in those people. As long as the franchisees kept the lines of communication open, told the officers at corporate what their plans were, paid even $5 a month, they'd all ride it out together. With Gail's accident, once overwhelming challenges seemed petty all of a sudden, altered by their new, radically different perspective. That was the silver lining. Everyone came together more strongly, the bonds that much tighter.

By March, Gail was out of the woods. She left the hospital, using a cane and support casts, but on her own power. It was one of the most remarkable recoveries the doctors and nurses had ever seen. Most people would have been content just to be alive; but Gail wanted to be part of the game again, and Liniger was not about to stop her. The annual RE/MAX convention was in Orlando, Florida, that year; and Liniger hired a special nurse and a special plane to bring Gail with them. When she was wheeled onto the stage on opening day, her head shaved on one side, her smile angelic, the cheering and crying was thunderous. The miracle was not only on the individual scale; it also gave a sense of possibility to all of them. RE/MAX had struggled and fought through so many desperate moments over the past 10 years that few outside the inner circle might have given it any odds of survival. There was a feeling, then, in the middle of the applause and tears, that the company that they had fought so hard to build had finally turned a corner. The only proof any of them needed was smiling at them from up on the stage.

Tails You Win

Gail and Dave Liniger never made it to the Chateau Pyrenees where Liniger had planned their surprise wedding. Instead, in 1984, they got married in the office. Could there be a more perfect place? The ceremony was conducted by Steve Woolley, one of their vice presidents, who happened to be a Mormon bishop. Liniger had hired him, they all joked, to keep God on his side. With their friends in attendance, Mr. and Mrs. Liniger spoke their vows, then everyone went across the street for dinner. The men played "Pac Man," the new video game that was all the rage. The whole event was low key, but beautiful just the same. The fact that it had happened at all made it truly special.

Liniger had changed; they all had. When you're in your thirties and struggling with something as glamorous as building a company, flying places, doing deals, staving off the enemy, you feel bulletproof. Gail's accident, on top of all the struggles RE/MAX had gone through, sobered and matured them, gave them a keener sense of mortality and life's meaning-fulness. They had an urge now to build the network not just for their own personal gain but for reasons of legacy, too.

But that didn't mean they still didn't like to have fun.

It had been a long, long time since Liniger had anything approaching an outrageous good time. Now that he was starting to get back into the swing of things, he missed that sense of energy. They were all so damn se-rious now. At lunch with Hachenberger, he complained about it. "I'm not having any fun anymore, Hack," he said. "We need a trip. Can you guys get away on Saturday? Let's go to the Bahamas. I want to hit the casino."

Saturday, Hachenberger thought? It was already Thursday. But when they got back to the office, Liniger made arrangements for a plane and some hotel rooms. It was an extravagance they could barely afford, but what the hell—they needed it. They flew down on the weekend, enjoying themselves in the plane cabin like it was old times—two couples, four friends. After dinner at the hotel, they spent a little time together in the casino. But Don and Glenda were not big gamblers like Dave and Gail, and they went to bed early. Around two o'clock in the morning, Hachen-berger woke up suddenly, hearing a pounding on the door between their adjoining rooms. "Hack! Let me in! Let me in!" It was Liniger's voice. *Gail,* he thought. *Something must be wrong with Gail.* He jumped out of bed, wearing only his underwear, and threw open the door. Liniger ran in through the open doorway, wearing his colorful Bermuda shirt, shorts, and sandals—covered in sweat, a mad gleam in his eye, both fists filled with money.

"I struck it rich!" he yelled and threw the money into the air. It hit the ceiling fan and scattered everywhere. Thousands of bills (nearly $20,000, in fact) flew this way and that, landing on the floor, the table, the bed. Glenda, still beneath the covers, started grabbing handfuls of money and shoving it under the sheets. "It's mine now!" she yelled. And Liniger, rising to the dare, jumped on the bed to try pulling the covers off. "I'm coming after it! I'm coming after it!"

They hadn't laughed that hard in years. It was just what the doctor or-dered. It almost made it possible to keep going.

Shortly after they returned to Denver, Hachenberger had his talk with Liniger. He and Glenda had postponed their plans because of Gail's accident; but now that things were settled again, it was time. In some ways, Liniger must have sensed that it was coming. "I'm going to resign, Dave. I need a change." RE/MAX was big enough, it didn't need him now the way it once had. He was an entrepreneur. He needed to do something that would get his juices flowing. He knew Liniger would probably take the news hard, but he was touched by what happened next. Liniger didn't try to argue him out of his plan or bully him into staying. Instead, he only expressed deep concern about what Hachenberger was going to do. "I'm not sure yet," Hachenberger answered. "I might sell real estate with Glenda. Sid Syvertson invited me to come to California and be a part of what he's doing, and I've got a couple of other things I'm looking at." He shrugged. That part was still up in the air. Thinking it through clearly had been difficult with the weight of resigning on his mind. Now, Liniger was not only freeing Hachenberger to worry about himself, but he was on his side, as any loyal friend would be.

"Okay," Liniger said. "I want to spend some time with you and work this out. It's almost four o'clock. Let's cut out of here and go to my house."

They left the office in separate cars and drove to Liniger's house. From four o'clock that afternoon until four o'clock the next morning, they stood at Liniger's bar and drank and talked. Liniger wanted to know everything that Hachenberger was thinking and feeling. "Tell me what's going on? Why can't we change this? What are we going to do?"

It became clear to Liniger over the course of the night that Hachenberger was leaving for real. "Hell," he said. "I want to keep you in the system. You can't just sell real estate. You've got all this knowledge and experience. I want you to be part of this thing. I need your help. It'd be a shame to miss out now, just when we're on the verge of really taking off."

Hachenberger didn't know. Maybe a clean break was better. He was all ears, but he didn't see any viable possibilities. He needed to find something new for himself.

"I got it," Liniger exclaimed. "I'll sell you Colorado."

Colorado was the prime franchise region in the country, and it was owned by Liniger himself. It was an absurdly generous gesture, but one Hachenberger couldn't accept. "Dave, I know what you're thinking, but you can't do that. Colorado's going too well. You can't afford to get rid of it, and I can't afford to buy it."

"Bull," Liniger said, refusing to give up, "there's got to be something we can do. Meet me back at the office at seven o'clock."

Seven o'clock. Hachenberger had time to drive 35 miles to the other side of the city, shave, jump through the shower, change his clothes, and head back to the office. Liniger was already there. It never ceased to amaze Hachenberger. The man had the constitution of a bear—able to outdrink everyone, raise hell, go for it in all situations, and still get in early, as if to punish himself or to prove how tough he was. In that particular contest, Hachenberger had lost to Liniger a thousand times.

Liniger brought Hachenberger to his planning room. He already had numbers and files spread out across the desk. "Okay, you're right. I can't afford to sell you Colorado. But, goddamnit, we've got some other regions. Let's find something else for you."

Liniger suggested the Northwest. It was just opening up: Oregon, Washington, Montana, Idaho. Hachenberger knew he was making the kind of decision he'd want to live with for the rest of his life. "Dave, honestly, it's the weather. And being so far away from family? I don't know if we could do it."

Liniger tried the Carolinas next, but Hachenberger wasn't sure about that either. Still, he'd gotten excited about the idea of owning a region in the meantime, and Liniger could tell he was hooked. "You just figure out what will work for you," Liniger said, "and let me know. We'll make it happen."

So Hachenberger went off and did some research on such things as crime rates and school rankings, knowing that his three kids would need the right environment for their own families as they got older. He did the numbers, looked up counties, populations, and projected growth for different regions. And when he went back to Liniger, he still hadn't figured out what he should do. Nothing really fit what he wanted. His best bet seemed to be Syvertson in northern California. Syvertson had even said that when he retired, years down the road, Hachenberger could buy him out.

But Liniger had done some homework of his own. "What about Florida?" he asked.

Florida had failed a half dozen times. "It never occurred to me," Hachenberger said. "It's cut into four regions."

"I can put them together," Liniger replied.

"I never thought we'd consider that."

"You do the numbers and see what it looks like. Then we'll make a deal," Liniger countered.

Hachenberger went off. He had a lot of thinking to do. He looked around the RE/MAX system and considered what worked best. The Canadians had the fastest growth in the whole network by far. So, Hachenberger called Walter Schneider and talked to him. Polzler and Schneider had just bought the New England region and were performing magic there again. Schneider gave Hachenberger some insights as to what worked well and what was a struggle. When Hachenberger had crunched some more numbers, he realized that the secret was the difference in the broker fee that was part of the Canadian system: 100 percent was great for the agents and great for RE/MAX International, but the obvious problem was broker profitability.

To Liniger, 100 percent was not just a number; it was a symbol that embodied a core principle. The *everybody wins* idea was at the heart of RE/MAX. It was the reason why Liniger had been moved to launch the company in the first place and why he had fought for it time and again. He was in it for the agents. Polzler's 95/5 had been a compromise based on a legal restriction. Hachenberger's argument that the brokers needed more benefit from the system worked on Liniger's head, but not his gut. And yet, Liniger had never been against experimenting within the system. (See Figure 5.1.) That was the beauty of RE/MAX. It was diverse and attuned to local conditions. The best ideas could be brought forward and shared widely.

In the end, Liniger relented. Hachenberger could buy Florida, as one region, and operate it under a 95/5 system. They shook hands on the deal, which was all either one of them ever needed to make a promise.

"All right," Liniger said. "Go out there and grow the hell out of this thing."

There would be other crises, other moments that tested the organization's endurance—trials, failures, crooked deals, mistakes, illnesses, marital problems. In 1988, a conflict erupted with one of Liniger's early regional owners who had bought three regions in the Carolinas, Maryland, and Virginia. But Liniger believed the owner wasn't pushing hard enough, and the

All organizations eventually face "dream siege."

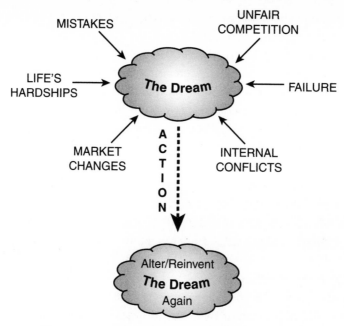

Figure 5.1 Theory of Unavoidable Consequences

competitors were passing him by. Liniger says he encouraged him, cajoled him, got angry at him; and the feelings between them broke down. Liniger was just trying to help; but apparently the owner worried that Liniger was trying to shut him down and filed a lawsuit. Liniger sued back. The other regional owners like Don Hachenberger interceded because the lawsuits threatened the legality of the entire RE/MAX system. The negotiations went on and on but were going nowhere. Finally, Liniger offered to settle everything, winner take all, under arbitration by a panel of regional directors—no attorneys, no advisors, just friends making a decision in the best interests of friends. Liniger won the debate, hands down.

The negotiations kept going, however, until a deal was finally struck. As the papers were about to be signed, Liniger says the man demanded one last thing. He wanted $250,000 cash from Liniger. It enraged Liniger. It could have been a deal breaker. But he went back into the room and confronted the owner face-to-face. "Let me understand this. We've already got a deal, right?" The owner said yes. "And you think I ought to pay you 250,000 bucks in addition to that?" He said yes. "All right," Liniger said, "I'll tell you what. I'll flip you for it."

Liniger was serious. Hachenberger had an oversized coin in his pocket that had been given to him by his great aunt after a trip to Las Vegas. He had carried it with him for good luck every day of his life since he was 12 years old. He took out the coin and handed it to Liniger. Liniger flipped it in the air and caught it on the back of his hand, covering it with his palm. "Let's make sure we understand this again," he said. "If I win, I don't have to pay you. If you win, I do have to pay you. But we have a deal either way." The owner said yes. "Okay, call it." The owner called heads. Liniger didn't even look at it and said, "Every man deserves a good piece of tail." And he uncovered his hand. Tails was the call. The new regional owners of the man's old territory would name their company "Tails Incorporated."

In Florida, Hachenberger was still part of the RE/MAX family, but he saw Denver from a distance now. As RE/MAX International took off and really began to grow, he and Glenda were part of that growth from a different angle, building up their own region beyond anyone's expectations. They had sold everything they owned to make the move to Florida, started over from scratch, and opened a small RE/MAX office above a TV repair shop. All the experience and knowledge they had gained working for RE/MAX International, all those years in the trenches, paid off. They began to build the system and make it grow. Within 20 years, Don and Glenda Hachenberger would have 195 offices with over 5,300 agents doing $19 billion in business. Their success story would be matched and surpassed by others like Sid Syvertson and Steve Haselton in California and Frank Polzler and Walter Schneider in North America and Europe.

RE/MAX achieved its incredible growth despite the fact that it should never have survived at all. There were too many obstacles, sharp turns, and sudden drops for anyone to reasonably expect that the small firm would last, let alone prosper. But the tenacity with which it overcame adversity, strategic mistakes, a lack of resources, personal tragedy, and unlikely odds makes the lessons for those launching their own great ventures all the more powerful. In the RE/MAX experience, if you stick to the dream and stay together, eventually you will win. There will be huge hardships along the way, struggles that you cannot even imagine. When you meet those obstacles, you need to believe in the dream and look out for one another, no matter what comes your way. If you give in, give up, or sell out, you will never know what you might have become. By endurance, you conquer.

Strategic Moves

Stay focused under fire.

The stability that RE/MAX exhibited during crisis is admirable. As an emerging, entrepreneurial organization beset with crises, it was able to maintain its focus on top-line measures and growth. Even while Dave Liniger stayed in the hospital at night keeping a vigil on Gail's recovery, he received top-line measure reports and sent notes back and forth to key members of his top team. With or without its two cofounders, the dream team executed flawlessly by placing one step in front of another.

- When your dream is threatened, establish a new goal around the dream for your team to refocus on and rally. Relentlessly focusing on an interim objective will provide your team with a sense of purpose and mission. (pp. 102–103)

- Approach adversity, mistakes, lack of resources, personal tragedy, and unlikely odds with tenacity. If you stick to the dream and stay together, you will eventually win. When you meet obstacles, believe in the dream and look out for one another, no matter what comes your way. By endurance, you will conquer. (p. 104)

- If you bring in people who truly say "yes" to the dream, they will support and stand by their leader in times of hardship and persecution. They will believe in the dream even when the leader is having a hard time believing and will help the leadership stay strong. (pp. 105–107, 116)

- Continue to invest in your people no matter what the company is going through and they will stay with you, support you, and be the force that allows your company to sustain itself. (pp. 108–109)

- Be vulnerable and honest with your people when your company is in trouble. You will earn their trust and loyalty. Ask their opinions—

they may have some great ideas for how you can run the company better. (p. 109)

- Pay attention to what your people need to improve their performance. Be eager for your people to succeed because the company will only succeed if *everybody wins*. (p. 109)

- Rely on those with whom you have shared the dream to carry you forward in crisis. They will keep the organization focused during dark periods and keep one foot in front of the other. (RE/MAX continued to stay focused on growth even after the plane crash.) (pp. 127–128)

- If key people are unhappy or dissatisfied with their job, spend time with them to find out what is wrong and then do whatever you can to find them a new role that will be a better fit. (p. 130)

- You need to be flexible to ultimately win, and sometimes you have to shift your goal to keep focused on the dream. (pp. 134–135)

Lesson

Keep unwavering focus on the dream, even in adversity.

There is an old saying: "Hard luck can be your good luck—if you let it." There is another: "When the tide is out, you can see the rocks" (John F. Keane, founder of Keane Inc., a medium-cap growth company that has endured for 40 years in the software services business). The tide will be out sometimes, and there will be "hard luck." How leaders face adversity and navigate at low tide determines survivability. Shackelton's story about endurance can be related to HG/HI organizations in many different ways. At RE/MAX and our benchmark companies, "endurance" has required the courage to survive in order to thrive. Some great growth companies no longer exist because they didn't navigate the rough times. (See Figure 5.2.) Digital Equipment Corporation, for example, stayed too long with a product, confusing it with the dream, and was consequently too slow to move.

When RE/MAX came under threat and faced adversity, its leaders huddled together and dug deep. The lessons around this include making sure that the organization has the capacity to focus and refocus in adversity. Figure 5.3 shows three focus-and-refocus methods from RE/MAX and its benchmark HG/HI companies.

When Under Attack

Do ← → Don't

Company	Action	Company	Action
IBM	Changed Business Lines	Digital Equipment	Denied Realities of Market Shift
Canon	Constantly Adapted Product Mix	Xerox	Waited Too Long to Change Structure
McDonald's	Responded with Higher-Nutritional-Value Foods	Enron	Exploited the Business
Intel	Reinvented Product Mix Twice	AT&T	Became Culture Bound
Gillette	Rebuilt Product	Bethlehem	Believed in Infallibility

Figure 5.2 Actions to Alter/Reinvent the Dream

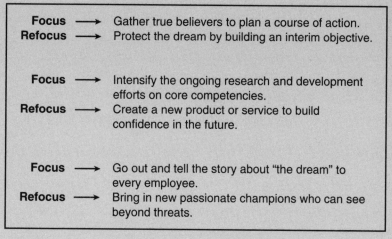

Focus ⟶ Gather true believers to plan a course of action.
Refocus ⟶ Protect the dream by building an interim objective.

Focus ⟶ Intensify the ongoing research and development efforts on core competencies.
Refocus ⟶ Create a new product or service to build confidence in the future.

Focus ⟶ Go out and tell the story about "the dream" to every employee.
Refocus ⟶ Bring in new passionate champions who can see beyond threats.

Figure 5.3 Under Threat or Attack: Focus/Refocus Methods

EAGLES DON'T FLOCK

Spreading the Principles of an *Everybody Wins* Culture

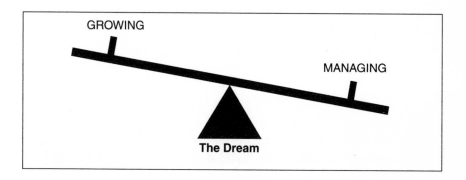

Leaders are like eagles—they don't flock . . . you find them one at a time.
—Anonymous

From 1977 onward, as RE/MAX spread across the map, the franchise owners flew to Denver for training. They came from cities and towns as diverse as Milwaukee, Wisconsin; Coppell, Texas; and Jefferson City, Missouri; and from as far away as Hearts Content, Newfoundland (right next to Hearts Desire and Hearts Delight). They signed on to the dream because they had a sense that the real estate world was changing and that RE/MAX was on the leading edge of the new way. Since the rise of the first national real estate firms, experts had been predicting that the real estate industry would converge and coalesce until it became dominated by two or three major players, like Pepsi and Coke in the soft drink industry. Perhaps it still would, but the franchise owners who came to Denver saw the world of real estate undergoing a different kind of realignment, splitting into two distinct models. In the traditional *broker-centric* firms, the agent was an employee and the vicious cycle ruled. The model of the future would be *agent-centric*, and it would bring with it an entirely different set of rules and strategies.

Feeling the undercurrent pressures of that emerging model, these brokers looked up and saw RE/MAX, an upstart firm that truly seemed to get it. Richard Mendenhall was a successful broker, a student of the industry, and very active within its mainstream associations. From the vantage point of various industry committees, Mendenhall had seen how fast RE/MAX was growing relative to the other franchise firms and knew that their agent-centric approach was the wave of the future. Ted Rowe, of Hearts Content, Newfoundland, saw the concept as totally different and utterly logical. He was tired of the revolving-door relationship with agents—hiring new people with promise, seeing them leave months later—and wanted to build a firm with a more solid foundation. He viewed RE/MAX as the vehicle to attract people with a professional orientation to real estate, people whom he could then groom and retain. Heather Skuce, in Ottawa, Ontario, faced the same challenge. She had seen the writing on the wall for the small independent brokers. The traditional approach to agent recruitment was, "If you have a desk, keep it full." But she knew that the time for such a philosophy was over, given the level of competition from the major brands. With her partners, she investigated every franchise model around and had come close to buying in to some, but something held her back. When a representative from Frank Polzler and Walter Schneider's group in Toronto presented the RE/MAX model, she and her partners looked at one another and realized: *This is it*.

Agents came to Denver because of the revolutionary idea, but they became passionate believers because of the culture. They ran into that culture head on. How could they not? With Dave Liniger, they met someone who matched none of their ideas about what the executive head of a burgeoning empire might look like. He was larger than life and rough and ready; but he had a savviness with people, a way of speaking simple truths with great impact, and an unstoppable energy for his vision. It was not a show or an act; the Liniger experience was for real. Ted Rowe remembers driving with him at high speeds through the streets of Denver, hanging on to the arm rest of Liniger's Corvette for dear life, as he talked about the future of real estate. The counterbalance to Liniger was the almost beatific steadiness of Gail. Her warm attentiveness to each person who came to

Denver made him or her feel more like a long-lost friend than a future business partner. Daryl Jesperson had the numbers, the financial arguments, the business plan insights, which they needed to operationalize the system. Bob Fisher had the glint in the eye of a true believer, but his matter-of-fact articulation of the vision bolstered and backed up Liniger's own. Don Hachenberger's laid-back, easygoing style made his commitment to the crazy energy of RE/MAX all the more convincing. Liniger had assembled a team of very different individuals with the cohesion of a family that provided a stabilizing force and was at the same time totally committed to the dream. It was a combination that made the RE/MAX culture instantly accessible for those who came into its realm.

Vinnie Tracey, boisterous as a teammate on the sidelines, excited to be meeting new apostles, led the training. *You're not in the real estate business anymore; you're in the real estate* agent *business.* That meant changing how brokers viewed their role as well as their relationship with agents—more selective, more personal, attentive to their needs. Brokers had to track the best, work on them over time, and convince them to come on board, transforming their jobs as well as their lives. It all started with recruitment, an activity that a few of the brokers found uncomfortable. In the clubby world of real estate, it felt aggressive to some, like a cross between proselytizing and telemarketing.

Heather Skuce was particularly beset by this challenge. She was more at ease with balance sheets, deal making, strategic thinking, and big ideas than she was with selling people on Liniger's dream. Vinnie Tracey pushed her hard during role-play sessions; but Skuce just didn't feel right going through the motions of recruiting someone in front of the others. "Heather," Tracey asked, "what are you afraid of?" She was uncomfortable talking to the people, she admitted. Tracey nodded. "Let me tell you something that will change the way you think about it." He described the Canadian real estate industry lay of the land. There were five major firms, all based on trust companies or banks, that dominated 80 percent of the market. Even more than in the United States, agents in Canada had no alternative to the traditional broker-centric way of doing business. RE/MAX, on the other hand, saw the agent as the customer. Heather would be offering people a career that would help them support and provide for their families in a new and better way. "You should never be afraid of talking to someone about coming to work with you at RE/MAX. *You've got the power to change people's lives.*" They were words that she would remember often during her own RE/MAX journey.

One of the most interesting aspects of the RE/MAX story is how successfully new franchise owners were able to absorb and spread the RE/MAX philosophy through the real estate markets in their own towns and cities. The RE/MAX culture and vision is based on a principle that would make capitalist thinkers from Adam Smith to Alan Greenspan proud—the idea of *enlightened self-interest.* Give people what they want, and you will get what you want in return. Find agents who are dedicated to customer service, provide them with what they need to succeed, and you will be rewarded in return. The brokers took the basic knowledge from their training seminars back with them, tested it under local conditions, and then shared what worked among themselves. The fact that their approaches and results were remarkably consistent says something about the power of culture to transcend geography and personality while staying true to a core belief system. Even if the brokers who came to Denver did not fully anticipate all the challenges they would later face, they left fired up to get out and change the world. As Jeff Benson of Milwaukee, Wisconsin, recalled, "We could have flown back without a plane."

Foundations for Individual Success

Over the years, the things that worked were kept, and the things that didn't were left behind. What became crystal clear was that the basic building block of the new RE/MAX franchise was the agent. One key to the success of the RE/MAX system was changing that agent's mindset about the nature of his or her business. The typical agent woke up each year, on the morning of January 1, with a problem. Somehow, over the next 12 months, she needed to make $100,000 in order to support her family, life style, and interests. Fear being a wonderful motivator, that agent got cracking. By the time the agent looked up again in June, she had made $70,000. Now, it was time to enjoy a feeling of respite. Somehow, for another year, she had made it, or was sure to make it, and would not need to panic and scramble to survive. The agent hadn't seen her family for many weekends in a row, hadn't enjoyed a vacation, and had put off buying that new car. Now, the agent was able to choose not to work on weekends when she might otherwise have attended yet another open house. It is not surprising that the agent's sales rate slowed during this down time. The anxiety or fear picked up again in the fall, and the scramble resumed. At the end of the year, the agent might come in a little above or a little below the $100,000 target; but one thing was certain: The hamster wheel was going to start spinning again come January 1.

Most agents found themselves caught in this loop. They had terrific sales skills but did not always have the business capability to build something more substantial and lasting out of their efforts. Even the best agents, able to make more than they needed in commissions, were limited by the targets they had set for themselves. Some were aiming for much higher earnings, others for membership in elite sales clubs; but their overall progress from one year to the next had a ceiling. Agents started each new year back on the ground floor wondering how they were going to pull it off this time.

To create the *everybody wins* culture, RE/MAX brokers first altered the environment in which agents functioned. The commission structure was the most obvious and boldest stroke—100 percent instilled a very different kind of thinking than a traditional split did. Another huge difference was personal promotion. RE/MAX agents put their own name prominently on their For Sale signs, and most had the opportunity for a private office and secretarial support. These were trappings that no other real estate firm provided at the time, and they helped create a more professional atmosphere.

The office space was a difference maker. When Heather Skuce went back to Ottawa to launch her RE/MAX franchise, she was typical of many RE/MAX brokers in that she seized the opportunity to open brand-new office space. When recruiting new agents, it helped highlight the different approach her firm represented. She could take those prospective agents to the new space and show them the layout, the color scheme, and the future location of each agent's office. The walls might have been imaginary still, and the floor covered in debris, but she was able to sell the agents just the same.

Another important innovation had to do with how those offices were run. Most traditional offices relied on secretarial-administrators or agent-managers for day-to-day operations. But this approach instilled a "me-first" attitude. Secretarial-administrators didn't always understand the nuances of the business, while agent-managers were naturally prone to favoritism in how the best walk-in referrals got doled out. By upgrading to professional administrators or managers who were responsible for running the office, recruiting new agents, and improving overall performance numbers, RE/MAX brokers injected fairness and team spirit into operations. Offices became more closely bonded as a result, driving for individual and group goals with a positive attitude characteristic of the brokers themselves.

The shift to fixed costs was another critical leap forward for the professionalization of the system. In the early years, brokers monitored and shared expenses with agents in an open-book fashion. But dealing with itemized expenses led agents to question each one and took up a great deal of the broker's time. Gary Thomas, a broker owner from California, couldn't stand focusing valuable energy on small details when he knew that everyone would be better off driving for more growth. A business manager in his pre–RE/MAX life, Thomas took all the nickels, dimes, and dollars and added them up on a yearly basis to determine the average cost that each agent incurred. This became the agent's fixed cost for the following year. From the perspective of developing a business mindset, agents benefited from knowing exactly what they were going to spend on fixed costs in the coming year and having that money taken directly out of their paychecks, rather than paying a bill at the end of each month. Suddenly, they had a baseline to move forward from and began to think more like businesspeople about growth.

Brokers like Gary Thomas were also instrumental in broadening the revenue streams of those business agents, adding escrow, title company, mortgage, and other services. It all comes down to thinking about the customer from the agent's point of view: How can that agent look better in the eyes of a potential customer? What services and capabilities will make it easier and more profitable for him or her to conduct business? What's going to make it more appealing for that customer to work with one of his or her agents instead of someone at one of the other major brands?

This overall professionalization—the fixed costs, the maximum commission-split structure, the use of personal promotion, the way the office was organized and managed, the array of services—all led to a different kind of environment in which top agents could grow and thrive. Most agents weren't going to thrive in a maximum commission-split system. For brokers, making room for top agents and raising the level of performance overall meant culling the ranks. It was an approach that could best be described as taking two steps backward to make a powerful stride forward. Having laid the groundwork, the broker owner could now turn to his or her real objective—encouraging new top agents to leave their current firms and come on board with RE/MAX.

They understood something about those top agents that other firms didn't always take into account. The essence of that understanding was encapsulated in a saying that Vinnie Tracey was fond of using: *Eagles don't flock*.

Top talent, like eagles, do not have the urge to run with the crowd. In other words, they only come to you one at a time. They fly higher than their peers. They are less afraid and more intimidating. They have different abilities. They need to be coaxed and encouraged rather than told what to do. They need to see a reason why one nest would be more advantageous to them than another. As far as they are concerned, all those nests are pretty much the same until proven otherwise.

RE/MAX brokers did not just recruit top agents; they actively scouted them. Imagine a company today—any company, in any industry—recruiting its people by identifying those with the right mix of capabilities and behaviors in other companies, watching their performance from a distance, getting to know them personally, discovering their individual wants and needs, and waiting for just the right moment to encourage them to jump ship. This isn't a sideline job for RE/MAX brokers or an occasional reason for them to look up from other important tasks. *RE/MAX brokers focus on this activity as their most important role.* They spend most of their time making calls, keeping records of conversations, calling again, meeting to exchange views and ideas, encouraging, enticing, figuring out what really matters for each individual, and calling some more. In doing so, they stock RE/MAX with the very best people.

RE/MAX brokers know what makes a successful RE/MAX agent. Numbers are not the only consideration; cultural fit is also critical. Recruiting an agent who doesn't fit the RE/MAX values—even if that agent is a star—would adversely affect the morale of the other agents just as severely as if the office had hired a subpar performer who couldn't keep up. Not every selection works out. Those who don't fit, as Gary Thomas put it, "get promoted to the competition as fast as possible." But a set of criteria, independently developed, seems to exist across the spectrum of brokers and nations. A premium is put on people who are entrepreneurial but not overbearing. The broker looks for someone who is positive and ambitious, who has high aspirations but is independently motivated. The firm's reputation for constant innovation, entrepreneurial zeal, and market-share drive does not attract people who expect to be fed their business or who are just in it for the status of belonging under the banner of a blue-chip brand.

Brokers are also concerned that they bring on people who are balanced, in other words, people whose career ambitions do not consume their personal lives. Perhaps the importance of this relates to other qualities that contribute to success as an agent. Top agents tend to be learners because they are engaged by and curious about their profession, which makes them more likely to seize on training and development opportunities that maintain their knowledge edge. They also tend to have strong interests in family, community, and recreational activities, which make them more empathetic to the needs of home buyers. Top agents aren't just gunning for a sale; they understand that it is more important to create the conditions for the *right* sale. Customers tend to make clouded decisions about their most expensive and important asset; a top agent is there to provide a measured balance of perspective, experience, and judgment. If the customer is satisfied months or years after a purchase, he or she is more likely to recommend that agent to a friend or a colleague. The true value of quality service is long term—to both the agent and the firm.

In order to identify those eagles, RE/MAX brokers track performance closely by analyzing local Multiple Listing Service (MLS) statistics and determining the number of transactions each agent is doing. An agent whose performance is steady is difficult to lure from a comfortable nest. An agent whose performance is accelerating or decelerating presents an opening. An agent who is up-and-coming may be improving sales numbers dramatically, but that agent is vulnerable because he or she probably isn't getting appropriate praise from a broker-centric agency. A call from a competitive RE/MAX broker may be the first pointed recognition that agent receives for his or her success. On the other hand, someone whose business has been tailing off is similarly vulnerable because it is likely that the firm has not been paying close attention to his or her needs or helping correct any problems. To the rising agent, the RE/MAX broker says, "You're a star. We can help your business get going even faster." To the agent who's in a downturn, the RE/MAX broker says, "We can identify what's wrong, help you turn your numbers around, and improve your performance by coaching you on how to spend your time and energy to obtain better returns." It's a powerful thing to sit across the table from someone who cares about how you are doing and hear them outline the ways in which you can get better.

Outside of that personal connection and the RE/MAX coach-to-success approach, the draw of one firm over another can be difficult to articulate convincingly. The numbers are there. A broker can show how a RE/MAX agent outperforms other agents in the market in terms of revenue. But most eagles think that they are totally responsible for driving their business, not their firm. Indeed, as commission strategies have converged, the money argument is increasingly difficult. The power of branding, referrals, and training is also difficult to convey before it has been experienced.

This is doubly difficult during good times. All real estate firms do well during upturns in the economy. When money is less tight and consumers are buying houses, it's easy for any agent and any firm to enjoy the ride. But notably, RE/MAX is an organization that thrives during downturns. In bad housing markets and adverse periods of the economy, average firms struggle or go bankrupt. Mediocre agents, seeing the writing on the wall, seek other career opportunities; solid agents gravitate toward offices that reveal themselves to be stronger, steadier, and more productive than the pack. For that reason, RE/MAX does better at attracting agents during tough times and has never experienced a month of negative growth in its 30-plus-year history. (See Figure 6.1.)

Often, recruiting an eagle comes down to understanding that person's particular wants and needs. What is it that thrills an agent about his or her work? What does he want out of life? Is it important for her to enjoy more time with her family? Maybe agents need systems that will help them work more efficiently. Is it important for him to build a bigger nest egg for his children? Maybe she needs coaching to improve her rate and level of sales. Is it important for him to be a leader in his community? Maybe she needs

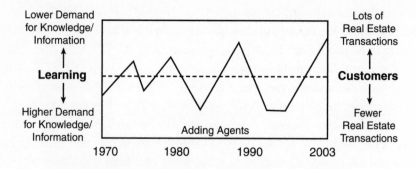

RE/MAX wins in both economies through consistent investment in learning. It continued to build learning (information and training) capacity, resulting in a steady influx of agents. In good times, leveraged listings; in bad times, leveraged customer acquisition.

Figure 6.1   Inverse Relationship—Economy and Agent

greater personal exposure. In an age in which many view business cynically or in purely financial terms, RE/MAX brokers are out to make their employees' lives better.

Heather Skuce, the broker who initially found the thought of recruiting to be distasteful, provides an example in point. After training in Denver, her business in Ottawa prospered and grew until she was the number-one broker in the region. The reputation of RE/MAX and her firm was stellar. Agents were coming to her as much as she was working to bring them in. It was time for her to make a strategic move that could only be described in chess terms as a checkmate.

Skuce's archrival was Royal LePage, the national real estate firm. Royal LePage's number-one salesperson, Bill Renaud, worked in her market. It took Skuce two and a half years to recruit him. Renaud was the kind of agent who did several million dollars in business a year. He was nationally recognized within Royal LePage and very happy in his niche. He would be a difficult eagle to lure in; but Skuce thought, "Nothing ventured, nothing gained." They met several times and got to know each other. Skuce was impressed by Renaud as a person and saw him as an equal in a professional sense. She realized that anything she could offer him in terms of money or perks would not be enticing enough. She knew that he could earn more than he believed possible at RE/MAX, but that wasn't the point; Renaud wasn't primarily motivated by money anymore. He had taken on a higher-level role in his firm as a teacher, expert, and success figure. He spoke frequently at Royal LePage conventions and got a great deal of satisfaction out of making a hall full of people believe in themselves. When Skuce thought about Renaud's motivations and what he was looking for in life, she understood finally what would sway him. "Bill, I can offer you something that Royal LePage can't," she said. Renaud waited, not really believing that she could, until Skuce said, "I can offer you the world."

Royal LePage was the second-largest firm in Canada, but it had no global presence. RE/MAX was the world's largest real estate firm with a presence in 49 countries. "You have knowledge that people in Amsterdam and Israel and South Africa would like to gain. And we can bring you to those people," Skuce said. Renaud didn't decide to join Skuce then and there, but he circled lower for a clear look. When he finally signed on, all the negotiations and arrangements were done in secret. It was the end of the year. They waited until Royal LePage announced that Renaud had been named their number-one salesperson in Canada yet again and then released their own news the next day: Renaud had left Royal LePage for RE/MAX.

The Canadian real estate industry was shocked. The local media pounced on the story. The news was a blow to Royal LePage and a boon to RE/MAX. Renaud ended up making more money at RE/MAX, and Skuce ended up with greater market share. But more important for Skuce, she had the acknowledged top salesman in the region on her team. For Renaud, he now had the whole world to draw upon.

The Value of Friendly Competition

The attention and effort taken to select and recruit top agents is difficult to understand from a broker-centric model. Building up market share, one top agent at a time, is not the way to rapid growth. An acquisition-minded firm can grow much faster in the short term, as can a firm in which any agent will suffice. Only careful, agent-by-agent recruitment results in sustainable, organic growth that becomes explosive in the long term. As Mark Wolfe of Coppel, Texas, has put it, "We created a RE/MAX culture by starting slow. We built a strong market share with strong agents from day one and continued to build on it, keeping that synergy and enthusiasm and sense of destiny going. And we never departed from that approach." The addition of top, smart, impressive leaders who fit the culture, whether in sales, administration, or management, has an accumulative effect that reinforces the strength and integrity of the group. It's a lesson for any company on the importance of careful selection at all costs and at all levels. Thinking long term and entrepreneurially encourages a leader to find the right people, groom them in the right way, and do everything he or she can to make sure they don't ever want to leave.

Top eagles can be difficult to manage, as one can imagine. They're independent, smart, ultraconfident, and successful; and they probably know more about the real estate business than the broker does. Richard Pilarski, a RE/MAX broker in northern Toronto, acknowledges that he earns more aggregate money, with less aggravation, from five strong performers than from one superperformer, so why bother? It's all about the culture of excellence that gets created as a result of having superperformers. As anyone who has been involved in sports can confirm, a competitive individual's performance improves when the overall level of play gets raised.

Eagles try harder when they are surrounded by other eagles. Why? First, the top performer himself is motivated to do even better. Chances are that he or she was the number-one salesperson back at his or her old office. Shifting to RE/MAX, that agent may only be number two. Time and again, Pilarski has seen that new agent shift into a higher gear as a result and far exceed his or her old numbers, *simply because of a new competitive environment.* Even agents who claim that being number one isn't important to them follow rankings and sales numbers with a keen eye and drive themselves harder, caught up in the thrill of friendly competition.

Second, others in the office, working shoulder to shoulder with such people, have a tendency to look up and think, *If they can do it, why can't I?* That's a question that RE/MAX brokers encourage their agents to ponder. Award ceremonies are one important means for doing so. One of Heather Skuce's more simple but powerful innovations was creating a yearly awards banquet for her own local group. She had a tough time convincing her managers that Ottawa should host its own event; most believed that the top agents would feel cheated by not getting a special trip to the "big show" in Toronto. But Skuce focused on creating an awards ceremony that was more intimate and meaningful for her agents. To everyone's surprise but her own, the event was a magnificent hit that allowed her group to celebrate and recognize the people who had made a difference locally. It motivated many average performers to try to reach that elite status the subsequent year. (See Figure 6.2.)

Richard Pilarski, at that big Toronto show, never fails to gather his group together on stage, pick up a microphone, and talk to the audience about the people with him. All are members of the elite Platinum Club of agents making between $250,000 and $500,000 a year. "Look at this group," Pilarski begins in his dry, acerbic humor. "Some are old, some are young. Some are tall, some are short. Some are fat, some are skinny. Some dress well, some not so well. Some speak English, some barely speak English at all. Do you know what they have in common? Last year, they averaged $366,000." After the banquet, he is inevitably approached by a dozen people asking how they can become more successful, too.

"That's where I get my jollies from," Pilarski says. "It's very rewarding emotionally. When I look at our group of people earning $500,000 and up,

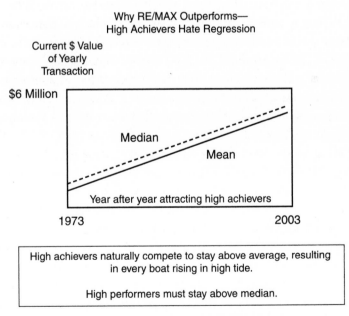

Figure 6.2　Achievement Motivation

I can think to myself, *Ten years ago, these agents were not making any money.* I don't want to say it's due to me, because I pour my heart out for the ones who fail to make a good living in real estate to the same extent that I do for the ones who end up earning a million dollars. But there's a satisfaction in seeing people grow. The RE/MAX system creates an environment where you stop working to survive and you start working to excel. I think that's crucial, because when you're working to survive, there's no value in that. All you're doing is surviving another year. For the other people who come on board, that's a very important perspective. They think, *Wait a second, these [Platinum Club] guys are doing numbers that are impossible. Maybe I can, too.*"

Jeff Benson, the broker/owner from Milwaukee, Wisconsin, feels the same way. "I'm really concerned about where our agents are going to be in five, ten, or fifteen years. When I bring them in, I let them know that I want to see them retire out of the business having built up something substantial financially, because most agents have to work hard right until the end." How do you raise your average sales price? How do you farm your name and get more referrals? Where do you place your money so that you are no longer living from commission check to commission check? How do you build a lasting business so that you're not starting from scratch on January 1? How can you take more time off and still be earning passive money? It's all part of the support and coaching that an office sets out to provide for an agent. "I still get a constant high every time I sign an agent," Benson says, "because it means that this person has realized that he or she has the ability to change his or her life. I don't really look at RE/MAX as a real estate company—I look at it as a *life success company.*"

Shifting into a higher gear requires coaching, training, development, and access to better resources. What gives an agent impetus to achieve that shift? In real estate, as in sales in general, personal perception has a tremendous impact on results. Many agents who are smart, articulate, hard working, and passionate about their careers find themselves stuck, often without realizing it, at a certain level of performance. When competitive people encounter others, not unlike themselves, who are doing better than they are, their perceptions are changed as to what is possible, and the process of eliminating limiting beliefs begins. Suddenly, it seems possible to move beyond a previous plateau.

The spread of the agent-centric culture at RE/MAX has reaped rewards on the local and global levels. RE/MAX balloons can be seen on billboards, bus stop benches, radio and TV commercials, brochures, mailers, and For Sale sign after For Sale sign in windows and on front lawns around the world. The intensity of brand awareness locally has created an interesting phenomenon: RE/MAX offices often get calls on listings that customers mistakenly swear are under RE/MAX signs. RE/MAX agents in established markets obviously benefit from this power of perception, and new regions have a leg up on the pioneers of 30 years ago. Opening a new franchise in Italy, Botswana, or Portugal, brokers find that the RE/MAX balloon has already made an impression. Mark Wolfe tells the story of speaking to an assembly hall of 100 first-grade students in Texas and explaining his duties as part-time mayor of the town. The children, naturally, asked him what he did with the rest of his time; so he mentioned RE/MAX. Suddenly, they were engaged and animated. "The balloon! The balloon!"

Market penetration and size have also created tremendous momentum for agents in terms of referrals. Unlike other industry leaders, RE/MAX International does not take a cut from the vast number of referrals it distributes to its network of agents. Considering the potential revenue involved, this seems a noteworthy demonstration of the *everybody wins* principle in action. The investment in Internet and satellite television technology for training and development purposes follows a similar line. RE/MAX was the first—and is still the only—global real estate network with in-house satellite capability and programming. Why would an organization tap its own capital to such a degree by providing a high-level service? We think that the technological advantages are enormous, but that only explains half the story. The primary motivation is consistent with Dave Liniger's early emphasis on constant upgrading and improvement of agent quality. *Give people what they need, and you will get what you want in return.*

Keep Peddling

The relentless drive for growth at the corporate leadership front and the entrepreneurial zeal at thousands of RE/MAX offices around the world are a formidable combination. A "never-rest-on-your-past-accomplishments"

attitude keeps everyone on his or her toes. And while there is great momentum behind the tremendous success experienced thus far, brokers express an awareness that RE/MAX is not an ocean liner or a jet plane,
but a bicycle that they can never stop peddling if they want to stay ahead
of the pack. They seem to be very conscious of the fact that 30 years after
launching their own franchises, they are no longer chasing the competition but being chased by it, a circumstance that brings different dangers. They talk about the difficulty of focusing on growth and innovation
when there is a strong temptation to spend energy looking over the shoulder to see how near or far the competition is. It's a very different kind
of challenge.

The quest for global market share has not diluted the intensity of efforts
at the local level. Many companies seem to lose their competitive juice
when they shift from small battles to grand ambitions. But real estate and
the RE/MAX structure seem to have made the system immune to such inclinations. If, as they say, all politics are ultimately local, then the corol-
lary has even more relevance in the real estate industry. What happens in
the local market, day by day, is the only thing that matters. For a broker
with ambitions to retain and grow market share, each win involves an individual agent's success. Few companies in any industry appreciate this incremental, customer-by-customer approach to growth in the same way
that RE/MAX does. And there is a sense, widely shared, that despite all
that RE/MAX has achieved and the momentum it has gained as a result,
the organization still has an incredible distance to go before achieving its
dream. In fact, the dream, as it is articulated by these smart, rational, mature businesspeople, just seems to grow bigger because they are truly caught
up in its importance.

The real estate world continues to change. In North America, sales
rates remain remarkably strong regardless of the business cycle. Some talk
about a housing bubble or the possibility of a return to higher interest
rates, but few think that real estate will revisit the struggles that it went
through in the late 1970s and early 1980s. In private, they don't view a
shake-up as necessarily a bad thing; the strength of local RE/MAX offices
is emphasized during tough times, attracting top agents from floundering
firms. Even in hard times, RE/MAX continues to hone its ability to adapt
to the world at hand, just like it did in the early days. Many brokers/

owners, independently and in shared acknowledgement of industry changes, have focused increasingly on bringing a new breed of agents on. Thirty years ago, being a real estate agent was a final career shift for the semiretired professional. Today, the industry is so lucrative and rewarding that real estate is frequently the first career choice of college and business school graduates and a midcareer shift for otherwise highly successful professionals. Many RE/MAX brokers now provide special training, mentorship, and team support programs for such people. The approach to eagles hasn't changed, just the means to the end. The brokers continue to *hire for attitude* and *train for results*.

Those brokers/owners have come a long way in 30 years. They took great personal risk when they embraced Liniger's dream, and many express wonder at how far things have come with a new generation of brokers coming into their own. Pamela Alexander, daughter of Frank Polzler, typifies this new breed. Her father is one of the most successful regional franchise owners in the history of any franchise company in the world. Alexander started in her father's office as administrator in 1979 and now directs the entire North American operations, with nearly 14,000 agents. She aims to become a nationally recognized expert on the real estate industry, addressing another kind of visibility to the RE/MAX brand.

Alexander sees that the real estate industry is in the midst of another shift. If the broker-centric model was the norm in the 1970s and 1980s and the agent-centric model became the leading force in the 1990s, then the customer-centric model is emerging as the wave of the future. Customers have more information and more choices than ever before. They want a seamless transaction in their real estate purchases, with a kind of one-stop-shopping capability. In response, RE/MAX offices have evolved in their offerings to include mortgage, escrow, title, and moving services; but this is just the beginning of a new wave of innovations on the horizon.

Strategic Moves

Build a learning machine to create a "Life Success Company."

From the outset, RE/MAX understood the connection between training and results. It saw that without creating a reproducible model for the intellectual capital within a service business, there would be no way to exploit the model for the dream. There are three principles that are contained as underlying assumptions within the following key points:

1. Everyone is responsible for learning—for his or her own sake and to share that learning with others.

2. Invest in the very best training and development materials and programs.

3. Training is a time saver and requires spending the necessary time on the front end to adapt the training to the culture.

An overarching belief at RE/MAX is that the very best people at the highest levels are responsible for delivering and overseeing the learning: training, coaching, and mentoring, as well as everyday support.

- You can't just bring people into a new culture and expect them to learn and adjust. In order for them to flourish, you need to provide training. (p. 141)

- If you are running a great company, recruiting is as simple as sharing that good news with others and inviting them to join you in an experience that will improve their lives. (p. 141)

- Give people what they want, and you will get what you want in return. Find employees who are dedicated to customer service, provide them with what they need to succeed, and results are the reward. (p. 142)

- Be open to creating positions that will enable a stronger team spirit for the entire group. (pp. 143–144)

- By investing time and money in building your people's professionalism and making them look better in the eyes of the customer, everybody will win. (pp. 144–145)

- Constantly keep your eyes open for the best people to bring into the company. (p. 145)

- Make sure the people you hire fit into the company's culture. Recruiting a person who does not share the company's values will adversely affect the morale of the other employees. (pp. 145–146)

- Learn what it takes to recruit the eagles in your industry. Identify who they are, take the time to understand each individual's wants and needs, and go about pursuing them with patience and persistence. (p. 147)

- Careful one-by-one employee recruitment is the recipe for sustainable, organic growth that becomes explosive in the long term. (pp. 149–150)

- Surround your eagles with other eagles who can challenge them through a healthy competitive environment. (p. 150)

- "The RE/MAX system creates an environment where you stop working to survive and you start working to excel." Believe that when you hire an employee, you are helping someone to change his or her life. Run a *life success company*. (p. 152)

- Continue focusing on growth and innovation, even if you are tempted to look over your shoulder as the competition tries to catch up. (pp. 153–154)

- When a company is truly focused on its dream, the dream continues to get bigger and bigger, even as you get closer and closer to accomplishing it. (p. 154)

Lesson

Link learning to strategy, people, and innovation to create "flow."

An everybody wins culture has "flow"—parts that fit together, each supporting the other. When one aspect isn't working, the whole thing falls apart. The big dream (RE/MAX in the center) has been increasingly supported each year by the flow of strategy (goal direction), new people (more dream sharers), and constant learning (leading-edge skill development). This flow builds an ongoing power, allowing innovation projects to emerge from all levels of the organization.

One reason that RE/MAX has continued to grow is that it has a culture that flows. It is "flow" that creates resuscitating power that fuels further growth. Flow is something that one senses in a company. When it clicks, speed is most apparent in decision making and in education. Flow allows the organization to stay balanced so that innovations are supported and not threatened—resulting in new ideas to improve the dream. With flow, the dream happens everyday. *Alignment*, a word little understood, is what others see when there is flow. Training is the supporting mechanism to flow. In today's world, flow is a key driver in decision making, in recruiting champions, and in spawning good new ideas. All the HG/HI companies we studied have "flow." (See Figure 6.3.)

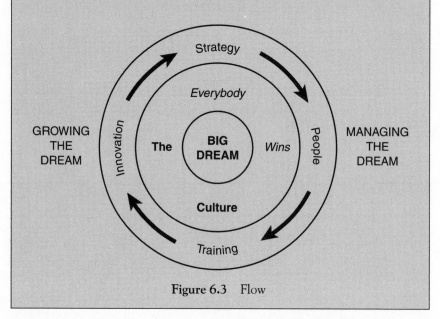

Figure 6.3   Flow

CHAPTER 7

CREATING A PACE-LINE PROJECT CULTURE

Turning Ideas into Growth

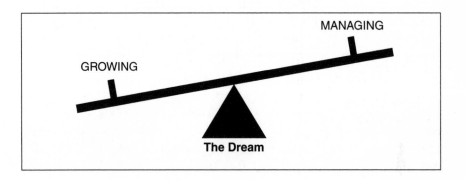

Innovation is the fuel for growth. When a company runs out of innovation, it runs out of growth.

—Gary Hamel and Gary Getz

In the summer of 2004, Lance Armstrong became the first cyclist to ever win the Tour de France six times. Most people know his incredible story—a cancer survivor who not only beat the disease that almost killed him but also went on to become one of the greatest athletes of all time. Armstrong's fans are aware of the brutal effort required to complete the Tour de France—a 3,390 kilometer cycling race over 21 days, up and down mountains in extremes of heat and cold, sun and rain, at the end of which the winner is separated from his rivals by mere minutes if not seconds. Many would argue that the Tour de France is one of the greatest tests of individual athletic accomplishment ever devised. But this emphasis on the individual challenge is missing a much larger point about how the Tour is actually won. As Lance Armstrong would be the first to admit, the Tour de France is *fundamentally and unequivocally a team event.*

The Pace Line

Some day, a book will be written about the significant leadership lessons that can be derived from the strategy, teamwork, and interteam alliances required to complete, let alone win, the Tour de France. For our purposes, we will draw on one such strategy, a simple leadership concept that team cycling illustrates vividly: the importance of the pace line.

If you watch the Tour de France for even a few minutes, you will notice just how closely the members of each cycling team ride together. Despite the amazing speeds and immense distances involved, cyclists of the same team "sit" inches from each other's back wheel, one bike after the other, in what is known as a *pace line*. They do so because of the physics of aerodynamics. The lead cyclist expends almost twice as much energy as his teammates by cutting through the air. This effort creates a slipstream that literally drags the rest of the team along in what is known as *drafting*. It's not unlike the way the lead duck flies at the apex of a flock of migrating ducks. When the lead cyclist is finally exhausted by his efforts, he falls to the back of the pace line to recover and is replaced by someone else on the team, who continues to push and drive the others with all his might. Together, the members of a cycling team create and sustain speeds unimaginable for an individual cyclist. In fact, a breakaway rider who is even 10 minutes or more ahead in the race can be caught easily by a strong team using this pace-line concept.

Lance Armstrong is one of the greatest athletes of our era, but that does not explain how he won an unprecedented six Tour de France championships. The secret to Lance Armstrong's success was his ability to form, lead, and be supported by the best team. As a group, Armstrong's U.S. Postal Service team stuck to its pace line with a discipline that no other team showed, exhausted all who tried to keep up with their blistering pace, and chased down and passed any rivals who dared to launch a challenge. When the Tour finally rode into Paris, Lance Armstrong, surrounded by his teammates, crossed the finish line having demolished all challengers over the course of three weeks.

One of the truly distinguishing features of a growth-oriented organization like RE/MAX is its ability to move from idea to project implementation faster than its rivals. Many have written about the importance of innovation in achieving growth; but a lack of ideas has never been any company's problem. Human beings are amazingly creative; and organizations are fertile grounds for useful, brilliant, even paradigm-shifting ideas. But very few companies seize ideas, transform them into projects, form effective teams, drive those ideas and implement them in a timely and competitively advantageous fashion the way RE/MAX does.

In explaining the difficulty of moving from idea to implementation, experts use terms like *institutional resistance, bureaucratic stifling,* and an *inability to capitalize on opportunity.* But no matter how you name it, the root cause is a *failure of leadership.* Too many leaders do not *get out in front* when it comes to project implementation. They allow leadership of ideas to reside at lower levels, as someone else's responsibility, or in a committee or a group where the idea is no one's responsibility. The reasons for this vary from organization to organization and leader to leader. Some leaders are simply not passionate about new ideas and have other organizational interests that move them. Some dislike getting their hands dirty when it comes to the task-oriented nature of driving growth. And some seem to worry that they will overwhelm or ruffle the feathers of the rank and file if they become too closely attached to a particular project. But in the great growth companies of our day, leaders at the very top do not hesitate to get out in front and drive the rest of the team. Michael Dell, Bill Gates, Charles Schwab, and Jack Welch, for example, are all leaders who know how to use their power, resources, and prestige to move their companies in new directions at a tremendous pace.

Similarly, Dave Liniger is not afraid to get out in front on a new project that is critical for his network. In fact, that's the role he enjoys the most. When an idea that will be useful for his organization enters his orbit, he is quick to recognize its importance and seize the opportunity for attack that it represents, like a cyclist who sees an opening in the road ahead or notices a weakness in his rivals. He does not delegate that leadership to others or submit to a committee for review or approval. Instead, he identifies passionate champions—people who believe in the idea just as much as he does, but who are more technically capable of executing it—and teams up with them, driving the idea forward at a blistering pace. With Liniger's leadership out in front, the team peddles with all its might to move from idea stage, to project implementation, to reality. Once the idea has achieved sufficient momentum, Dave Liniger moves off the front of the pace line and lets those passionate champions take over. (See Figures 7.1 and 7.2.)

"You're Going to Do What?"

One such passionate champion is Mike Ryan. Mike was from a family who for generations had lived, worked, and been laid to rest in northern Kentucky. If you'd told him that he'd ever pick up and move to Denver, Colorado, one day, he never would have believed you. Then he had a meeting with Dave Liniger.

Ryan was director at a company called MAC Productions. Over the years, Ryan had led some big media production jobs for some very big clients—Ford, GE, American Express, Anheuser-Busch. He had even done some work with RE/MAX, helping produce their international conventions. He knew that RE/MAX had a corporate culture that was very different from that of the GEs and IBMs of the world. The RE/MAX people Ryan met were not corporate blue-suit types but rebels—spontaneous risk takers who always seemed to be in a good mood no matter how fast they were moving. Visiting their headquarters in Denver on a Friday put the icing on the cake when it came to that impression.

Sure, Ryan knew RE/MAX had a Wild West, frontier-outpost kind of reputation, but this was ridiculous. Everyone in the organization, from the senior officers to the receptionists, was in a cowboy outfit—10-gallon hats, pearl-buttoned shirts, blue jeans, and boots. Ryan didn't know it then, but

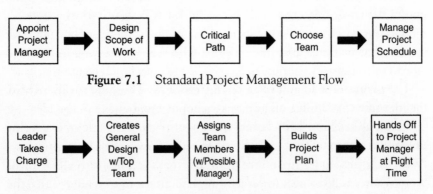

Figure 7.1 Standard Project Management Flow

Figure 7.2 Pace-Line Project Management Flow

he had stumbled onto a tradition at RE/MAX. On Fridays, you needed to blow off a little steam. Some Fridays, they did big barbecues in the parking lot or had fashion shows. And if the mood struck them . . . well, they just dressed up like cowboys.

The beautiful mountains, the Western garb, the size of the possible project . . . Ryan was intimidated to be meeting the chairman of RE/MAX. He entered the corner office, shook hands with Dave Liniger, and sat at one of the two empty leather chairs before the very clean, very large desk. "Mr. Liniger," he said, in his best understated bravado, "I understand you are thinking about starting a private television network."

Liniger hesitated a microsecond, and then Ryan got a sense of what it would be like to be tossed into Liniger's maelstrom of activity. "First of all, call me Dave," Liniger said. "Second, we're not thinking about it—we're doing it. It's a great idea, and I'm one hundred percent behind it. We are going to be on air four hours a day, five days a week, every week of the year." If Ryan had any trouble digesting that declaration, then Liniger's next words absolutely floored him. "And," Liniger continued, as though tossing in an afterthought, "our first broadcast will be in November."

It was May 1992. Liniger wanted to take a brand-new satellite network from idea to launch in just under six months and throw in four hours a day of programming to boot. Not a camera had been bought, not a staff member had been identified. It was quite simply the craziest plan that Mike Ryan had ever heard. He loved it. The cowboy hats. The rebels. The chairman sitting across the desk who told him to call him Dave. There was something great about to happen here, and Ryan knew he wanted to be part of it.

"I'm in," Ryan said.

Liniger gave him a grin.

The idea itself had germinated for some time. The need it represented had been an irritant in Liniger's oyster shell for years.

RE/MAX had long been vulnerable to one particular criticism: its training. Other firms said that because RE/MAX *only* hired experienced agents, it didn't bother to provide any training. The claim was nonsense, but it bugged the people of RE/MAX and Dave Liniger, in particular, just the same. Although RE/MAX did not provide entry-level training at that time, that was because it didn't have entry-level agents. Instead, RE/MAX offered higher-level training commensurate with the needs of its top agents. In fact, it didn't just sprinkle some training around, as many firms would, to make itself look good; it went all the way. Liniger believed that leading-edge, continuous learning was critical to the success of RE/MAX, and he pushed that idea personally, like a man on a mission, to make it a core competency. Since the inception of RE/MAX, Liniger had taken any real estate course available, sifted through that information with his encyclopedic understanding of the industry, and taught the critical points at every opportunity to RE/MAX agents and brokers all around North America. He argued for training constantly, pushed agents and brokers on the need for it, gave them statistics and research comparisons to show them how they would benefit from the effort, and arranged for countless courses and certification tests, all in an effort to ensure that RE/MAX had the *best-qualified and best-trained agents in the business*. Understandably, it galled him to no end when outsiders used the "lack of training" argument to try to dissuade people from the RE/MAX brand. Nevertheless, while baseless opinions about RE/MAX would never have driven him to engage the resources of the firm toward a new challenge, something else most definitely did—a compelling idea from the field.

Liniger and the other leaders at RE/MAX listened closely to what people in the field thought and said. It was one of the key attributes of the leadership team. Liniger knew plenty about real estate, but he was humble about not having all the answers, and he ran the organization like a volunteer group, not a dictatorship. In the early days, when he and the original franchise managers and agents were struggling to keep the dream alive, Liniger said the same thing to them constantly: What would you do? How do you think things should be? What ideas do you see working? It wasn't false modesty; it was a blend of curiosity, an openness to new and better approaches, and an enthusiastic willingness to embrace and incorporate good ideas. Over the years, the proof of that approach had struck him again and again. The best ideas don't come from the top. *The best ideas come from the field.*

That's not to say he embraced, believed in, or even agreed with all the ideas that came from the field. Plenty of times he thought a particular idea was wrong, plain nuts, not worth it, unworkable, or even damaging to the brand. Sometimes in his own rejection of an idea, he was flat out wrong, as was the case with Bill Echols and the RE/MAX balloon. But at such junctures, he was not intractable; and people knew that if they believed firmly in an idea, he was not going to stop them. Liniger encouraged RE/MAX to function as a mass laboratory of ideas. There were always experiments going on here and there—and RE/MAX saw that as a good thing. The brokers and agents were incredibly entrepreneurial and threw tremendous passion and energy into doing what they felt was right. Why stifle that commitment and creativity? The brokers and agents were the ones with local knowledge. They were the ones grappling with the competition, house by house. In an *everybody wins* universe, people needed free rein to act in their own best interests under the rubric of clear principles. That didn't mean Liniger had to endorse every idea. He had too much responsibility for the system as a whole to tilt at every windmill. In fact, RE/MAX was such a vibrant marketplace of ideas that Liniger's very act of looking favorably on something was bound to tip the balance and send other brokers and agents scrambling to follow suit—not unlike what would happen if Alan Greenspan were to recommend one particular stock over another. In other words, Liniger had to be careful in his stewardship of this community of very eager entrepreneurs.

To exercise this caution appropriately, Liniger had learned to take on a persona that people referred to as "the pope." Liniger turned a blind eye to many experiments in the field that he did not necessarily want to endorse but also did not want to squelch. Only when he thought something was harmful to the values and the brand of the network did Liniger ever step in and use his considerable powers of persuasion to avert a wrong move. He was fiercely protective of the brand, and he was a formidable foe to those who tread on the RE/MAX flag. But unless important lines were crossed, Liniger did not exert a heavy hand because he wanted to encourage people to be creative and energetic in their pursuit of success. Whenever he did see something that he thought would be valuable to the rest of the organization and deserved public sanction, he gave his blessing, like the Pope. At such times, ideas would be picked up and spread quickly through the various communication channels at RE/MAX—its host of conferences, conventions, audio tapes, videos, and speaking lectures.

And then there were those times when an idea was so important that it deserved and needed the full force of Liniger's attention. The germ of the idea for the satellite television network was one such moment. Several key brokers and agents had come to Liniger a few months before Mike Ryan visited Denver on Western Day. They were at Liniger's house brainstorming about various critical matters when Bob McWaters, the co–regional owner for RE/MAX of the Carolinas, raised the issue of teleconferencing. "You know something," McWaters said, "teleconferencing is really hot. Some of the best training programs in the country are being done that way by companies like Wal-Mart and General Motors. The real estate industry is so complex that we need to be learning all the time. But it's also hard to do all the travel. It's expensive, it takes time out of our business, and we've all got families now. Maybe RE/MAX should put together a satellite network or cable channel or something."

Liniger didn't fall in love with the notion right away, but he agreed to look into it. He worried that an investment into a RE/MAX-operated cable or satellite channel would be an immense cash drain and a diversion. Did it make sense for the network? They were just gaining size enough, at that time, to be able to put together some really impressive resources; but was this the best use of all that power? Despite his doubts about the feasibility or worthiness of the idea, Liniger made good on his word. He followed through by asking his director of information technology (IT), Bruce Benham, to examine the possibilities.

Benham had been hired only recently as the new director of IT. In terms of title, it was a step down for him, but a move he made because he had a hunch about the future of RE/MAX. He had been working very happily as vice president for a national franchising organization, well on his way to being a senior officer someday, when a friend at his golf club, who happened to be a headhunter, gave him a call and told him about a new opportunity. Was he interested in considering a new position? Not really, but maybe if he knew more about it. To his surprise, his friend was constrained in what she could tell him about the position and couldn't even let him know the firm's name. All she could say was that it was a Denver-based franchising business looking for someone to lead their new information technology push. Without a name or a context to consider, Benham didn't feel like pursuing the idea any further. But a few weeks later, his friend called again. "Come on, Bruce," she said. "Trust me. This organization is going to grow like crazy over the next ten to fifteen years, and you're the best person they could possibly find. I think you should look into it." Benham held his ground, however, until the nameless organization relented and finally let its name be known. When he learned that it was RE/MAX, his interest took a considerable jump.

And why not? His own wife was a RE/MAX agent. She had been one of the agents with Van Schaack when the final group of superagents there had decided to make the leap to RE/MAX and open its own franchise. Deborah Benham had gone with them, and she loved what RE/MAX was all about. Once he knew it was RE/MAX, he acceded to his headhunter friend's encouragements and agreed to go in for a series of interviews.

Despite RE/MAX's interest in him as a potential hire, Benham found that it was not the kind of organization to oversell you on the positives in order to lure you inside the door. Instead, RE/MAX was more interested in evaluating Benham for how well he would fit its culture and how badly he wanted to climb on board. Its approach to bringing on new people was still the same as it had been when Dave Liniger had interviewed Gail Main, Bob Fisher, Daryl Jesperson, and Vinnie Tracey—RE/MAX was looking for people who said "yes" to the dream. In Benham's first round, he faced what he called a RE/MAX "gang interview" comprised of Jesperson, Fisher, Tracey, and a new up-and-coming senior officer, Margaret Kelly. Despite being so outnumbered, Benham found it a pleasant experience. They asked really good questions, mostly about his philosophy on various matters. When Benham left the interview, his excellent impressions of RE/MAX were reinforced. He thought to himself, *Those are good people. This is a good organization.*

But he wasn't quite ready to make the leap. In terms of bottom-line details, RE/MAX wasn't offering the moon. It was characteristically guarded in its promises—the kind of place, Benham would learn, that needs to let people in the door only a little at first, in order to see what they're like under fire and what kind of person they really are, before opening up with the unreserved trust, friendship, and responsibility that serve as the medium of speedy decision making at top levels. To establish his own feelings of trust and confidence in RE/MAX's intentions, Benham still needed to have a powerful conversation under his own terms. He asked to meet with Jesperson and Fisher, quietly, to get to the heart of the matter.

"This is a really big decision for me," he told them, and began to discuss all the worries he had. It was Jes and Fish's way of answering those concerns that finally swayed him. They wanted him badly, but they didn't let their own needs outweigh Benham's. Nor did they try to "sell" Benham on jumping ship. Instead, they were simply honest and grounded in their discussion. They talked to him about the challenges he'd be facing. The IT staff was raw and would need to be built up. The resources were not free-flowing. It would take some time before Benham gained the credibility to accomplish everything he would want to do. He'd be in charge of the RE/MAX IT challenge and would be independent to a great degree in what was clearly a very unstructured corporate culture; but he wouldn't be given carte blanche, and he would still have to report to somebody. Benham had been involved in corporate politics enough to know that this honest assessment of his future role was a refreshing change. He felt like he was getting the whole truth—an expression of trust in and of itself—and he respected that immensely. Moreover, he felt like he would fit in with this group. His relationships at his old company had been solid and functional, ranging from respect to friendship, but this culture was different. Joining them, he couldn't help but admit, felt a little bit like coming home.

When Benham walked in the door on that first day, he was well aware of the extent of the job that awaited. In technological terms, RE/MAX was stuck in the age of moveable type. Moreover, it was growing explosively, at an exponential rate, and was in desperate need of leapfrogging to an entirely new level of data management and communications technology. That was the exciting part of the challenge. RE/MAX had around 30,000 agents in its system at the time and was expecting to reach the mid-70,000s within five years. Personally, Benham thought those expectations were a little nuts; but it seemed like a worthy goal, and it certainly gave him a battle cry to create major change. (Little did he know that RE/MAX would hit those numbers dead on.)

He was given more trust and latitude than he might have expected, considering the reserved promises of the interviews. He didn't have an open checkbook; his approach needed to be very methodical, over a period of time, without creating too many shock waves. But at the end of his first six months, his objective feeling about RE/MAX was, yes, he had made a very good move with lots of potential for future growth. Then he had an opportunity to see RE/MAX under fire and realized just how special a place he had come to.

The occasion was the first big convention of the year, held in Las Vegas in 1993. Every member of the senior leadership team was on hand. Benham was witness to an amazingly simple but profound moment of corporate culture. There was a problem with one of the handouts that needed to be distributed in every conference delegate's bag. Five thousand of the bags had already been packed with the faulty handout. The delegates couldn't receive those bags in that state; something needed to be done. The late-night meeting to discuss the problem included Dave and Gail Liniger and all the senior officers. Fisher said, "Guys, we've got to get in there and fix that mistake. This needs to be one hundred percent right." The next thing Benham knew, every single one of the senior officers, including Dave and Gail Liniger, got to work. They spent the rest of the night changing the handouts in the bags before the 5,000 RE/MAX brokers and agents showed up the next morning. If Benham needed an example of the roll-up-your-sleeves, everyone-here-is-good-enough-to-get-to-work culture of RE/MAX, he got it in technicolor. It was an experience he would never forget.

But it was when he got swept up the ladder into Dave Liniger's world that Benham finally understood what made RE/MAX click. After the RE/MAX brokers and agents suggested the idea of a cable or satellite channel, Liniger turned to Benham to check things out. This was not an off-hand request—Liniger chooses his early explorers carefully, knowing how critical it is to get accurate scouting reports of the terrain ahead. In fact, although Benham was not aware of this, Liniger had been watching him closely. He had talked to the key officers who were getting to know Benham's approach, style, and character. Liniger may not have worked closely with Benham yet, but he had plenty of information about Benham and was ready to go to battle with him.

Over the next nine months, Benham and Liniger would get to know each other well. They accomplished their due diligence in a few short months and knew that the satellite channel was going to be an extremely good move. They could see the strategic value, almost regardless of the cost. Done right, the satellite network could be the firm's learning, training, and communications hub, binding a global brand together like no other medium or technological approach.

There were big stakes involved, serious dollars and a huge sense of mission. Moreover, Liniger wanted to accomplish this project in time for the National Association of Realtors (NAR) annual convention in November. It was a timeline that was two to five years faster than any other organization would even consider. Why so aggressive? Liniger learned that the NAR was investigating the possibility of creating its own satellite network and wanted to beat them to the punch. And he also wanted to counter those persistent and annoying claims that RE/MAX did not provide training with an astounding demonstration of how serious RE/MAX actually was about the issue. Like a championship cyclist in the Tour de France, he aimed to put on an intimidating burst of speed over a difficult mountain climb that would create enormous distance between him and his rivals and blow them away psychologically. He had a competitive athlete's innate sense of when to go for the win.

He also believed that RE/MAX could pull it off. As a privately held firm with a strong leadership team, RE/MAX could turn on a dime, attack aggressively when it wanted to, and make lightning-fast decisions with committed follow-through and quality results. RE/MAX did not need to form study committees or to make long-range plans involving all its constituents before moving forward. It got its buy-in for critical projects by communing with key leaders, assessing the pluses and minuses, throwing the appropriate amount of weight into the push, and selling everyone on the absolute need. In that respect, Dave Liniger himself was the firm's secret weapon, one it could bring to the front of the pace line whenever necessary.

Benham saw this firsthand. Whenever he pulled critical information together, Liniger wanted to get his hands on it immediately, dig through the details, and really understand the significant points. He wasn't the type to say, "Make this happen, and let me know when it's done." Instead, he rolled up his sleeves and participated personally. They flew all around the country together over those next few months, attended important meetings as a team, shared ideas, assessed challenges, set critical objectives, and made things happen. Liniger had a dominant and aggressive style but not a domineering approach. They were creative collaborators, joined in common cause, equally passionate about the possibilities; and they were having fun at the same time.

Mike Ryan saw exactly the same thing when he joined in after Liniger decided to go forward. Benham had recommended him; Liniger assessed the suggestion, liked what he saw, and signed him onto the project. As an outside contractor, Ryan was in awe. The corporate headquarters buzzed with excitement. The teamwork, tenacity, and focus was like nothing he had ever experienced, and Ryan got swept up in the magic. Every department became engaged in the battle cry: RE/MAX was going to launch the first private-business television network in the industry. Dave and Gail Liniger held meetings at the RE/MAX planning center. It was an off-site location where ideas were sacred and strategy discussions were top secret. Nothing that was said in that room was repeated outside of it until the time was right. As the team came up with ideas, Liniger filled out pastel-colored three-by-five index cards and pinned them to the wall. Soon, they had a master timeline that looked like multicolored wallpaper—green, yellow, blue, and red ideas checkering the entire wall. The race was on to meet the fall deadline.

Liniger dropped everything else for the next three months once the Go decision had been made. Liniger, Mike Ryan, and the RE/MAX team jumped on airplanes and flew to different factories and companies that were using satellite television. They negotiated satellite time and developed their own content ideas more fully. Every moment waiting for a plane or a meeting was filled with talk, a constant bantering of ideas back and forth. They were benchmarking the best, and it was exhilarating to be caught up in such a well-disciplined pace line. The excitement was contagious, too. Across the system, brokers and associates opened their doors and minds to share their own ideas, needs, and experiences. In this way, the project became an embodiment of something they all wanted—and wanted to see succeed.

The content ideas came fast and furious. They didn't want talking heads and cheap production standards. No one would watch a form of downscale community access television. If RE/MAX Satellite Network—or RSN as it became known—was going to be a success, it needed to be a high-level product, with high-level content and great speakers. They divided that content into various areas. They wanted to teach technology, knowing, even before the Internet, that computers were one day going to be an important part of an agent's success. They wanted to train assistants and secretaries on how to do word processing and spreadsheets. They wanted to teach sales and motivation. They wanted to teach brokers how to run their businesses and agents how to do advertising and networking. All that content had been available at conventions for years. This was an opportunity to go live with the learning culture of RE/MAX all around the world.

The first broadcast of RSN was unveiled on the floor of the annual National Association of Realtors convention in Anaheim, California, in November 1994. No one in the real estate industry had ever seen anything like it. Instead of the usual exhibit hall booth, RE/MAX had built a TV studio with camera operators, makeup experts, and a director. Liniger approached the best instructors at the NAR convention to appear on RSN and began to sign some very big names. *We won't pay your fee to appear on RSN; but if we feature you, we'll help sell your books and spread your message. It's a win-win deal.* Most of the other real estate networks had resisted letting industry gurus gain too much credibility and exposure before their agents, fearing a pied piper effect. Liniger felt just the opposite. He told those experts, "You have the keys to my success. How can I help you?" He was willing to go to their events and speak for free in return for their support of RSN.

The emphasis on training made an incredible impression on the 20,000 NAR conference attendees, and the competition was shell-shocked. On the second day of the convention, handwritten signs were displayed at some competitors' booths claiming that they would be offering satellite television by next year's event. (None of them would succeed.)

The push to go live at the NAR convention paid off many times over and serves as an example of the productive use of speed in today's competitive business world. In one bold move, RE/MAX created an insurmountable impression in the minds of Realtors: *RE/MAX was the leading real estate firm when it came to training and coaching.* A year before, few would have given RE/MAX such top-of-mind recognition, despite all its legitimate offerings. Sensing the benefits as well as the inevitability, NAR soon embraced the new RE/MAX distance-learning tool as a vehicle for distributing its own content. By the year 2004, over 60,000 North American RE/MAX associates had the capability to obtain proprietary professional designations, continuing education programs, and live prime-time coaching, right in the comfort of their homes and offices. If this had been a race to conquer outer space, RE/MAX would have most definitely won—they had built the most advanced training system in the history of the real estate industry, using pace-line management to pull if off in record time.

Moreover, the satellite network had been designed and built to reflect the people and the spirit of RE/MAX, further boosting the sense of cultural cohesion that could easily have diminished in an organization that was growing in leaps and bounds. RSN was not an ivory tower pulpit or an airbrushed facade; it was a tribute to the entire organization, comprised of tens of thousands of RE/MAX business people openly sharing their trade secrets, while personally promoting themselves and benefiting everyone in the process. Despite its new technological capabilities, RE/MAX remained aware that it was not in the real estate television business; it was in the *real estate agent* business.

Switching Positions in the Pace Line

Once the RSN project was successfully launched, Dave Liniger no longer needed to be at the front of the pace line. Mike Ryan had been working side by side with Liniger for 12 hours a day for more than three months. He traveled with him, stayed at his house, enjoyed his skills on the barbecue, played rounds of golf with him, and had total access—no matter the interruption—to Liniger's insights into the training, education, and communication services the RE/MAX membership needed. Then Liniger was gone, but not before he made one last move.

Ryan had felt tired but torn when the exhilarating launch of RSN was finally accomplished. He and RE/MAX had been in battle together, and now he felt it was time to leave. But Liniger had other plans for him. He had seen Ryan up close and knew what kind of manager he was and what kind of leader he would make. He wanted Ryan to move to Denver and come on board the RE/MAX team as the head of RSN.

It was no longer such a tough decision to contemplate. Yes, Ryan and his family had been born and bred in northern Kentucky, but they would be a welcome part of the RE/MAX family. Knowing it would be a hard move with his daughter a senior in high school, Liniger made the transition easier by offering Ryan an apartment so that he could continue to commute back and forth until life was settled. Ryan agreed. Once he had secured Ryan's leadership, Liniger felt free to release the project into his care and let him take his place at the front of the pace line.

This left Liniger free to move on to his next creative endeavor. Inserting himself into projects as needed keeps him fresh and rejuvenates his energy, while feeding his insatiable technical curiosity. In fact, we suspect that monitoring the day-to-day operations of RE/MAX as closely as a good manager must would drive him nuts. Liniger is well aware of this and has always sought to balance his focus on constantly growing the dream by finding those people who are more skilled than he is at managing individual aspects of it. In his projects, Liniger works as hard at putting the right team together as he does on any other aspect requisite to its success. If he doesn't have all the leadership pieces assembled from the beginning, he picks up those pieces and readjusts them along the way. By the time the project is done, he has formed a core group of outstanding leaders who now have the capacity to run the show themselves. Liniger sees his primary role in the pace line as getting out front early to ensure that the project has the necessary momentum and a team that can execute it with the RE/MAX signature quality.

Once the project has sufficient forward motion, he lets others take it the rest of the distance and gives them the resources and the mandate to improve it every day. No leader has unlimited time, particularly in an organization growing as fast as RE/MAX. Liniger tries to accomplish the big things, get them to the point where everybody has a thorough understanding of the goals and financial parameters, then hands the model over to those who can lead it further and make it better.

Bruce Benham saw this from another perspective several years later when RE/MAX leapfrogged into the Internet age. His work at RE/MAX had been incredibly challenging and exhilarating. During one multiyear project, he migrated the RE/MAX database to a new network, creating a critical system that tracked every piece of information about how the firm did business. He was impressed again at how closely Liniger observed this project. For someone whom everyone referred to as an idea guy, Liniger kept his finger on the pulse of what was going on much more than one would expect—an indication of how important he thought information technology was to the future of the RE/MAX network. From the beginning of the development of Mainstreet, the RE/MAX extranet, Liniger shifted back into his slot at the front of the pace line; and everyone else in every other department got ready for another high-tempo ride.

Since 1992, with the advent of electronic bulletin board systems, RE/MAX had seen the value of computer-to-computer communication as a means by which agents could share information, ask each other questions, and archive good ideas. When the Internet was first developed, RE/MAX was already very familiar with the principles behind e-mail and web sites. Liniger and the other RE/MAX leaders resisted the lure of investing too heavily in the unrealistic promises of the medium, understanding that its true value was more practical. After a great deal of assessment, careful thought, and idea sharing, RE/MAX decided that its foray into the Internet should follow the pattern of RSN—develop a vehicle that would provide information, training, and resources for the service of RE/MAX associates.

Kristi Graning was on Bruce Benham's team and became Liniger's co-collaborator in the development of Mainstreet. She had joined RE/MAX directly out of high school at age 18 as an administrative assistant in the IT User Support group. She had risen rapidly in the ranks until she was co-managing the IT department. Again, as with Ryan and Benham on the development of RSN, Graning got the experience of serving as key lieutenant in the Dave Liniger pace line. Liniger cut out the bureaucracy, streamlined the departments, brought the checkbook, and rode the team hard. Graning knew that she did not have to go to Benham for permission to devote herself fully to a new cause; and she also knew that Benham had been there before and understood that once her time on the project was over, she would return to the normal activities of her role. In the end, Mainstreet was another monumental leap forward in technological capability, all done in service of the RE/MAX agent community. At the close of 2004, the majority of agents in the RE/MAX network had been enrolled as users, a virtual community without parallel in the industry.

There have been many other initiatives over the years, but the pattern of the pace-line project culture is the same. It is the means by which RE/MAX accelerates its growth and puts distance on the competition. Although Liniger is a person who likes certainty and holds strong opinions, he is not afraid of ambiguity, complexity, or change. And he looks for those kinds of people in his own leadership team. It's a frame of mind that makes one predisposed to being open to new ideas—the kind of attitude embraced by an organization that understands the importance of listening to the customer in the field. The critical ingredient required for such a mindset to work effectively is trust. Liniger has created a trust-rich environment among his senior team. The people within that team think of each other as family. Deep, connecting conversations about important matters inside and outside the parameters of the job are commonplace. It's this intrinsic trust that enables the team to work together flawlessly and that translates into speed.

Indeed, Liniger's ability to turn away from the daily concerns of RE/MAX and to focus so intensely on critical projects is its own form of trust. He created a leadership team capable of running the network as well as he could in his absences, with just as much commitment and passion. The time he spends on critical projects is time in which the team members can flourish in their own roles without Liniger's oversight. Everyone recognizes, with good humor, that he is a restless and energetic person who needs the engagement of new challenges. Without it, we suspect he would have the bored and sullen disposition of a teenager with nothing to do. As a leader, Liniger knows that it is not his job to tell people how to do their work, unless they need help to succeed. Everyone has his or her own methods and approaches and needs room and space to grow. When Liniger is deeply engaged on a project, his leadership team is most happy, because they know they will be left alone to do their own work the way they see fit. Conversely, they are most anxious when Liniger goes on vacation—not because Liniger's presence is so missed, but because they are terrified of what new ideas and projects he will come up with when his mind is given the chance to float and dream.

Jokes aside, we are not suggesting that Liniger is disengaged from the day-to-day operations of RE/MAX when he is immersed in a project; but like most great multitaskers, he is able to sense the pulse of the organization through the input he gets from his key lieutenants, the more than 30 reports he reads each week, and the 400 or 500 e-mails he receives each day—more than enough data to know where and when his more precise attention might be needed. Despite the capabilities that he has collected in his leadership team, no one in the network has the same breadth of understanding into the nuances and history of all the relationships and events that turn up on his radar. That knowledge gives him quick insights into trouble at the first sign of its development.

Perhaps Liniger's project obsession can be fully explained with one more nuance. In Liniger's view, part of what makes life special is finding something that you can be passionate about. More than his wealth or his accomplishments, the ability to discover new interests is what makes Liniger feel as though he is the luckiest man alive. There's more to life than accumulating power and possessions. The people who enjoy life the most are those who develop—because of an avid sense of curiosity—a fascination with the world around them. They get involved in new endeavors because they quicken their imagination.

When you have big dreams, Liniger believes, that creative passion fires your soul. It gives you the enthusiasm and the hope to look forward and see beyond the trials and the humdrum of everyday life. When Liniger engages with a new project—whether it be the launch of a satellite television station, the development of a wildlife art museum, or the building of a NASCAR race team—he is most intensely alive. The kaleidoscope of ideas and machinery and people makes him even more curious about why things work, how they can be better, and what makes them so fun.

Is it any surprise, then, that Liniger couldn't resist the chance to fly a balloon into outer space?

What Really Mattered

The idea to fly a balloon around the world was not new. In fact, it had been a dream of many explorers over the past two centuries. In the 1990s, the race to be the first to successfully circumnavigate the globe in a balloon heated up, fueled by the charismatic personalities of several larger-than-life participants like Richard Branson, head of Virgin Group. The Earthwinds Hilton team, led by Larry Newman, made attempts from 1991 until 1994 but failed. Richard Branson's *Virgin Challenger* tried to lift off several times from Morocco but got no farther than Algeria. The *Breitling Orbiter*, piloted by Betrand Piccard, left from Switzerland and stayed up for a record 10-day flight, until China refused permission to fly through its airspace. American Steve Fosset set off from South Dakota in a solo attempt aboard the *Solo Challenger* but landed in eastern Canada three days later because of technical challenges. Fosset made it from St. Louis to India in his next attempt aboard the *Solo Spirit*, breaking distance and duration records, but again failing to make it around the world.

All of those attempts involved highly scientific variations of the classic Roziere balloon, the helium-filled envelope lifting a basket (or capsule) that most of us think of when we imagine balloon flight. The technical difficulties of such a system were enormous, but the biggest challenge by far was the global weather system. Balloons, of course, have no power on their own and need to catch the wind to travel any distance. The giant Roziere balloons require incredible winds in order to make it around the world. Their lift-off locations were no accident; each was chosen because it gave the balloon team the best opportunity, in their view, to rise high enough to catch hold of one of the fast-moving slipstreams that circle the earth. The problem, however, is that weather systems at that altitude could turn ferocious, ripping the balloon to shreds. That's what happened to Steve Fossett when he made another attempt in the *Solo Spirit*, this time leaving from Argentina. He set a new world record but was forced down by a terrible storm in the middle of the ocean and was rescued in his life raft off the Australian coast.

The idea to fly a balloon around the world caught Liniger's imagination like nothing else before. Of course, the image of a balloon soaring around the world was basically synonymous with the RE/MAX brand; but more than that, there was something Shackletonian about the adventure. It was one of the last great expeditions available to mankind. Indeed, Liniger had even contemplated the challenge more than 20 years earlier.

In the late 1970s, a friend in the ballooning industry had been convinced it would work and wanted to sponsor an attempt; but its program was set back by various circumstances. Watching the many attempts that were made in the 1990s, Liniger could not help but ponder how a better mousetrap might be built. The Roziere-style balloons, with their mix of helium and hot air, were at the mercy of the weather. If a thunderstorm struck, it couldn't go high enough to avoid it, and it certainly couldn't go any lower without abandoning the attempt. Never one to think conventionally about challenges, Liniger's instincts were to avoid the capricious difficulties of the weather system altogether by piloting a balloon in the stratosphere. As was his way, Liniger began to do some research and then met with his senior officers. He had developed his concept and believed it could work. The dangers were real. Subspace altitude was a very hostile climate. Any technical problems involving rapid decompression would mean instant death. But despite their worries for his safety, the leadership team knew that Liniger was a complex pilot, a skydiver, a deep-sea scuba diver, and a race car driver who put safety first and insisted on scientific thoroughness in planning every stage of a project. In the end, everyone was for it. After all, RE/MAX always did say it was *Above the Crowd!* With their unanimous buy-in, Liniger began to develop the project.

After a year of due diligence, the RE/MAX team concluded that stratospheric balloon travel was possible, and they were on track with a viable plan. That's when they were approached by another group in Albuquerque, New Mexico, with the exact same concept, but no funding. Here, Liniger made a mistake: His usual move in the pace-line project culture would be to use a key, trusted lieutenant to investigate further; but he sent a lower-level person instead. The news was phenomenal; and that person's advice was to join forces. Then Liniger made his second major mistake: Rather than dig in deeper personally, he relied on that advice and made an agreement over the telephone with the team in Albuquerque. Only when he went down to their laboratory himself did he discover that the RE/MAX team's new partner was far behind RE/MAX in terms of scientific know-how. Having made a promise, however, Liniger couldn't back out. Instead, he took over the project and brought the new group along with him.

The setback aside, RE/MAX put the financial and managerial resources into the project and plowed ahead. What evolved was a scientific adventure beyond anyone's imagination. Sixteen hundred scientists from around the country volunteered their expertise to help Liniger's mission succeed. Martin Marietta (the aerospace company), Colorado University, NASA, and the U.S. weapons command all contributed to the efforts required to build a space capsule that could achieve a cabin altitude of 14,000 to 18,000 feet. It was an opportunity for those groups to conduct their own scientific tests and to further the knowledge of high-altitude research.

Spending the required time in a capsule at that altitude would be comparable to climbing Mount Everest. Liniger would need to train vigorously. He had a personal coach from the Olympic bicycling team in Colorado

Springs. But there was still the matter of space travel. The best training facilities available for civilians were the cosmonaut centers in Russia. The man who designed Liniger's space suit had made Yuri Gagarin's suit for the first manned space flight. The training, which took him to Russia, was hard, risky, and dangerous. One tear in the space suit or break in the capsule seal meant instant death.

Nevertheless, the project absorbed Liniger completely, and the mission seemed to achieve higher levels of intensity with each passing day. RE/MAX ambassadors made diplomatic visits to each of the 18 countries over which the capsule would pass during the global flight. RE/MAX created an education curriculum for students from kindergarten through grade 12 with studies on geology, geography, weather, balloons, and airplanes, all in four different languages. Liniger spoke to more than 40,000 school children in 1999. Graduate school programs were incredibly excited about the opportunity to conduct atmospheric experiments at an altitude that was too high for most manned aircrafts but too low for spacecrafts. From such an altitude, Liniger and the accompanying RE/MAX team would be able to see the curve of the earth and the dark of outer space.

As time went on, Liniger made friendships with some of the greatest leaders he had ever encountered. Colonel Joe Kittinger, a Vietnam pilot who had set a world record for making the highest altitude parachute jump from a balloon, called to try to talk Liniger out of the attempt. "You'll be killed," he said, "if even the slightest thing goes wrong." Liniger talked to him about the dangers, and Kittinger could tell how prepared he was to face them. Impressed, Kittinger joined Liniger's team as a volunteer. Former naval aviator officer Dan Pederson, the founder of Top Gun Academy, agreed to be launch commander. The head of the Russian space program, who had been a fighter pilot in Vietnam, became a drinking buddy. Liniger and he couldn't quite believe that 40 years later, two former enemies could sit side by side, drink vodka, and talk about the world as friends. All in all, the project involved an extraordinary gathering of passionate and curious adventurers, leaders, and scientists; and it affected Liniger deeply. It was a leadership experience beyond compare.

Liniger gave his RE/MAX senior team and board members one more opportunity to deter him before proceeding with the countdown to launch. A 6,000-pound space capsule. A 1,000-foot-tall, 40-million-cubic-foot,

NASA–style helium balloon. Incredible danger. The people in the room refused to do a secret vote and rose to their feet in applause instead. More than 200 of Liniger's friends and supporters inside and outside of RE/MAX flew to the launch site in Alice Springs, Australia, to see them off. That's where the stratospheric winds, which blew around the equator four weeks of the year, could be caught, starting in the last week of December.

Mike Ryan, as head of RSN, directed the crew that set up live TV feed to capture the events as they unfolded. His team was up day and night broadcasting interviews around the world. Liniger was with them during every transmission, even as they waited until two or three in the morning to set up interviews with CNN or the major U.S. networks. The two-week period in which the launch date had been scheduled extended to five and a half weeks as the weather patterns and atmospheric conditions refused to cooperate. Every day and night, the RE/MAX team counted down the launch sequence with the NASA balloon crew, only to postpone. To Ryan, it was as though they were stuck in a remake of Bill Murray's *Groundhog Day*—each morning they woke up to find that nothing had changed! No one lost faith or got demoralized, however, despite the 100-degree outback heat. Mike Reagan, another senior leader at RE/MAX, organized a cricket tournament. Daryl and Nan Jesperson delivered food at breakfast and lunch times. The senior officers literally swept the floors of the Quonset hut.

One last attempt to launch was made. The balloon crew did interviews and sat for photographs; then the launch commander escorted everyone out of the room and made time for family members only. Liniger sat with Gail and his sons and felt humbled by the perils he would soon face; but he was utterly confident and optimistic, blessed by everything that had brought him to this place. Finally, it was time to make their last preparations. Before the launch, the team needed to breathe pure oxygen for at least eight hours. Underneath their spacesuits, they wore silk undergarments because any static spark from cotton or nylon could have blown them up. The capsule door was shut and locked down. Then the capsule was raised at the end of its long tether by a crane. Liniger was upbeat and positive, despite all the problems that had been encountered thus far. "I'm ready," he said. "I can fly this bird." He knew every control panel in the dark. He could move in an inflated spacesuit, on the ground or in zero atmosphere. He was in the best shape of his life.

The launch was scrubbed just after daybreak. Technological problems had been noticed. The weather was still not cooperating. After three years of scientific work, nine months of hardcore planning, and five weeks of waiting for "Go," the Team RE/MAX Global Balloon Mission was fated to remain grounded. Looking out the capsule window, Liniger could see the entire area surrounding the airport, where almost 20,000 people had gathered starting at about midnight, lighting bonfires and waving Australian and American flags. It was extraordinary to see; and for the first time during the entire emotional roller coaster, Liniger hurt badly. It took a lot not to cry in front of his friends and team when he stepped out of the capsule.

A week later, the final decision was made to cancel the expedition. Mike Ryan felt heartbroken, too, but not for the same reasons as Liniger. Walking around the facility on the dirt road that night with Liniger, they discussed how to handle the press conference the next day. Liniger apologized for the fact that Ryan's production crew had to miss Christmas with their families, brave the desert for weeks, and essentially waste their lives for the past nine months. Ryan couldn't have been more stunned. That wasn't how he felt at all. There was no mistaking that missing Christmas had taken its toll on everyone's family, but the past nine months was anything but a waste of everyone's life. The number-one mission of Team RE/MAX had been to keep the balloon crew alive. The number-two mission had been to participate in a scientific adventure that would help the world. And the number-three mission had been to generate publicity for the RE/MAX brand in line with its rapidly expanding global presence. On all accounts, the mission had been a success. The team was safe, young people around the world had their education brought to life through a terrific learning opportunity, and Ryan knew that the publicity had been incredible. In fact, a media study conducted later would show that the branding achievement had been off the charts.

But more important than all of these things, in Ryan's view, had been the sense of teamwork. Ryan had never been more proud of being part of a team. The corporate officers had delivered meals. The president had swept floors. The CEO had dropped by one morning to pick up Ryan's dirty clothes on the way to the laundromat. Ryan had joined RE/MAX long after all of the dramatic life-and-death moments of the firm's Wild West early years. He had heard about those legendary events, but the firm had become so sophisticated and successful in recent years that it was not the same as living those times. But now he felt as though he had experienced what it must have been like in the old days. That's what the balloon project meant to him—a chance for him and the other members of the next generation of RE/MAX leaders to live and breathe the dream. RE/MAX was the kind of family where you won together and you lost together. The winning or losing didn't count, except in the short run. It was the "together" part that mattered.

Strategic Moves

Project leadership is different from project management.

Productivity on important projects is a function of fast start. This is a well-known principle of project management. At RE/MAX, getting traction on high-leverage projects is all about senior leadership involvement. What Dave Liniger models and other leaders follow at RE/MAX is a "come play golf with me" approach. Rather than telling people what they should do to get projects started, Dave takes the lead, showing the way, becoming a "pace-line" leader. In order to make this happen, he clears his desk of other things; gets the right people involved on the project; sets aggressive schedules; and then, at the right time, when the project has torque, steps aside and becomes a cheerleader and supporter of the project manager and the team. His approach demonstrates the difference between project leadership and project management. We think this is a critical way in which leaders get high-leverage projects off the ground.

- Leaders *get out in front* and drive the rest of the team when it comes to project implementation. (pp. 160–161)
- A great growth-company leader is open to hearing the ideas of others, recognizes an idea that will be useful, and seizes the opportunity to drive the initial momentum of the project. (p. 161)
- The "pace-line" leader identifies passionate champions—people who believe in the idea as much as he or she does but are more technically capable of executing it—and teams up with them, driving the idea forward. (pp. 161–162)

- Once you decide to lead a project, be 100 percent behind it from the get-go. (p. 163)

- Emphasize and pursue development in your employees. Make it a priority for your company to have the best-qualified and best-trained people in the business. Use your project pace line to test and to develop leadership in others. (pp. 163–164)

- Run your company like a volunteer organization, not a dictatorship. Listen closely to what your employees out in the field think and say. (p. 164)

- The best ideas don't come from the top. The best ideas come from those closest to the customer. (p. 164)

- In an *everybody wins* culture, people need free rein to act in their own best interests under the rubric of clear principles. Encourage people to be creative and energetic in their pursuit of success. In a high-trust, entrepreneurial environment, this will only benefit your organization. (p. 165)

- When looking into a new idea, choose your early explorers carefully. It is critical to get accurate scouting reports of the terrain ahead before sending a team into a project. (p. 169)

- Create an exciting environment around a project. Make it a place where people can feel welcome to share their ideas, needs, and experiences. The project will become an embodiment of something that everyone wants to see succeed. (p. 171)

- The finished product should reflect the people and the spirit of the company, thereby strengthening the corporate culture. (p. 173)

- Dave Liniger is a project-oriented leader. He is passionate and energized by new endeavors, which feed his insatiable curiosity and in turn excite and energize everyone around him. (p. 174)

- Liniger's focus is always on growing the dream; however, he balances that with people who are more skilled than he is at managing the dream. (p. 174)

- When leading a project, put the right team together. If it is not right from the beginning, readjust the team until it is the best it can be before handing the project off to its new leaders. (p. 174)

- The leader's primary role in the pace line is to get involved early to fully understand the issues, to create momentum for the project, and to ensure that it has the signature quality of the company. Once the project has the momentum it needs, let the team take it over. Then the leader's role is to provide the resources and the mandate for the team to take the model they created and improve on it every day. (p. 174)

- Through its pace-line project culture, RE/MAX is able to accelerate its growth and put distance on the competition. (pp. 175–176)

- Create a trust-rich culture. A trust-rich environment is one in which senior officers are able to flourish in their roles while the leader is consumed in a project. (p. 176)

- HG/HI leaders have great curiosity and a fascination with the world. Big dreams fill such leaders with hope and excitement. (p. 177)

- The most rewarding part of large-scale projects is the sense of teamwork and pride that they produce in the organization. (p. 183)

Lesson

Become a pace-line leader.

Pace-line leadership is a metaphor for describing how leaders can most effectively spend time on projects. All leaders face the same difficult quandary: how much to be involved in projects. RE/MAX has figured out how to leverage Dave Liniger's time on projects. He plays the pace-line leader on major projects that will make a difference to the business. He gets involved early on high-leverage/high-payoff projects that have a direct impact on growing or managing the dream. Then he jumps in and spends up to 90 percent of his time on leading the charge. When he does, he exerts all the might of RE/MAX resources across the network. He gets clear definition on acceptance criteria and gets the right people involved at the right time (great project management principles). When it builds momentum and has to be run as a project, he appoints the person who has been closest to him on the project, lets go of the reins completely, and applauds from the sidelines.

This is a big idea for senior leaders. There are thousands of books on project management but none of any note on project leadership. The role of top leader involvement is to provide muscle without interference so that projects can get a "fast start" (e.g., allocated resources, priority status, and overall focus). The other significant moment of project leadership is the "handoff" at the right time, to the right lieutenant, and with the right resources.

The last significant point of this lesson is to pick the right projects to be involved in. Such projects should be top-focus areas that have measurable impact on growing or managing the dream and that will be unifying—adding to pride and positioning. Figure 7.3 shows a map to help with this from the view of the RE/MAX case on how to pick projects for leaders to be involved in.

	Growing the Business	Managing the Business
High-Impact Projects 80%	• Geographical expansion • New products and services • Partnership alliances	• Mentoring key people • Supplying • Recruiting
Low-Impact Projects 20%	• Product enhancement	• Researching and developing

Figure 7.3   Pace-Line Project Leader Guide Time Map

CHAPTER 8

SOARING ABOVE THE CROWD

Staying True to the Dream across Borders and Generations

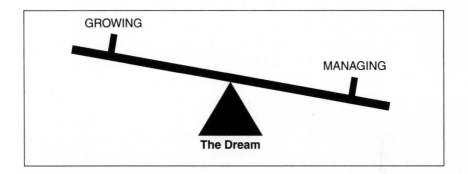

So many of our dreams at first seem impossible, then they seem improbable, and then, when we summon the will, they soon become inevitable.
—Christopher Reeve

Vinnie Tracey came back. He left RE/MAX in the spring of 1982 because there were no new franchise owners out there to train. It was one of the hardest decisions of his life, but he made the most of it. He found a good, solid company—an IBM–like leader in the medical technology field—and brought his considerable skills to the job as a top salesman. Like others who had left the organization over the years, Tracey could not help but compare everything else to his RE/MAX experience. Like many of those people, he would find a way to return because no other company came even close to feeling so much like home.

In the fall of 1982, the phone rang. It was Liniger. "Vinnie, we're starting to sell franchises again," he said. "I need your help, buddy." Tracey had only been with his new company for a few short months and had already received a promotion to take over a top territory. He couldn't just jump ship, could he? "Let me call you back tomorrow, Dave," Tracey said. He

187

and his wife, Michelle, who had been Liniger's assistant at one point in her own RE/MAX career, needed time to think about it. They stayed up the whole night, drank a bottle of red wine, and talked about their future and what they wanted and needed right now. In the early morning hours, they made a decision. Leaving their new home and Vinnie's new job just wouldn't be right at this point.

Liniger took the news in typical fashion. He swore at Tracey, called him terrible names, told him he never wanted to see him again for as long as he lived, and asked him if he'd be coming home for Christmas. Tracey laughed and said that he and Michelle would be visiting her parents in Denver. "Good," Liniger said. "Make sure you stop by the office." Then he swore at him a few more times and said goodbye.

That next year, when Tracey heard about Gail Liniger's plane crash—two hours or so after it had happened—he called Liniger on the phone and told him he was ready to drop everything. Liniger said it was okay and not the right time.

Three more years went by. Tracey continued to do superbly well at his new company, but work just wasn't the same. The difference became crystal clear on one of Tracey's most successful days on the job. The president of the company came to town to observe Tracey in action. Like any good salesman, Tracey had lined up a bunch of sweetheart accounts that would be easy to land. But he decided to take a chance. "Sir, I can give you a dog and pony show if you like," he said. "Or we can roll up our sleeves together, and you can help me sell to three doctors whose business we don't have. We'll need to put on scrubs and get into the operating room with them, but I think it will be worth it." The president of the company was all for it—he hadn't been inside an operating room in years. Together, working side by side, they turned two of the three doctors into new accounts.

The success broke the ice between them. It was rare at that company to have any friendly contact with the senior group. Maybe, Tracey figured, he had finally pushed through. At lunch, celebrating their win, Tracey asked the president all kinds of questions about the future of the medical technology industry and the company: What's coming over the horizon? What are the new products going to do for people? Where do you see the big changes happening? It was the kind of talk he had loved engaging in at RE/MAX with Liniger and the senior team. But the president didn't feel the same passion. "Right now, I'm not thinking about the big picture. I've got retirement in about three years," he said, "and then I'd like to open up a bookstore somewhere."

The conversation deflated Tracey and left him feeling lost. He couldn't help but wonder what Liniger would have said. There was so much energy at RE/MAX and so much focus on the future. Every day at RE/MAX he had come to work wondering what they could do just a little bit better: How can we recruit another agent? How can we sell another franchise? What's really going to make a difference in the race against the competition? It was then that Tracey understood that he wasn't cut out for a company that didn't work on honing and driving its vision every single day.

He missed his RE/MAX family. He missed the culture. He called Liniger up and asked if he could come home. Liniger told him to wait until Christmas and call back—he'd need some time to see what he could line up. Christmas season came, and Tracey called again. Liniger invited him to his house to meet with Daryl Jesperson and Gail where, to Tracey's surprise, they interviewed him for a job. The lesson was clear. Cultural fit was the most important criteria at RE/MAX. It didn't matter who you were or how close everyone felt to you. Liniger, Jesperson, and Gail needed to know how Tracey's experiences at his recent company would contribute to the RE/MAX future. More important, they needed to know if Vinnie Tracey was the same guy he'd always been.

When the interview was over, they shook his hand and hugged him and welcomed him home. Tracey was back at RE/MAX—just in time to help take it to the next level.

Ten Years—Then Boom!

Something amazing was happening at RE/MAX. After 10 years of incremental but steady growth, RE/MAX began to exhibit signs that a powerful momentum was forming. The rate of growth continued apace, but now those numbers were really starting to build. In 1983, the year of Gail Liniger's plane crash, the network had just under 5,000 agents. Ten years later, at the end of 1993, RE/MAX had seven times that number—35,000 agents—making it one of the largest real estate networks in the world. By 1998, RE/MAX had more than 50,000 agents and began to open offices in a few overseas countries. During the next five-year interval, RE/MAX reached just under 90,000 agents with offices in 45 countries. By the end of 2004, that number will reach 100,000 agents in 52 countries. Dave Liniger's stratosphere balloon may not have made it around the world, but the RE/MAX balloon certainly did. As if overnight, RE/MAX became one of the most successful franchises in the world. Surely, people must wonder, "Is this 20-year period of tremendous growth the real story? Shouldn't the point from which the business finally took off be the moment that we begin to learn about what RE/MAX did differently?" Well, that in a nutshell is our problem. Because when we analyzed what RE/MAX did differently during the 20 years when it grew like crazy (compared to the first 10 years when it barely survived), we find ourselves at a loss for explanation. You see, RE/MAX did nothing differently.

Yes, RE/MAX had become a much more sophisticated organization. It had the best technology, the best training, the best brand, and the best agents. But none of those leaps were revolutionary; they were just progressions along a path that had long been taken. Indeed, the RE/MAX growth story is just as remarkable for what *did not* happen.

- *RE/MAX did not change its core leadership team.* Although new leaders did come on board, they did so gradually and organically, becoming part of the original family over time, growing into their roles as family members do. How many companies retain their core leadership over a 30-year period? We know of very few.

- *RE/MAX did not change its core strategy.* The core strategy evolved according to changing conditions; but the premise of agent-by-agent growth, driven by broker owners in regional territories, remained fundamentally the same.

- *RE/MAX did not change its dream.* The vision had always been to become the biggest real estate network in the world by providing agents with maximum commissions. The shift from a straight 100 percent commission split to a system in which 95 percent of the commission goes to the real estate agent and 5 percent to the broker/owner is, in our view, completely consistent with that dream. In 1973, when RE/MAX started, the cost of launching a real estate office was no more than $10,000. As the industry changed and became more cost heavy, the 100 percent formula stopped working because the broker/owner could no longer afford to provide the services that made the agents more successful. The 5 percent fee paid to the broker allowed the broker to be profitable while still providing necessary services. Moreover, the focus on continuous learning, human development, and life success, which was so critical for the agent, had been part of the plan since the beginning; but the technology for accomplishing those objectives had improved even as it also became more costly.

- *RE/MAX did not change its brand.*   The RE/MAX name, the red, white, and blue colors, the RE/MAX balloon, and the *Above the Crowd!* slogan felt less like revolutionary ideas and more like a natural manifestation of its identity. The brand never changed. Despite its increasing national and international heft, RE/MAX never veered from its fundamental strategy of building brand awareness agent by agent under local conditions. Agents and brokers relied on personal promotion and individualized marketing strategies to grow their own business all over the world.

- *RE/MAX did not change its growth formula.*   The seesaw approach to managing the dream and growing the dream remained the same. Dave Liniger actively sought to surround himself with two types of people: growth engines and great managers. He was ferociously aware of the need for dynamic balance. Those growth engines and great managers put their hearts into driving that seesaw with all their might.

- *RE/MAX did not change its core principles.*   The radical reward-sharing idea became the *everybody wins* principle at the heart of the dream. Liniger understood that RE/MAX would be successful only by making its people successful. The true RE/MAX customer is the real estate agent associate. If RE/MAX works hard every day to make that customer satisfied and successful, then home buyers will be satisfied, too.

So is that how a company leaps into greatness? By changing nothing about its dream over a 30-year history? By sticking to everything it believed in during its long years of struggle, no matter what? By maintaining the same leadership ideals regardless of setback and challenge? We think so. In fact, the sudden explosive growth shown by RE/MAX after 10 years of steady, incremental growth fits the model presented by Jim Collins in his book *Good to Great: Why Some Companies Make the Leap . . . And Others Don't.* In that work, Collins profiles a host of remarkable companies that showed no extraordinary promise over their early years and then realized a strong and sustained upward surge in growth, describing that shift as "a truly revolutionary leap in results but *not* by a revolutionary process." While we have drawn some different conclusions as to how RE/MAX managed this "truly revolutionary leap in results," we are struck by the similarity in the pattern of growth between Collins' case studies and RE/MAX.

Indeed, the fact that RE/MAX stuck to its core principles and growth strategy consistently was aptly demonstrated when the network expanded internationally.

Across Borders

In 1989, Peter Gilmour wanted to bring RE/MAX to his native land of South Africa; but in Liniger's view, South Africa under apartheid wasn't ready for RE/MAX. So what did Gilmour do? He learned everything he could about RE/MAX and bided his time until his country changed. Then he tried again.

Gilmour was from Cape Town, the country's beautiful capital city. He had an accounting background and worked with Deloitte & Touche, an international accounting firm. Then, in 1974, his father asked him to join his own local real estate company as a bookkeeper for a few months, until full-time help could be found. Those few months would end up lasting several decades; and Gilmour's partnership with his father would continue all their lives, until three months before his father passed away.

They ran the firm very successfully on a conventional 50 percent commission model. By the early 1990s, after Gilmour joined in partnership with his wife, Val, the firm had grown to 100 agents with seven offices throughout greater Cape Town. Despite that success, Gilmour knew that more was possible. His firm had long experienced the typical vicious cycle: It recruited good people and trained them to be top performers, only to see them leave to create their own businesses. As a student of real estate, Gilmour had given much thought to this issue and to how a firm could create a more sustainable market advantage by focusing on the niche of top agent service.

Around that time, Tom Dooley, a noted speaker in the real estate industry, came to South Africa to talk about the buyer brokerage movement. Gilmour listened closely to what Dooley had to say about his experiences with the large franchising firms. Gilmour's initial approaches got him nowhere fast; so he turned his attention to RE/MAX, sending personal letters to Daryl Jesperson and Bob Fisher. Gilmour told them he would be visiting the United States later that year and would like to see one of them to talk about the possibility of bringing RE/MAX to South Africa.

It was 1989. If Gilmour had been excited about that possibility before, he was positively fired up about it once he had the chance to meet with Fisher and Jesperson in person. They were passionate people who believed in the RE/MAX dream. It was the kind of dream Gilmour wanted to be part of, and the RE/MAX people were the kind of people Gilmour wanted to work with. Fisher and Jesperson felt the same way. They invited Gilmour and his business partners back to the United States for further discussions.

In 1991, at the RE/MAX convention in Las Vegas, Gilmour and his partners returned to the United States and got the full RE/MAX experience firsthand. They saw the passion and the success of the dream played out with thousands of different agents and brokers. They wanted to say "yes" and climb on board. The only hitch was Dave Liniger. Ferociously protective of the brand, Liniger was wary of launching RE/MAX in a country besieged by political upheaval, where the majority of the population didn't even have the opportunity to participate in society. It just wasn't what RE/MAX was about. In the end, Gilmour was sent home empty-handed but not without hope.

Three years later, shortly after apartheid was abolished, Val and Peter Gilmour came back to the United States and attended another RE/MAX convention. This time, Liniger was the one who said "yes." How could he turn down a group that wanted to be part of RE/MAX so badly? The deal was finalized; and later that year, South Africa joined Spain as one of only two countries outside North America to have a RE/MAX franchise.

There would be many more countries added to that list in the next few years.

On January 1, 1995, just as South Africa's renaissance was beginning, the Gilmours and their two partners got to work. It was an amazing period in their country's history to be building a business. For the first time in their lives, black South Africans could own homes and participate in the above-ground economy. The international sanctions against the country were dropped, and the entire world opened up for an isolated people. South Africans could finally travel abroad more freely, and investment capital could come to South Africa unimpeded. International brands came flooding into the country, including the RE/MAX red, white, and blue balloon. Being *international* was an appealing thing for a brand in those days, a symbol of change, progress, and freedom.

Still, the Gilmours and their partners had their work cut out for them. All four were experienced real estate people, well-respected in the community; but they faced the same difficulties that every pioneer in RE/MAX faced. The general real estate community had never heard of this radical reward-sharing idea before. The Gilmours became evangelists, spreading the RE/MAX idea to anyone who would listen, working 18 hours a day to get the word out. They did everything they could to draw attention to RE/MAX. They held open houses to speak with agents directly, and they used the RE/MAX balloon at every opportunity to gain awareness for the brand. Billboard bylaws were strict in those days, but no one had ever considered advertising on a balloon. The RE/MAX balloon showed up all over Cape Town. At a nationally televised cricket match, it rose up and down in the field behind the stadium, captured on camera over and over, while the RE/MAX people barbecued below it. Traffic helicopters made a habit of pointing out the balloon whenever they spotted it floating around the city. The RE/MAX balloon was doing its job.

The pioneers of RE/MAX South Africa did not simply transplant what had worked for RE/MAX in the United States. Although the *everybody wins* principle remained the same, many aspects of the business plan needed to be altered to fit local conditions. RE/MAX had always operated that way, wherever it went, understanding that real estate is a profoundly local phenomenon. (See Figure 8.1.)

But the kinds of adaptations RE/MAX undertook in South Africa and

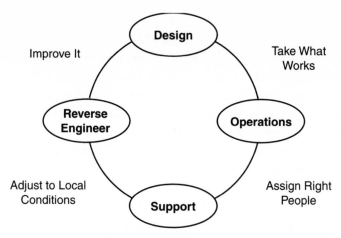

Figure 8.1 Operations Model

the type of change the brand represented were magnified by the cultural differences and the period in history. For instance, the traditional real estate firms in South Africa had applied a great deal of control over their agents; but RE/MAX emphasized personal promotion, self-reliance, and entrepreneurial energy. To the real estate agents of South Africa, the RE/MAX message was: *You can take yourselves as far as you want to go.* After years of corporate and government restrictions, this kind of freedom was truly radical. For years, real estate in South Africa had been closed to most nonwhites. This reality did not change overnight for most traditional firms. But RE/MAX was in the business of recruiting and training top agents, regardless of sex, race, or belief system. After decades of apartheid repression, Gilmour and RE/MAX South Africa were open for business to anyone who said "yes."

In the first few years, RE/MAX South Africa went through many of the same growth patterns that RE/MAX had experienced in the United States. The terrific momentum in years one and two was completely stifled in the next few years by a period of incredibly high mortgage rates. But then came the breakthrough: Eight years after Dave Liniger signed up South Africa, RE/MAX became the number-one real estate network in the country; and Peter Gilmour's firm was named RE/MAX region of the year by RE/MAX International.

South Africa was the engine of growth for the entire southern African region; and under Gilmour's leadership, RE/MAX soon spread to Namibia, Zambia, Botswana, and Mauritius. A few years later, Peter and Val Gilmour got an offer from Dave Liniger they couldn't refuse. *Come to Denver. Teach the rest of the world how to do what you've done. Travel to Europe, Australia, South America, and Asia, and work with them to make RE/MAX a success around the world.* RE/MAX offered to buy back their region, one of the most successful in the world. Without signing a contract or even negotiating an agreement, the Gilmours packed up and moved halfway around the world to join the team at RE/MAX International. Having grown up in a country closed to the rest of the world, the opportunity to travel that world and share their RE/MAX experience was a dream come true.

Frank Polzler Returns to Austria

Frank Polzler had left Austria as a young man with $35 in his pocket. He returned with Walter Schneider to bring RE/MAX to his native Europe.

Polzler and Schneider had blazed a trail for RE/MAX in Canada. They were the guys who saved RE/MAX during the lowest economic moments of the early 1980s. When they started in 1980, all of the Canadian banks had real estate arms and dominated the national scene with 60 percent of the market. Within seven years, RE/MAX was number one in the country; and the giant banks and trust companies left the business, unable to compete.

Polzler had been in the plane accident with Gail Liniger in 1983; but even while in the hospital, he continued to strategize about growth opportunities extending from his stronghold in eastern Canada. Some of the regional owners in the United States had failed during the economic downturn, and Polzler and Schneider were eager to make headway now that the economy was finally improving. As we mentioned in Chapter 5, they asked for New England, and RE/MAX International signed it over. Shortly thereafter, Wisconsin was struggling, so Polzler and Schneider picked that up, too. When Minnesota and Indiana came available, they acquired those as well. Their timing was impeccable. The U.S. economy began to pick up. Polzler and Schneider focused on what needed to be done, marketed the franchises, got key lieutenants in place, and started recruiting agents. Specific goals were set and became milestones that absolutely had to be met. But the overall goal was always the same—grow, grow, grow.

In 1992, Polzler and Schneider were invited to speak about real estate and the RE/MAX story in Vienna, Austria. Polzler couldn't resist the chance to go home. There were 700 delegates in the audience, grey-haired, elderly gentlemen, for the most part, who seemed to be drifting off to sleep after the heavy lunch. The RE/MAX presentation went over like a lead balloon. Dinner that night was at one of the ornate palaces in Vienna. Polzler and Schneider attended, more for the ambience and experience than for any business development opportunities. To their surprise, their table was surrounded by a small group of younger real estate people who had heard their speech. Unlike the elderly men, these people were eager to learn more and desperately wanted RE/MAX to come to Europe. Polzler and Schneider looked at each other. This was the sign they had been waiting for. "Well," Polzler said in his understated way, "I guess we shall have to do something in Europe."

Polzler was hungry for the challenge. Like Liniger, he was a builder, not an administrator. As a leader, he liked to hack a path through the wilderness with a machete and allow others to follow behind him to remove the fallen brush and make the trail. He let Liniger know about the interest they'd seen in Europe. "Why don't you guys just do it?" Liniger said simply. By that point, Liniger knew exactly what the two men were capable of.

Although comparable in terms of economic might to North America, Europe was a very different market. Forty-seven countries, a thousand or more tribes. The typical RE/MAX franchising rules simply wouldn't work in that environment. For the next year, Polzler and Schneider tried to work through complex contracts with RE/MAX International but got nowhere. In the fall of 1993, they ran into Liniger at a RE/MAX event and pulled him aside. "It's not working," Polzler confided in him. "We need more flexibility than your people are willing to give. No one at RE/MAX International understands Europe the way we do. Get them out of the way, and let's do a deal." Liniger understood. Within a week, he had hammered out an agreement with them for a vast territory stretching from Iceland to the Polish/Ukrainian border and including Turkey and Israel. There were

500 million consumers within those boundaries. Everyone of those people needed a place to live, and Polzler could see no reason why RE/MAX shouldn't be the firm that those consumers went to for guidance. It was as though RE/MAX were starting all over again in a brand-new world.

Facing the opportunities of that brand-new world brought familiar feelings, echoes of their first days with RE/MAX. *Now what do we do?* Remembering Liniger drawing a grid on the dusty table in the Harbor Castle Hilton, Polzler and Schneider divided Europe into regions. They planned to market those regions to territorial franchisors, allowing people with local real estate knowledge to run franchises in their respective countries. RE/MAX International, by that time, had moved away from selling regions to selling individual franchises. But Liniger understood their reasoning and okayed the strategy.

Despite the fact that both Polzler and Schneider spoke German, the first franchise region they sold was not in Germany, Austria, or Switzerland, but in Spain. Thus, in 1994, RE/MAX International truly became international with the launch of Spain and South Africa around the same time. Germany was next, then Israel and Italy. For the first five years, the going was extremely rough. Frank Polzler lost his wife to cancer and stepped back from the charge for a time while Schneider took over; but then he was at it again—his "retirement hobby"—trying to grow a region almost double the population size of North America.

In 1999, they were advised to pack it in. RE/MAX simply wasn't going to fly in Europe. There were too many differences in business and in home-buying culture to make it work. But Polzler was like a dog with a bone, and they gradually and steadily turned the corner. He had learned a lot from Liniger about leadership. The path to success was not in dictating direction from the top, but in finding the right people and providing them with the opportunity. A leader needs to be there with his experience and know-how, but his job is to transfer that knowledge, help those individuals grow, and then stand out of the way. *Do what you have to do to be successful. If you make mistakes, you can always fix them later. If something doesn't work, try something else. Anything goes as long as you never mess up the brand.*

Polzler was also not hesitant about helping people leave RE/MAX who did not fit the dream. You needed to recognize the weak spots and deal with them right away in an *everybody wins* system. But that was an active part of managing the dream, not something that one could predict or plan for. Despite all their years recruiting and training, neither Polzler nor Schneider could accurately identify a good RE/MAX person from the outset. Some of the best real estate minds didn't make it; while others who barely met the grade did incredibly well. Polzler himself was a case in point. Liniger never would have predicted that he would lead a RE/MAX charge in North America and around the world. Polzler had seen many people fail in RE/MAX, but he always believed it was not the RE/MAX system that had failed, but the people themselves. They got into the business for the wrong reasons. They thought it was a license to print money. They didn't realize the need to work hard everyday, with incredible effort and determination. Polzler knew that there were a lot more negatives than positives on any given day, that you need to recognize and focus on the positives as you go along. The motivation and determination comes from the top and gets amplified by those at ground level.

After 10 years in Europe, Polzler and Schneider saw the hard work finally pay off. Including their 700 offices in North America, their territory worldwide numbered 1,600 offices of the 5,000 RE/MAX offices total. The opportunities for growth in Europe remain virtually untapped. *The dream is just getting started.* The secret to success in Europe was not the RE/MAX system, but its principles.

In 2004, Polzler had a chance to bring Dave Liniger and Margaret Kelly to Vienna, his birthplace, to speak to his brokers owners and agents and to see the operation firsthand. Polzler was like a king there, a conquering hero, and it was fun for Liniger to see how this former baker who started with $35 in his pocket was honored by his countrymen. For his part, Polzler wanted to impress upon Liniger how much potential existed in Europe. He didn't have to say much; Liniger could tell right away. The energy of the economy was palpable. The new rules governing the European Union were allowing the younger generation of Europeans to move anywhere they wanted in search of good opportunities, building lives, trading up. "I can feel it," Liniger said. "This is the next great growth region for RE/MAX." He grinned and added, "Until I get China going."

Proud to be introducing Liniger to his dream, Polzler felt emotional. "Dave," he said, "you know how some of the regional people complain about how much money gets sent to RE/MAX International? Well, I've never felt that way—ever. You gave Walter and me opportunities we can never repay you for." He meant the chance to transform lives, including their own, to see people provide better for their families. And he also meant the chance to change an industry, leaving it better than they found it.

Dave was struck by that and by the enormity of the distance they had both traveled. Not only had Polzler and Schneider saved RE/MAX, but Polzler had also been in the plane crash with Gail and handed over his $20,000 insurance claim to help with Gail's recovery. Every year, on the anniversary of the crash, Gail calls Polzler and wishes him Happy Birthday—it was, after all, the first day of the rest of their lives. Liniger was deeply grateful for everything that Polzler had done for him, too. "I've always respected you for that, Frank. But has it never struck you how you talk about everything I've done for you, but what about everything you've done for me? You guys saved RE/MAX. You grew your regions in North America. You're building Europe. And you write RE/MAX checks for tens of millions of dollars every year and never complain."

"I'm looking forward to the day I get to write you a check for one hundred million dollars," Polzler said. "Then I'll know I've really done something special."

Liniger knew it was true. It never had been about the money. It was always about growing and becoming number one.

The New Generation of Leaders

In Margaret Kelly, Liniger must have seen the kind of sophisticated managerial and leadership sensibilities that Gail Liniger brought to the equation when RE/MAX first started. In the succession of RE/MAX presidents, Gail Liniger had given way to Bob Fisher after her plane accident. Then, after Bob Fisher retired, his old roommate Daryl Jesperson had taken the helm. When Jesperson became CEO and Margaret Kelly was appointed president, everyone could see that Kelly was bringing with her a talent and an approach exactly right for RE/MAX. She was the organization's first humanitarian president.

That didn't mean Kelly had come into the job without ever having gotten her hands dirty along the way. Almost everyone in the top leadership team at RE/MAX has had some personal experience with hard physical work, and Kelly was no exception. She grew up in Detroit and worked for her father, who owned a machine shop. Kelly's job was to make nuts and bolts. It wasn't easy being a teenage girl covered in machine oil, surrounded by truck drivers; but it taught Kelly a tremendous ethic—work hard, have a good attitude, and do whatever it takes to get the job done. In fact, it was that same work ethic that first got her noticed at RE/MAX.

She came to RE/MAX in an inauspicious way. Kelly was married and living in Denver, where she was the manager of the financial analyst department in a hospital system. In 1987, at the same time that Kelly and her husband had their first boy, Kelly's job moved to Texas. Rather than follow it or shift roles, she decided to resign and take time off to be with her son. She enjoyed that change in life. When it came time to return to work, she decided that she didn't want the stress of a management job anymore and kept her eyes open for something simpler. She saw an ad in the paper for a financial analyst position at a little firm called RE/MAX.

RE/MAX hired her and put her in the accounting bullpen with the other number crunchers. Her attitude and hard work got her noticed. One day, Elaine McCain, her boss, called her into Dave Liniger's office. She'd never really spoken to him before, and suddenly he was offering her a new position as a member services representative. "I've heard excellent things about you," Liniger said. "I know you're a hard worker. Would you like this position?"

"I'd love it," Margaret Kelly began. Before she could get the next words out of her mouth, Liniger said, "Great. Congratulations. Elaine, let's go get lunch. We need to talk." And Liniger and McCain strode out of the office, leaving Kelly to try to figure out how to undo what had just happened.

Margaret Kelly was pregnant and would soon be taking maternity leave. She had only recently found out, and now she'd accidentally misled the CEO. Once McCain and Liniger returned from lunch, Kelly approached McCain, white as a sheet, and explained why she was upset. "It happened so fast," she said. "I tried to tell him, but I couldn't get it out quickly enough. I won't take the job." RE/MAX was a young organization. No one else had been in Margaret Kelly's situation before. McCain said, "Don't worry, it will be fine," and she went off to explain matters to Liniger. Kelly stewed for another week before she met Liniger personally at a Friday barbecue. "Hey," he said, "you want a beer?" And then gave her a look. "Oh, hold on, I guess you can't have one," he joked. Then he high-fived her in congratulations.

So, having a child at RE/MAX was no problem apparently. But Kelly vowed to not let her pregnancy be too disruptive. She worked right until her due date and returned to work five and a half weeks after delivery.

She grew into her new role, got promoted, became a vice president, then led the Colorado region, and after that became Zone Director, rising steadily within the ranks. Not once did she ever ask for a promotion or even expect that one was on the horizon. In fact, she had no idea how closely her performance was being watched, nor how carefully the senior team was placing her in new and challenging stretch assignments. Once, when she turned down a position because she did not think she was ready for it, Liniger approached her. "Don't you understand I wouldn't offer it to you if I didn't believe you could do this?" Kelly was surprised. "We all believe it," Liniger continued, "and we're going to support you. But you've got to believe in yourself, too." It was something for her to hear. She'd known that Liniger saw things in people that they didn't see in themselves. "If I could buy people for what they think they're worth and sell them for what I know they're worth, I'd be a rich man," Liniger once said. His belief in her was very motivating. She wanted to live up to it by working even harder, even as she feared going too far overboard and losing the balance with her family. She was senior vice president of external operations at the time, in charge of everything that happened outside RE/MAX International. The work was thrilling.

Then, in 1990, she was diagnosed with breast cancer, and she learned just how supportive and special an organization she really worked for. It was terrifying and life changing. Three weeks after diagnosis, she was scheduled for a mastectomy. Liniger approached her privately and told her to take time off. "Don't worry about anything. Take the time you need."

Some people thought she would quit after that; but she believed in her heart that if she did quit, the cancer would win. She came back to RE/MAX after four weeks. To her surprise, her job responsibilities were increased when she returned. It made her nervous, but it also meant that they still believed in her.

A year later, RE/MAX and two large regional brokerages were locked in a court battle in Ohio. It was one of the fights of Liniger's life, and he wasn't backing down. Margaret Kelly was scheduled to testify when she got a call informing her that her father had just passed away. She sent a note to the court explaining what had happened. Liniger left the courtroom in the middle of the proceedings, got her a private jet, and had her flown to Detroit to be with her family. As was the tradition at RE/MAX, the senior leaders all joined Kelly for the funeral. Under Dave Liniger's watch, nobody spent a night in a hospital or attended a family funeral alone. The organization had your back, in good times and bad.

They say bad luck happens in threes. In the fall of that year, Kelly learned that she had cancer again and would need more surgery. Two cancer diagnoses. A father dying. One year. It was too much. She asked for a six-month leave of absence.

"I'll take your responsibilities," Liniger said. "Your people will report directly to me. You take the time off and don't worry about it."

During surgery, Kelly's back was somehow injured; and eight weeks later she needed more surgery, this time to repair a ruptured disk. The RE/MAX team knew the drill. They brought her lunches. They spent time with her. Kelly's husband spent nights with her in the hospital; but by morning, he needed to be back for the kids. Someone from RE/MAX was always there to see her through the day.

It took nine months for her to recover and return to form. No one expected her to come back to work. But she knew, deep down, that she had opportunities at RE/MAX that she could find nowhere else. Six months after her return, Margaret Kelly was made president of RE/MAX International.

Each president added something at the right time. Gail Liniger had built the backroom and the feel of RE/MAX, even as she created the sense of a RE/MAX family and kept the creditors at bay. Bob Fisher had grown the dream with his entrepreneurial drive. Daryl Jesperson had brought sophistication to the organization just when it was ready to go global and become world-class.

Margaret Kelly, like Gail Liniger before her, brought a heightened awareness of what the people of RE/MAX needed to feel part of the dream. Times were changing. The hard-charging, hard-partying ways of the original RE/MAX generation were from another era. The network was global,

and its people were diverse. Fun and competition were still at the core of
the culture, but the definition of work hard/play hard had evolved.

In the old days, Liniger, Fisher, and Jesperson knew almost everyone in
the organization personally. With nearly 100,000 associates and 52 countries in the network, that was no longer possible. Yet, Margaret Kelly ex-
celled at creating an environment in which people felt part of the culture.
As president, she was responsible for the organization's ongoing efforts at
being the industry leader; but Kelly also saw her role on a human level. She
was there to touch every person she possibly could within the RE/MAX
family. She knew that a simple moment of recognition or mutual sharing
lasted a very long time and reinforced the message about what was important at RE/MAX. It was a belief that Liniger shared and had also practiced
in his own more private way.

Women had always been at the forefront of the RE/MAX success story.
In a world in which women found it hard to make as much money as men,
real estate was an industry in which women often made more than men.
Gail Liniger had started a tradition called Ladies' Day in the first few years
to recognize the special contributions of women in the back office. Margaret Kelly adopted Ladies' Day and came up with themes that were critical to women's lives, like safety, health, and self-protection. Soon after
Kelly became president, an employee was raped and two others were physically beaten by their spouses. Kelly, with Liniger at her back, saw to those
women's needs, helping get them out of their abusive conditions and into
shelters and hospitals, arranging for restraining orders, counseling, and
care. On another occasion, an agent's client was raped in a vacant house.
It was every real estate agent's nightmare—to enter an empty home and
find danger. With a law enforcement officer that Liniger knew, Kelly created a program on safety awareness. The program spread throughout the
RE/MAX network, and the feedback from agents and brokers was pure
gratitude. They knew it had nothing to do with real estate and everything
to do with what's important.

In a similar vein, there were charities and funds and shelters that
RE/MAX contributed to, some of them in a high-profile way, others behind the scenes. Giving back had always been part of the community-
focused perspective of the network. RE/MAX had long been a contributor
to the Children's Miracle Network, an alliance of hospitals treating sick

children, and became the second largest corporate donor, after Wal-Mart. In 2001, Kelly led RE/MAX to become a major supporter of the Susan G. Komen Breast Cancer Foundation. To Kelly, that's what drew her back to RE/MAX after her illnesses. It was an organization that was not too big to care. She knew she could continue those very personal efforts, inside and outside of RE/MAX, and it made her want to be a better leader.

All of the network's new generation of leaders were groomed in the same way as Margaret Kelly. Diane Metz worked for a Denver competitor that was obsessed with measuring its own performance in the market by tracking RE/MAX. The company lacked a formula or a dream, in her view, and the constant comparison with RE/MAX only reinforced what was missing. During one particularly frustrating meeting, she vowed to herself that she was going to call Dave Liniger personally and ask for a job. Her mother had been a RE/MAX agent, and Diane had met Liniger at various real estate functions and knew him well enough to give it a try. Although she expected to get his voice mail, Liniger answered the phone in his usual manner. "Hi, this is Dave." Surprised, Metz said, "Dave, my name is Diane Metz. I'm over at Metro Brokers. You don't know me, but . . . " Liniger cut her off. "Sure, I know you." Another surprise. "Well, I'm frustrated over here, and I can't help but look at RE/MAX as the place to be. I've just heard all about the RE/MAX Satellite Network and everything else you're doing, and I'd like to come work for you." Liniger told her that he'd set up a meeting for her with two vice presidents, Margaret Kelly and Jack Kreider.

By many measures, it was a successful interview. Metz would end up in Margaret Kelly's role as external vice president nine years later, and she would end up marrying Jack Kreider. But it took her four months of badgering Liniger, Kelly, and Kreider before they finally brought her on board. She tracked RE/MAX in the press with great interest, sent them clippings of their accomplishments, commented on how advanced RE/MAX was compared to the rest of the industry, and "wore them out until they had no choice but to hire me." That was the RE/MAX philosophy. Find people who want the dream as badly as you do. Hire a good person with the right attitude, even if there's no position or title waiting for them. Don't always tell them what you have in mind. In fact, Diane Metz felt so lost that first week at RE/MAX without a title or a job that she locked herself in the restroom and cried, wondering if she had made the biggest mistake of her life. She didn't realize that Dave Liniger had a master plan, and she was now part of it. She soon saw that plan come into action and met every challenge they sent her way.

Nick Bailey hunted RE/MAX down, too. If ever anyone had felt a calling for the real estate industry, it was Bailey. He grew up in northern Wyoming, had his own listing book when he was seven years old, and even made business cards by pasting his picture onto a rectangle of paper. After living in Colorado, he moved back to Wyoming to get into the real estate industry as an agent for a few different real estate companies. He became curious about what really made a great firm. Once he realized that RE/MAX was the franchise he wanted to work for, he picked up the phone and called the human resources department. They told him that there was nothing currently available. He shot off a resume anyway and got a call two weeks later asking when he could come in. Two interviews and eight days later, he had a job. Jack Kreider and Diane Metz asked him at one point during that process what aspect of the job advertisement had appealed to him. Bailey was confused. "I never saw any ad," he said. "I picked you, you didn't pick me." Kreider and Metz understood. RE/MAX was an organization people were drawn to.

Once on board, Bailey experienced the same intense series of stretch assignments. He didn't always know how closely he was being watched. On business trips, Bailey, like other young leaders of promise such as Adam Contos and Kerron Stokes, was often intentionally paired with senior leaders—in taxi rides, during golf games, over dinner—without realizing it. All of it was scripted, structured, and designed to maximize the learning experience. Those senior leaders—Jesperson, Kelly, Liniger—assessed what they saw, discussed new information, probed for weaknesses, created developmental plans. Some of those plans required new challenges, coaching, or even a formal mentoring program. They were always pushing their young leaders and watching them closely, even though the management or oversight style at RE/MAX was completely hands off. It was an approach to nurturing that could be described as "leadership by high expectations." They push you to be better than you think you are.

At the same time, the RE/MAX leadership team, starting with Liniger, was never afraid to stretch itself. Liniger seems to believe fully in the adage that *you should not be afraid to hire way above yourself.* He wants the best people with the most talent—as long as they have the right attitude, passion, and common sense.

An outsider might worry that an organization with a strong founder, still in an ownership position with great responsibility and authority, could crumble quickly when that founder finally left the stage. We looked for such cracks and found no signs of them. In fact, we were surprised by the seriousness with which Liniger and his senior team are actively looking to replace themselves. The original group of Dave and Gail Liniger and Daryl Jesperson are still in positions of ultimate authority, but they have bridged to other generations, starting with people like Vinnie Tracey, Margaret Kelly, Bruce Benham, Joe Reynolds, Diane Metz, and Jack Kreider.

Indeed, people we talked to inside and outside of RE/MAX commented on the depth of this leadership bench. The source of that depth is the organization's culture. Starting with Gail Liniger's accident, Dave Liniger learned that when he stepped away from daily operations, others stepped up and took over. When Liniger seizes a project, the same thing occurs. Liniger's attitude is that the number-two person in any position should be fully capable of assuming the number-one role on a moment's notice. Because of the level of trust and the close personal relationships fostered within the family atmosphere of the senior team, this kind of interconnectedness seems consistent with its long-term survivability. RE/MAX leaders rarely use the word "I" in conversation and seem to naturally speak of "We." They have great pride in what that "We" can accomplish. They are down-to-earth and plainspoken in a way that shows a distaste for corporate politics or showmanship. It is still next to impossible to find an organizational chart anywhere in the organization. It is still a group that believes job descriptions do not tail off at "and other" but actually begin there.

Bill Soteroff is an example of new leadership at the regional level. Until 1994, he worked for a large, established corporation. The focus on profitability over people did not feel right to him, but he enjoyed the trappings of three-piece suits and high-powered business trips. When Walter Schneider approached him to start up the fledgling New England region of RE/MAX, Soteroff realized that those trappings were golden handcuffs. What appealed to Soteroff about RE/MAX was the entrepreneurship and the opportunity. In an organization attuned to local regions and circumstances, there was no single strategy of success. He loved the camaraderie of a group of business leaders from different areas of the world who were focused on growth in their own regions, sharing what worked and what didn't openly with each other. The culture of ideas and success was a pleasure compared to his experiences in a more traditional top-down company.

That didn't mean RE/MAX was an environment in which mediocre performance was tolerated. Walter Schneider brought an incredible discipline and focus to the operations in New England. At a meeting at Foxboro Stadium in Massachusetts, where the new New England Patriots' quarterback Drew Bledsoe was making his debut, Schneider taught some lessons that Soteroff and the regional broker owners would never forget. The battle cry for growth came down to the following: "Recruit, Retain, Charge Enough, Collect, Gain Market Share." If each group did those things, it would create a collection of work environments driven for growth. It was not the responsibility of one person or one president to execute; it was up to every person in the system to do his or her bit. Those efforts didn't need to be flawless, but the effort itself was critical. If each individual at each level followed that battle cry, then growth would result.

Walter Schneider hired Bill Soteroff because he believed Soteroff could lead that growth charge. At the same time, Schneider drove Soteroff to push past his own limitations of what he perceived possible. Schneider was not the type to bask in the glory of past accomplishments; he was always moving on to the next audacious challenge. It was as though he believed that taking a moment to reflect on how far you've come gave others an opportunity to pass you by. When Soteroff first started in New England, the region was selling six or seven franchises a year. It was a number Soteroff was proud of. He had logged 50,000 more miles on his rented Jeep Cherokee than his leasing agreement allowed. But Schneider said, "That's not going to cut it. You need to find a way to organize differently so you can get those numbers up. What are you going to do to sell twenty-four franchises next year?"

That was Schneider, always pushing people to the next level. Seventy-two hours later, Schneider called Soteroff in follow up. "So, what's your plan?" Soteroff knew that Schneider was totally supportive of hiring the right people and buying the right technology to succeed. "I know I can't do everything myself," Soteroff said. "So I'm going to recruit two new franchise salespeople, a service person, and a better administrator." Schneider pushed him further. "Not enough. It won't get you to your plan. You're going to need four or five new franchise salespeople, and you need them immediately, not six months from now."

Two years later, Soteroff's region began an eight-year run of selling no less than 24 franchises a year. RE/MAX of New England went from 60 offices to more than 250 offices with over 2,500 agents, making it the number-two real estate firm in the region. When the head of the oldest firm in the region retired, he phoned Soteroff and acknowledged defeat. "You beat me," he said. "I thought I was the best business manager around. But I can't compete with a group of people who manage and own their own businesses." Soteroff knew that what he really couldn't compete with was the idea of *everybody wins*.

Schneider pushed Soteroff every step of the way. The challenges that Schneider gave him were not just about numbers; they were about breaking through preconceived limits. New England, as a region, only had seven million people; but it managed a level of agent growth second only to California. It was also a region with diverse local conditions that Soteroff somehow brought into alignment. Schneider perceived he was ready; he tapped Soteroff to come in and shake up Europe just as he'd done New England.

Schneider and Polzler had chosen local managers in Europe, people who knew the native culture and conditions firsthand. Soteroff did not see the same kind of drive, passion, and commitment to the brand in them that he knew in New England. When he met the regional managers, they were polite but standoffish—as though they expected Soteroff to only last a short time before he went home again. Soteroff stood in front of the group and gave them the kind of push Schneider had always given him. "You're not doing very well," he said. "If this was a traditional organization, we'd be looking for new managers. We need to do better. But if we want to change things, we are going to have to think very differently. Take the next five minutes and consider whether you really want to be here or not. Whether you want to work with me. Whether you want to go through the difficult days and nights ahead to grow this business. If you want to leave, no problem. I have some mutual release forms right here. There will be no hard feelings. You can go home today." And he sat down.

The eyes of 20 European managers widened. They watched him carefully, none of them moving. One of the managers later told Soteroff that he was afraid to breathe. After five long minutes, Soteroff spoke again. "Okay. If this is where we are, then we will go forward together from this point. We're going to work hard, and you are going to be successful."

Soteroff's five-minute stare was the turning point for Europe. Growth became the battle cry. Every success earned a congratulatory handshake from Soteroff, followed by a Schneider-like question. "Okay, how are you going to get to the next level? What's your plan?" With the hard push and the hard work came the growth, and also the pride. From Iceland to Turkey, brokers/owners became proud to wear a RE/MAX pin. The idea of owning and operating a real estate business with international connections was new and innovative in Europe. In their communities and cities, these RE/MAX leaders were viewed as great businesspeople. One manager in Portugal recruited 900 agents in 18 months and was given an award by the government of Portugal for building the fastest-growing business in the country.

From Denver, Liniger tracks the growth in each region and sees the big picture, too. His prediction for RE/MAX is audacious—100,000 agents in 2004, 115,000 in 2005; 2 countries in 1994, 52 in 2004. We see no sign that Liniger's team is resting on their past accomplishments. Indeed, we see convincing evidence that RE/MAX is focused on the next wave of growth. Many of the regional owners are nearing the end of their run. Some have children or leaders they have groomed who are ready to pick up the torch; others are looking for an exit strategy. Roll-ups are the rule of the day. Brokers/owners are joining with other brokers/owners to increase the size of their businesses, further systemize their operations, and prepare for the possibility of a buyout. RE/MAX International is ready to bring more of those businesses inside the big tent, as if coiling up and preparing to spring.

What It's Really All About

Liniger has mellowed over the years but never lost his fire or his restless drive for growth. He slipped into success in a very comfortable way, as though it was always meant to be; but he does not exhibit the trappings of privilege. He has always been a very caring person, beneath a gruff exterior. He seems to accept the responsibilities of leadership without pretense, as though he feels humble to realize how much impact he has on people's lives. If his world has grown immeasurably large because of the distance he has traveled, his curiosity and sense of obligation seem to have grown proportionately, too.

He and Gail keep looking for more ways to give back. As people of great prosperity, they do not want to be consumed by the need for more and more. How many houses can you own? How many cars can you drive? How many steaks can you eat? They try to combine giving with ideas that mean something to them and to the people of RE/MAX—a world-class golf course built to host charity tournaments; a wildlife museum to preserve nature and educate children; help for hospitals, shelters, and treatment centers—because he and Gail understand what it means to be in need of care.

Liniger has never lost his shyness, but he seems to have grown in presence on the stage. He has become accustomed to people looking to him for vision. What will the next 10 years look like? What should we watch out for? How are we going to get there? He has a sense of that future, an unwavering optimism about it and a clear-eyed view of the challenges between here and there—a way that feels very Shackletonian.

We asked him what he thought the entire RE/MAX journey was all about. He said that for years he had believed firmly that he knew the answer to our question, and then one day it hit him that he was all wrong. He told us more about that insight.

When Gail Liniger was injured in the plane crash, Liniger had bought her a glass terrarium. Within the small space, there were little plants and moss. Over the next three years, as Gail spent many days in and out of the hospital, Liniger took care of her terrarium and watered it. He did not have a green thumb. The roots became covered in algae and the dirt looked unhealthy. He told Gail that he wanted to throw it out. "I've ruined this one," he said. "I'll buy you a new one." Gail wouldn't let him. "You can't. That's my terrarium," she said, "ever since I got hurt." Liniger tried hard to convince her, but it was no use. Finally, he said, "Okay, at least let me replant it."

He took the plants that had never been outside their enclosed space and repotted them. Free from their walls, the plants began to grow. Today, those plants press up against the ceiling of their house in Denver, close to 10 feet tall.

Thinking about that remarkable change, it finally struck Liniger. *That's the significance of RE/MAX.* He had believed that the meaning of RE/MAX was all about recruiting top producers and gaining market share, but it was much more simple and profound than that. It was really about giving people the space and the care to grow. When Liniger took away the barriers and the impediments that were inherent in the traditional real estate system, he gave agents the freedom to become something bigger. His message was simple: *Promote yourself. Advertise as much as you want. Negotiate your own commissions. Decide your own deals. Grow your business the way you know how to grow it.* Without restrictive boundaries but with the support of others dedicated to their success, the agents had the ability to succeed beyond what they had ever thought possible.

It is a view of the world in which *everybody wins.* And it is a belief that we think can make the world a better place.

Strategic Moves

Stick to the *everybody wins* formula, and you will win.

RE/MAX has an uncanny knack for operations. Walking through its culture, there is an apparent quiet calm—total engagement—no panic. It leads change with precision as if it were practicing John Kotter's eight-point model. At the same time, the organization has a backup for every position. The strength of its systems approach is that the organization stays balanced and aligned. Leaders know that operations are core to strategy, that "everyone carries the boxes," starting with senior leaders. Most important, we find in our research that lots of organizations forget that *hand over* means passing on responsibility and accountability. There is no throwing things over the fence at RE/MAX. We believe this is a good model for organizations to consider.

- An organization must work to hone and drive the dream every single day. Leaders create and reinforce a corporate culture where employees are motivated by continuing the refinement of the dream. (p. 189)

- Even if you know a person, interview him or her thoroughly before you hire to ensure that you have the best fit for the organization's needs and that the person truly believes in the dream. (p. 189)

- Exponential growth does not happen overnight. By maintaining the same core leadership team, strategy, dream, brand, growth formula, and core principles and by working diligently and patiently until its time had come, RE/MAX went from "good to great" after 10 years of hard work. (pp. 190–191)

- Be open and flexible to altering details of the business plan when expanding globally. Your organization may need to alter small factors in order to function well within a new environment. Principles are the only nonnegotiables. (p. 194)

- "Do what you have to do to be successful. If you make mistakes, you can always fix them later. If something doesn't work, try something else. Anything goes, as long as you never mess up the brand." (p. 198)

- Let the people go who do not fit the dream. In order to have an *everybody wins* system, recognize the weak spots and deal with them right away. Keep your eyes open for those who are buying into the dream for the wrong reasons. (pp. 198–199)

- Watch the potential future leaders very closely. Be intentional about placing them in jobs and assignments that will stretch and challenge them. Groom and train them carefully for their future and the company's future. (p. 202)

- Wise words from Dave Liniger: "If I could buy people for what they think they're worth and sell them for what I know they're worth, I'd be a rich man." Believe in employees more than they do to encourage and motivate. (p. 202)

- Once you find a prince or a princess, support him or her through any extreme or personal hardships. Treat princes and princesses like the invaluable treasure they are. (pp. 202–203)

- As a leader, connect with as many employees as you can. Know that a simple moment of recognition or mutual sharing can last a very long time and will reinforce motivation and drive toward the dream for employees. (p. 204)

- Give your people what they need to feel supported in their lives, not just their jobs. At RE/MAX, safety, health, and protection information demonstrated caring above and beyond the boundaries of work. (p. 204)

- As an organization, give back to the community through charity and philanthropy. Not only will it show the public and your employees that you care, but it will motivate their work in a different way. (pp. 204–205)

- On business trips or in other work situations, intentionally pair up potential future leaders with senior leaders in taxi rides, for meals, in games or projects to maximize the learning experience and to create mentoring relationships for younger leaders. (p. 206)

- Don't be afraid to hire above yourself. Hire the best people with the most talent—as long as they have the right attitude, passion, and common sense. (p. 207)

- Actively look to replace yourself and your senior leadership team. Mentor younger leaders and build bridges to the younger generation so that there will be a smooth transition when any of the current leaders leave. (p. 207)

- Create a "we" culture rather than an "I" culture. (p. 207)

- Prepare successors ahead of time. Create an environment of trust so that others can step in and take over a project when someone leaves or in a personal emergency. (p. 207)

- Leadership is about giving people the space and the care to grow. (p. 212)

Lesson

An operational mindset requires formulaic persistence resulting in exponential surges in growth.

Sticking to the formula and principles of *everybody wins* is an operational mindset. As RE/MAX has learned again recently in Europe, success doesn't happen on a straight line. The investments in growing and managing the dream require time to build infrastructure, for passionate champions to ramp up, and for branding concepts, like OMD, to gain hold. Keeping it all together, holding the leadership strong, providing constant focus and attention to all the implementation details, consistently upgrading people, always believing and selling the dream: Those are the factors that create explosive growth and unstoppable momentum. It has been this focused drive model that has made RE/MAX exceptional and worthy of study. (See Figure 8.2.) After all, it's easier to grow at 20 percent per year when you have 5,000 associates than when there are 100,000.

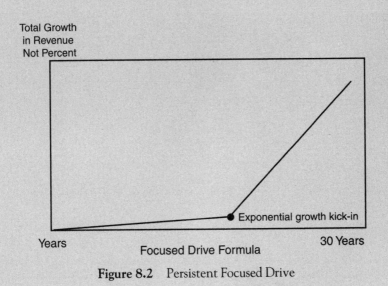

Figure 8.2 Persistent Focused Drive

CHAPTER 9

THE RESEARCH STUDY

While we were deeply involved with our study at RE/MAX, we ran a parallel analysis of what we believed to be the best HG/HI (high-growth/high-impact) global company benchmarks. This chapter is a synopsis of the pertinent conclusions that we learned from our selected study of these six HG/HI benchmark companies: Wal-Mart, McDonald's, Nokia, BMW, Toyota, and Canon. HG/HIs are publicly traded, global brand companies that have had 30 years of consistent revenue and employee growth and that have not principally grown through acquisition. Our hunch was right; we found valuable insights that brought us beyond the conclusions that we reached in our analysis of RE/MAX.

Our Criteria

We started the research for this book some three years ago. At that time we were convinced that internally generated growth for organizations was and would continue to be challenging. It coincidentally was at the beginning stages of the economic downturn of 2000–2001. While it proved to be one of the more challenging economies of the past 30 years and still plagues many parts of the world as of this publication in 2005, it was an opportune time for us because it became a laboratory for our research. Of interest, experts, economists, and other forecasters were blindsided by the swift onslaught of this dour financial gloom-and-doom economy, which many now see as having been caused partly by a loss of focus on internally generated growth. We wanted to better understand what HG/HI companies do to generate better-than-average growth results consistently, despite all that influences organizations to regression toward the mean (the natural forces that make organizations prone to average performance over time).

Moreover, we had a theory that best-in-class organizations, ultimately the ones that we believed were HG/HI, could and do grow through all economies, including economic downturns, beating business cycles. We further speculated that some organizations may have a winning formula and certain practices that ensured higher rates of growth. We wanted to learn from these organizations and report our findings. We knew that there were growth companies out there, mostly giant companies like Wal-Mart and Home Depot in the retail space, that were growing at an unbelievable pace. However, we resisted the urge to go with the standard, apparent success stories, such as General Electric and Microsoft. Rather, we took a more analytical approach, starting with a clean slate. We wanted to avoid companies that just had consistent bottom-line growth, knowing that many companies achieve growth principally by reducing costs without adding organic revenue. We wanted companies that had primarily achieved their growth by adding products, services, markets, and geographies. We felt that expansion by merger and acquisition would cloud our ability to make determinations on how organizations accomplished internally generated "pure" growth. Our goal was to identify the best global examples of companies that truly had the most consistent runs of top-line growth and that were also considered to be high-impact organizations. We chose publicly traded companies so we could get the information we needed.

With this in mind, we researched growth companies, read their annual reports, and discussed growth with high-impact leaders from around the world, always looking for the edge on identifying HG/HI organizations. With so many organizations to look at, we recognized the importance of honing in on criteria that we could use to find the best HG/HI companies.

After careful review and study, we narrowed our definition to include the following five criteria that we believed HG/HI organizations must be/have:

1. *Global*, conducting business around the world, with a presence in many countries and on at least three continents.

2. *Continuous growth*, defined as growth year after year without fail (we made a few exceptions, which will be further explained) for a minimum of 20 to 30 years (preferably 30).

3. A recognizable global *brand*.

4. Trying to become *number one* in their industry.

5. An *organic growth company*, meaning that growth must be primarily without acquisitions or mergers.

Our criteria proved to be very high hurdles for organizations to leap over, and very few made the cut. We ultimately reduced our list to the Top 20, and even then most companies could not measure up to the standard we set. Table 9.1 shows the "Top 20" list of companies by region and the criteria that caused them to be eliminated from our study.

The truly challenging part of this search, we discovered, was finding companies that have grown year after year for 30 years without acquisition. Because we wanted this study to be international in scope, we decided to include in our study six companies representing three different areas of the world. We had set out to select two from North America, two from Europe, and two from Asia. One of the major difficulties was finding European companies that did not grow as a result of acquisition. For example, we found that all 20 of the companies on the list of European High-Growth Value Adders (Stewart, "Champions of Profitable Growth") had to a large extent grown as a result of acquisitions or mergers. Also, *Fortune*'s "Europe's Top 50" in "The 2004 Global 500" revealed that 48 of the 50 companies succeeded in growth mainly through acquisitions. Of the few that did have strong organic growth, these did not have a strong enough brand or reputation to be used as a comparison company for this study.

We determined that global business at the turn of the twenty-first century is an acquiring world with an accretive mentality. Most companies we studied, it seemed, were primarily focused on making profits rather than on scaling the value of their products or services. Over the past 10 years, we

Table 9.1   Top 20 Comparison Companies

	Company	Continent	Outcome
1	General Electric	North America	Eliminated, Criteria 5
2	Wal-Mart	North America	Accepted into study
3	McDonald's	North America	Accepted into study
4	Johnson & Johnson	North America	Eliminated, Criteria 5
5	Pfizer	North America	Eliminated, Criteria 5
6	Exxon Mobil	North America	Eliminated, Criteria 5
7	Procter & Gamble	North America	Eliminated, Criteria 5
8	Intel	North America	Eliminated, Criteria 1
9	Nestlé	Europe	Eliminated, Criteria 5
10	GlaxoSmithKline	Europe	Eliminated, Criteria 5
11	BP	Europe	Eliminated, Criteria 5
12	BMW	Europe	Accepted into study
13	Nokia	Europe	Accepted into study
14	Munich de Group	Europe	Eliminated, Criteria 3
15	Robert Bosch	Europe	Eliminated, Criteria 3
16	Toyota	Asia	Accepted into study
17	Sony	Asia	Eliminated, Criteria 5
18	Honda	Asia	Eliminated, Criteria 1
19	Canon	Asia	Accepted into study
20	Nippon Telegraph & Telephone	Asia	Eliminated, Criteria 1

speculated that most of the revenue gain that companies have generated has been through acquisition rather than organic growth. This was even more prevalent in Europe. Overall, it may be more significant from an economic standpoint than we can report on here.

Why is it that this trend of growth through acquisitions is so prevalent in European countries? Here is an explanation:

European companies are smaller and more regionalized within their individual countries. The European marketplace has not been united. For instance, California is the world's sixth-largest economy; it is larger than more than 90 percent of the world's developed countries. The smaller European countries without a united larger European economy have had fewer ways to compete with larger economies, such as the United States and Japan. As a result, European companies perhaps have merged and acquired as a defensive strategy.

With this conclusion, we chose European HG/HI companies more on year-after-year growth over 30 years. We still held firm for companies with strong single brands that are global and determined to be the best in their industry and geography. We chose to study BMW and Nokia as the European comparison companies for this study.

In selecting our finalists across all three major regions of the global economy, we concluded that consistent, real growth is hard to find. It seemed to our research team that companies that are consistently focused on increasing and improving the strength of their brand and the value of their product and/or service and on striving for overall global expansion are rare. The key word is *consistent*. Fortunately, the fact that there are some organic HG/HI companies that passed our tests is noteworthy and interesting. How do they do it? Is the trend changing from acquisition mindedness to organic growth? Our study seems timely. This makes companies like RE/MAX, our case study, and companies like Wal-Mart and McDonald's, who are part of our study group, even more exemplary with their high growth, strong brands, and great reputations within their industries.

Findings and Our Study

With a great deal of work and some small concessions here and there around our criteria (which we have noted) so we could stay on course to have two North American, two European, and two Asian companies, we arrived at what we believe to be the six best HG/HI companies that we could benchmark. To follow are our analyses and conclusions.

Our early research proved very valuable in that we immediately saw that the companies that performed better during down cycles clearly had a dream and a major focus on internally generated growth. That observation, however, although interesting, was not enough for our research team. We wanted to get under the covers and know more. Was there a common formula, as in RE/MAX? Were there underlying principles by which these companies operated that allowed these organizations to beat the odds? The more we dug, the more we observed a fundamental pattern of how these six companies operated. *HG/HI companies know how to focus on the critical few and believe that they can and will succeed in all economies.*

It became clear and simple that organizations that are consistent in growth have the ability to create a *major focus* on growth. They believe that they can grow despite downturns. Of course, these companies did better when the wind was at their backs. Yet they all have strategies on how to keep sailing when there is no wind or, worse case, when the wind is against them.

Six Companies Chosen for Study Companies

Of the six companies that we identified as HG/HI (Wal-Mart, McDonald's, Nokia, BMW, Toyota, and Canon), only two of these companies have grown every year for more than 30 years: Wal-Mart and McDonald's. The other four have had great growth runs over 30 years but have had explainable slips. They are all high-impact companies, global, with strong brand names, aimed at being or becoming number one in their industry; and they have grown without major acquisitions. One fact that has become obvious to us is that year-to-year growth over a long period of time without acquisition is an incredibly rare thing to come by. Figures 9.1 and 9.2 show the revenue growth and the employee growth for the six benchmark HG/HI companies by year and percentage growth.

We prepared the High Growth/High Impact Score Sheet (Table 9.2) based on our criteria for the six HG/HI companies plus RE/MAX. There

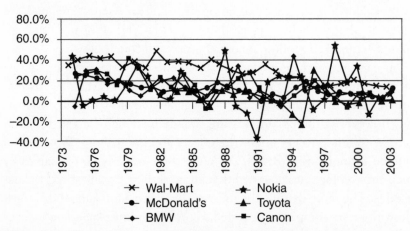

Figure 9.1 Revenue Growth for Selected HG/HI Companies, by Year and Percentage of Growth

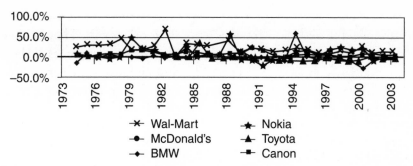

Figure 9.2 Employee Growth for Selected HG/HI Companies, by Year and Percentage of Growth

are some surprises. The chart was prepared by our researchers using objective criteria and, whenever possible, third-party indexes so that we could have objective and valid conclusions.

We created an HG/HI rating system and ranked each company according to our five criteria. Each company received a ranking of 1 to 7 based on where they fell in relation to the other six companies, with 1 being the best. Those rankings were then added up for each company's total score. The final scores are in Table 9.2. RE/MAX and McDonald's tied for the #1 spot. It was surprising to us that Wal-Mart came in as #3 in the final rankings. We would have expected it to be either tied with RE/MAX as #1 or in the #2 placing. The reason for Wal-Mart's #3 placement is the fact that it has not expanded as far globally as our other benchmark organizations. In the category of global presence, Wal-Mart got last place (7 points) because it is only in 11 countries worldwide. Also, as a result of not being as global a company as the others, Wal-Mart does not have the same global brand awareness that the other organizations have. These two categories brought in scores for Wal-Mart that moved it down to a #3 ranking on our HG/HI Score Sheet.

Table 9.2 Our High Growth/High Impact Score Sheet*

Company	Global	Growth	Brand	Goal to Be #1	Acquisitions
BMW	71 countries 6 continents	#17 Europe high-growth value adder	#17 Global Brand #15 Most Admired	#74 *Fortune's* 2004 Global 500	Rover, Mini, and Rolls-Royce
Total points: 20 Ranking: #5	#1	#7	#6	#4	#2
Canon	42 countries 5 continents	#6 Asia high-growth value adder	#35 Global Brand	#45 The Info Tech 100	None
Total points: 22 Ranking: #7	#5	#6	#7	#3	#1
McDonald's	119 countries 6 continents	Over 30 years of year-to-year growth	#7 Global Brand #2 in Brandweek America's Top 2000 Brands	#7 Franchise 500 #114 Fortune 500	Bought stakes in Chipotle, Boston Market, Donatos Pizzeria, and Pret A Manger
Total points: 8 Ranking: #1	#1	#3	#1	#2	#1
Nokia	50 countries 6 continents	#7 Europe high-growth value adder	#8 Global Brand	Consumer Products: Gold Award Annual Design Awards 2004	Many acquisitions and mergers over history
Total points: 21 Ranking: #6	#4	#5	#4	#5	#3

224

	Countries	Growth	Advertising/Brand	Franchise/Fortune	Dependencies
RE/MAX	52 countries 6 continents	Month-to-month growth for 31 years	Will have spent $5.5 billion on brand advertising by the end of 2004	#1 Fastest-growing real estate franchise in the world	None
	#3	#1	#2	#1	#1
Total points: 8 Ranking: #1					
Toyota	27 countries 6 continents	#1 Asia high-growth value adder	#9 Global Brand #8 Most Admired	#8 *Fortune's* 2004 Global 500	None
	#6	#4	#5	#3	#1
Total points: 19 Ranking: #4					
Wal-Mart	11 countries 4 continents	#2 America high-growth value adder over 30 years of year-to-year growth	#1 Most Admired	#1 Fortune 100 and Fortune Global 500	Few, and would have continued growth without them
	#7	#1	#3	#1	#1
Total points: 13 Ranking: #3					

*The lower the number of total points, the higher the HG/HI score.

How HG/HI Organizations Grow

What has allowed these companies to become HG/HI over a 30-year period? We identified five consistent themes:

1. Enormous focus on top-line growth through major product- and service-line expansion.

2. The ability to create alignment.

3. Brand awareness.

4. Balance between innovation and operations.

5. Charismatic leadership.

1. Enormous Focus on Top-Line Growth in Major Product and Service Lines

Each of the six HG/HI companies knows how to focus and to create vigorous energy around its core products and services. Each one also, in addition to being incredibly focused, has a continuity of equally focused leaders.

Among the six benchmark companies, Wal-Mart, the largest retailer in the world, takes first prize for top-line growth. It has such an enormous focus on growth that people don't know whether to love Wal-Mart for its low prices or hate it for the empire that it has developed, which scares competitors and sometimes suppliers. Regardless of what people may think about it, it is hard not to admire the fact that Wal-Mart excels in its ability to focus on top-line growth. "The company is so ruthlessly efficient that 4 percent of the growth in the U.S. economy's productivity from 1995 to 1999 was due to Wal-Mart alone, researchers at the McKinsey Global Institute estimated last year. No other single company has had as measurable an impact. Wal-Mart also has forced competitors to become more efficient, driving the nation's productivity—output per hour of work—even higher." (Goldman and Cleeland, "An Empire Built on Bargains")

We discovered that when our HG/HI companies lost focus, they also lost ground in top-line growth. BMW's acquisition of Britain's MG Rover group in 1994 caused it to experience significant brand and marketing challenges, which cost it revenue and growth. But BMW knew that top-line growth through the strength of its products was the most important thing and that the Rover line was affecting its ability to focus on that. "Since BMW sold its stake in Britain's MG Rover Group in 2000 and gave up the notion of acquiring a mass-market brand, the $50 billion auto maker has carefully added one hit model after another, from premium SUVs to sleek coupes and zippy roadsters. Each addition stoked growth, with revenues up 11 percent since 2000 and profits up 61 percent." (Edmondson, "BMW: Crasing the Compact Market") The biggest lesson that we can gain from BMW's experience with Rover is that BMW had much better success when it concentrated on its core areas of focus and on the products and services that represent what BMW does best—luxury cars, not mass-market brands.

This was also observed at RE/MAX. Dennis Curtin, one of its very successful leaders, compared his experience at RE/MAX to his past corporate business life in this way: "We've had over thirty years of straight growth. We only talk about recruiting and retaining and gaining market share, and that in a business environment is so pleasurable because you don't have to spend any part of your life or your existence worrying about the downsize. All of your problems can be resolved and solved by selling more or recruiting more people—growing your business by twenty or thirty percent a year."

2. Alignment

All of our benchmark companies create alignment. All six companies have the unique ability to focus on their core areas of strength. These core areas are supported by their core competencies (what produces competitive advantage), which are linked to specific capabilities that each company and its people have. We uncovered an interesting truth among the benchmarks. *HG/HI companies are dedicated to learning, but not about everything; they are focused on continued learning around the areas that will differentiate them in their market.*

All six companies consistently measure and report on their core areas. They *measure the critical few*, always concentrating on their specific areas of focus. They can articulate their growth competencies and capabilities because they are constantly measuring their progress in their focus areas.

RE/MAX weighs in as a good example of alignment. It reports only on what is critically important to its growth, and it measures that efficiently and often. If you walk into Dave Liniger's office, his desk is always completely clear except for one report, which he receives every day. This report measures the number of offices, the number of associates, the production of the offices, and the production by associates. These are the only numbers that Liniger needs to determine whether RE/MAX is growing in its core areas. If RE/MAX associates and offices are growing and creating revenue, Dave knows that RE/MAX itself is growing.

Great companies all have their own unique ways of measuring their growth. McDonald's for years measured the number of hamburgers, now visibly displayed under the Golden Arches as "Billions served." Wal-Mart measures the average cash register receipt per customer and the number of customers per day. BMW and Toyota measure car orders per dealership. These are their core areas, driving top-line growth.

3. Brand Awareness

Each of our six HG/HI companies understands how important its brand name is and knows how to leverage it. All six of our study companies are ranked brand companies, either on *BusinessWeek's* 2003 Global Brands Scoreboard or on *Fortune's* 2004 Global Most Admired Companies list, or on both. These rankings can be seen on our HG/HI Score Sheet. Our research shows that there is a strong link between growth and brand. Our conclusion is that *companies that focus on their brand have the highest opportunity for exponential growth around that brand.*

A turbocharger for growth companies is their ability to leverage their brand in everything they do. From day one at RE/MAX, even when there was little money to spend, there were dollars expended for signs, pins, and anything else that represented the RE/MAX Balloon.

McDonald's emerged in our study as the #1 brand leader of the world. Its brand is the most widely recognized on the planet—96 percent of American schoolchildren can identify Ronald McDonald, and the Golden Arches are now more widely recognized than many religious symbols. McDonald's does get its share of negative press, though. When it is attacked, as it has been for supplying low-nutritional-value food, it immediately revises and improves its product line to satisfy its customers. Then McDonald's uses those changes to fuel a campaign to revive its brand image.

Canon has been rewarded for its focus on brand. It is a company that has been recognized for inspiring brand loyalty in its consumer base. *Forbes* recently reported,

> Canon U.S.A., Inc., the nation's market share brand leader in black-and-white and color laser copier/printer solutions, today announced that *Brandweek* magazine has ranked the digital imaging leader number one in the "Office Copier" industry category as part of the 2004 *Brandweek* Customer Loyalty Awards, powered by Brand Keys. . . . Canon has dominated the black-and-white U.S. copier market, owning the number-one share position for 21 of the past 22 years. It has also dominated the U.S. color copier market, with the number-one brand share position for the past 17 consecutive years. (*Brandweek* Names Canon No. 1)

Nokia was the #6 Global Brand in *BusinessWeek*'s Global Brand Scoreboard in 2003. It is a European company that has not only established great brand awareness in the United States, but is also actively pursuing to continue to build its brand globally. Nokia is a great example of a European company that has produced a growth engine worldwide based on brand awareness.

4. Balance between Innovation and Operation

Each of the six HG/HI companies has consistently invested in product development and product improvement, while still expanding geographically. These six organizations are deliberate about staying balanced; they recognize that focusing on growth alone will put a company out of business. Maintaining the balance creates consistent growth over long periods of time. Toyota is a great example of how to balance growth while continuing to improve products and services every year. One *Fortune* article (Taylor, "Toyota's Secret Weapon") reported, "The merest hint of a problem—any problem—instantly registers on the corporate radar. When Toyota's longtime lead in quality over all its rivals began to narrow in the past year, it immediately began to reexamine all manufacturing and engineering processes." Toyota has mastered the practice of creation, destruction, and evolution. It is constantly balancing its focus on growth, innovation of new products, and refinement of its current product lines.

We found that *the balance between innovation and operations requires a corporate culture of innovation and learning in which employees can thrive and develop.* Each of the six HG/HI companies puts an emphasis on new and better, as opposed to just focusing on being more efficient and effective at what it already does. Sumantra Ghoshal, who was at the London Business School, believed that the most successful companies in the world grow year after year because they produce 25 percent of their revenue from new products, programs, and services. His "525 rule" stated that 25 percent of a company's sales revenue should accrue from products that have been launched during the past five years. This is an incredible concept for companies to explore when considering the value of their revenue and the ability to sustain growth over time. Canon's CEO, Fujio Matarai, is an example of how new products and services drive growth. "Mitarai says the way Canon pushes incremental improvements into products is at the heart of the company's success. More than 60 percent of the products it sells today have been introduced within the past two years." (Holstein, "Canon Takes Aim at Xerox")

5. Charismatic Leadership

Each of our six benchmark companies has a founder or a current leader who is a "charismatic leader." We don't mean *charismatic* in the traditional sense of the word. The type of leaders we saw at RE/MAX and in our other HG/HI companies is charismatic in the following ways: *high energy, action oriented, connected, and committed, with a pronounced focused drive.* These leaders are not just company heads. They are truly leaders who believe in sharing the dream, communicating the vision and culture of the company, motivating their employees, and creating the energy around the focused drive for growth. Dave Liniger perfectly encapsulates this type of leader—rather shy and not at all a people pleaser, rather a charismatic leader who drives the culture and growth of RE/MAX. Our HG/HI benchmark companies provide some clear examples of charismatic, visionary leaders.

Sam Walton was the founder of Wal-Mart. He had a dream to open discount stores in towns all over the United States, passing on price reductions from smart retailing to the customer. Even though he passed away in 1992, his influence is still present and strong within the company. He is often quoted by Wal-Mart managers and employees, and his creeds still form the foundation of how the company is run and what a customer's shopping experience should be like. One of his better known quotes is, "There is only one boss. The customer. And he can fire everybody in the company from the chairman on down, simply by spending his money somewhere else." His vision of customer treatment is the dream that he has shared with Wal-Mart's 1.5 million employees across the United States and around the world.

Ray Kroc, a cofounder of McDonald's, saw the McDonald's restaurant in California in 1954 and knew that this was a model that he wanted to perfect and multiply.

> When Ray Kroc secured the master franchising rights to McDonald's, he didn't go to work "in" a McDonald's "restaurant." He went to work "on" McDonald's "the business." To Kroc, the first McDonald's restaurant was just a model or prototype that could be reproduced again and again in cities and towns all over the world.
>
> Instead of personally rolling up his sleeves to run the joint, he instead began analyzing every operational function of the original McDonald's from purchasing to prep to the cooking and cleaning. Without changing the essence of the concept, he made refinements and proceeded to develop a comprehensive set of standards and procedures, essentially a SYSTEM for running a hamburger stand "the McDonald's way."
>
> Ray Kroc told his franchisees that following the McDonald's system would enable them to give their customer the same food and service as the original McDonald's AND give them the best shot at becoming successful business owners. We now know that it worked, almost without exception! (Laube, "Lessons from Ray Kroc")

Kroc's drive and perfectionism allowed McDonald's to reproduce restaurants all over the world with the same taste, the same cleanliness, and the same culture as his first model restaurant. It was his never give-up-or-give-in attitude that drove the dream forward.

Canon has a type of leader that is different from that of most Japanese companies. Fujio Mitarai, the current CEO of Canon, spent time in the United States, running Canon, USA. "However it's described, American CEOs with whom he interacts believe he is a different kind of Japanese business leader. 'What you find in many Japanese companies is that the CEOs are often ceremonial, just figureheads,' says Steve Appleton, head of semiconductor maker Micron Technology, a Canon customer and supplier. 'That's not the case with Mitarai at all. He's active in leading the company. He's pretty driven.'" (Holstein, "Canon Takes Aim at Xerox") Mitarai doesn't think that his management style is necessarily an "American" style of leadership. He believes that it is the winning style for growing a company.

These leaders are all charismatic in a way different from what we normally picture—*they are charismatic about running their company well.* These high-impact leaders never stop their hard work, and their energy and passion don't falter. They have total focus around the goals that they have set out to accomplish—that's the dream. Even to this day, with RE/MAX as the number-one real estate network in the world, if you call Dave Liniger's office at 7 A.M. on Saturday morning, you will be greeted with, "Hi, this is Dave." The huge lesson to be learned here is that these leaders have the ability to focus their organizations on the right things. Their focus communicates to the whole organization where they should be spending their time. All of the benchmark HG/HI companies had focused, driven leaders who could get the entire organization to allocate its time around the company's major focus areas.

Conclusions

There is so much that we learned about HG/HI companies from our research of the benchmarks and also from our field study of RE/MAX. We have included all the major points and lessons at the end of each chapter. We have also placed in the Research Results detailed summaries on each of the six benchmark companies. We give you here our top-five points, which are not easily found in other books or studies. Each is immediately implementable and could turbocharge your organization's growth.

1. Big Ideas

There is no shortage. Our conclusion is that you have to hone ideas into workable solutions and then work the process—hard—to get to a sellable dream. Follow the process at the end of Chapter 1 for converting ideas into dreams. It worked for RE/MAX and in all of the benchmark companies. Read the Research Results on the companies and compare those companies to RE/MAX. You will notice that all of the founders of each of the companies spent considerable time and sweat on development of the big idea. They then worked the ideas into dreams that were sellable. We could see so clearly in our study that so many good ideas get lost or go nowhere. It's as if they get hijacked. Sometimes good ideas get lost for other reasons, too: They go to implementation too fast; they skip steps; they fail to connect ideas to other ideas already in the works; and too frequently there is just too little testing. After talking with leaders about what they most learned in converting ideas into sellable dreams, we conclude that a critical success factor is to stay on course with the dream, not blindly, but rather tweaking the dream to fit reality and then, like Winston Churchill, "Never, never, never give up."

2. Recruit Dream Sharers

There has been plenty written about how to hire the right people. What we found at RE/MAX and in the benchmark companies is something different and perhaps new. The added concept here is somewhat of a reverse technique of recruiting. Instead of determining what you need, recruiting the best talent, and then selecting and finally selling them on your dream, try this approach: Recruit for skills and knowledge, select finalists for values and attitude, have finalists sell themselves on why they want the dream. What's different here is who is selling whom at the end. RE/MAX spends a huge amount of time on recruiting, and it does sell its dream up front. That's the recruiting process. However, what is different and a key to its success is that it selects at a higher retention rate than others because it selects only those who buy the dream. This has also worked for other successful companies like Southwest Airlines, Goldman Sachs, and Intel.

3. Create Flow and Balance

We suspected from the onset of our research that *focus* is a key lever in growing great companies. In a recent conversation with Mike Ruettgers, chairman of EMC, an amazing growth company over the past 17 years, we asked him what was the key to success in growing great companies, particularly during economic downturns. With a seasoned CEO expression and in a clear voice, he said, "*Staying focused.*" His emphasis was on "staying." The conversation solidified our conclusion that all companies, even the strong growth companies that have demonstrated above-average focus, sometimes get out of alignment. This out-of-alignment dynamic creates a constant struggle in creating flow and balance. We think it is this struggle for balance that stifles growth. It seems that companies have a natural tendency to shift their focus, sometimes more toward growth and sometimes more toward tightly managing the business. During the growth mode, more focus on innovation and productivity results oftentimes in expansion and overall growth. Unfortunately, frequently during these times, efficiency and effectiveness suffer, resulting in bottom-line erosion. Leaders appropriately react, shifting to realign by refocusing attention on profits. However, high-impact leaders, who are focused on both growing and managing the business, recognize that staying focused requires vigilant attention on growth initiatives even when there are shifts. They accomplish this by never, ever letting up on operational excellence, maintaining balance between managing and growing the organization.

4. Brand Dominance

Many companies that we looked at failed to make our list of benchmark companies because they didn't have brand dominance. It was very clear that the HG/HI companies we studied love and protect their brand. However, all the companies that made our Top 20 list (Table 9.1) had developed a worldwide brand. What we are sure of from our study is that brand awareness, as in the case of RE/MAX or McDonald's, can become the growth accelerator for a company. Organizations—whether public or private, profit or nonprofit, even government services—can create brand dominance. Brand dominance occurs when the visual images, the stories, and the first thoughts about the company create an image. When brand awareness is combined with a strategy for growth, as in RE/MAX (Premier Market Presence—PMP), then brand dominance is possible. It's noteworthy that all the HG/HI companies we studied had a consistent brand awareness investment practice. Consider BMW. What's the first thought that comes to mind? Now consider Toyota. Each is obviously different, each powerful—that's brand dominance.

5. Pace-Line Project Leadership

This last point is a major takeaway. It may be significant enough for further study because it could change the way that leaders think about allocating their time to projects. As we dug deep into what type of leaders are managing our HG/HI companies, we observed that all had a pace-line leadership style. They are charismatic (as defined earlier), not politicians, but rather hard-charging, focused, driven leaders who take the helm on major efforts leading as part of the team. We love the concept of pace-line leadership because it purports that senior leaders should get involved in important projects in an active way, riding alongside, taking the lead whenever necessary to win the race. How leaders spend their time is always a question. Larry Bossidy, one of the authors of *Execution: The Discipline of Getting Things Done* and famed Honeywell CEO, when coaching senior leaders, always asks, "How do you spend your time?" Time is all leaders have. When to get involved, how much to get involved, when to move to the front and lead, and when to lay back, as in the Tour de France, is part of strategy. It involves a prescriptive, well-constructed plan and a lot of practice. What is different about pace-line leadership? It's the simple notion that leaders can and should create *fast start* by getting out in front on big projects early—clearing the way for others to lead, ensuring that they are there for the team to take them to the finish line, as Lance Armstrong did six times.

Concluding Statement

After all the work in preparing this book, we are left with one simple conclusion: *Growing organizations is a function of leadership.*

We learned that dreams can come true by converting really big ideas into believable dreams that can be shared and then sold by pace-line leaders. When combined with the ability of organizations to stay focused, *everybody truly can win.* We believe this and we hope you do, too.

For training in creating an *everybody wins* organization and becoming pace-line leaders, please contact Linkage at www.linkageinc.com or call 781-402-5555.

RESEARCH RESULTS

Top Six High-Growth/High-Impact Companies

BMW

Revenue Growth for BMW Corporation, by Yearly Percentage Growth Rate

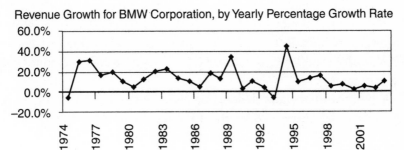

Employee Growth for BMW Corporation, by Yearly Percentage Growth Rate

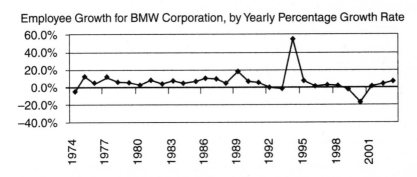

BMW began in 1913 when Karl Rapp opened an aircraft-engine design shop near Munich, Germany. In 1917, he named it Bayerische Motoren Werke (BMW). When World War I ended, German aircraft production ceased, and BMW moved to making railway brakes until the 1930s. In 1932, BMW debuted its first motorcycle—the R32. Then in 1933, BMW launched a line of large cars; but the company built mostly aircraft engines for Hitler's Luftwaffe in the 1930s and stopped all of its production of motorcycles and automobiles in 1941. After World War II, BMW's factories were dismantled, and it survived by making kitchen and garden equipment until 1948, when it introduced a one-cylinder motorcycle.

BMW did not do well in the 1950s until 1959, when Herbert Quandt bought control of it for $1 million. The new BMW focused on sports sedans, which came to be a successful niche for the company. In the 1970s, BMW's European exports soared, and the company opened a distribution subsidiary in the United States. BMW launched its luxury line of cars in 1986, which began the BMW-Mercedes rivalry that continues today.

BMW is a company with a strong brand name, a great reputation, and growth over a long period of time. It has made a few acquisitions in its history, the least successful of which was Rover in 1994. Rover turned out not to be a financially advantageous acquisition; and in 1998, BMW had to cut jobs at the money-losing Rover unit. Rover's plants continued their downward trend in 1999, which had an affect on the overall revenue of BMW in 1998 and 1999. When BMW sold Rover in 2000, revenue began to go up again.

Despite the financially challenging period involving Rover, BMW has remained a high-growth company in Europe. In 2004 it was #74 on *Fortune's* Global 500 and #17 on the list of European high-growth value adders from *Harvard Business Review's* "Champion's of Profitable Growth." BMW also has maintained its strong brand name over the past 30 years. It was #19 on *BusinessWeek's* 2003 Global Brands Scoreboard, moved up to #17 on the 2004 Global Brands Scoreboard, and was #15 on *Fortune's* 2004 Global Most Admired Companies.

BMW continues to strive to be the best in its industry, led by its current charismatic leader. "There is a real dynamism in Europe these days—and it comes from exceptional corporate leaders performing exceptionally well. Sure, BMW CEO Helmut Panke has been helped by U.S. consumers' almost insatiable appetite for cars like the BMW Mini. But the real key to BMW's success has been Panke's leadership skills and his meticulous attention to manufacturing and marketing details" ("Stars of Europe, *BusinessWeek* online, July 5, 2004).

Canon

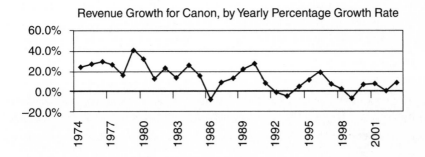

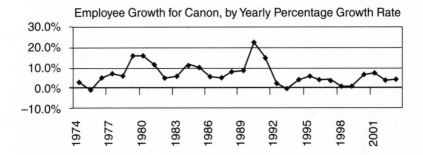

In Tokyo in 1933, Takeshi Mitarai and his friend Saburo Uchida started Seiki Kogaku Kenkyusho (Precision Optical Research Laboratory). They created Japan's first 35 millimeter (35mm) camera, which they introduced in 1935 under the name "Kwanon," the Buddhist goddess of mercy. Later they renamed it "Canon." In 1947, they named the company Canon Camera Company as its brand name gained popularity. In 1955, Canon opened its first overseas branch in New York. It diversified from just cameras and began making business equipment. In 1969, Canon dropped "Camera Company" from its name.

Throughout its history, Canon has been an innovator and inventor of business and office equipment and cameras. It has been in head-to-head competition to be the world's number-one camera maker since it ran the first TV commercials for a 35mm camera in 1976. Mitarai died in 1984; and in 1993, his son, Hajime, became president and began a process of expanding product development. When Hajime died in 1995, his cousin, Fujio Mitarai, a 34-year-old Canon employee who served as the head of Canon, USA, in the 1980s, was named president and CEO. He is still the leader of Canon today.

Canon is a company that inspires brand loyalty. It has maintained growth for 30 years without any acquisitions and at the same time expanded throughout the world, while still being innovative in its technology and environmental focus. Canon was #6 on the list of Asia high-growth value adders on *Harvard Business Review*'s "Champions of Profitable Growth" and #45 on *BusinessWeek*'s 2004 Information Technology 100. It also was #35 on *BusinessWeek*'s 2004 Global Brands Scoreboard, up from #39 in 2003.

Canon strives to be the best in its industry, not only in growth but also in its products, services, customer loyalty, and environmental awareness. It is able to focus on its core competencies around its products and services, which contributes to Canon's position as an HG/HI organization.

- "Most of Japan's top manufacturers deal with high domestic costs by making as many of their products as possible overseas. Not Canon, Inc. So far, the strategy at Japan's biggest office-equipment maker [is]: Focus on the product, not the manufacturing location. . . . Canon wants to 'preserve its core competence' by retaining as much manufacturing as possible in Japan. . . . Canon, by contrast, has a target of keeping about 60% of its production in Japan, despite generating more of its revenue—about 75%—overseas. Earlier this week, the company said it would spend 80% of its capital outlays over the next three years in Japan in order to strengthen research and development of products. That compares with 75% spent in Japan this year." ("Canon Manufacturing Strategy Pays Off with Strong Earnings," *Wall Street Journal*, January 30, 2004.)

- "'At Canon they know exactly what their strengths are, and they keep concentrating on them,' says Shin Horie, a Goldman Sachs analyst in Tokyo." (Holstein, "Canon Takes Aim at Xerox," *Fortune,* September 19, 2002)

- "Canon's strength is all the more remarkable because so many other icons of Japanese high tech are floundering. Hitachi, Matsushita, Toshiba, NEC, and Fujitsu all posted losses in the fiscal year that ended in March. Canon earned $1.4 billion on revenues of $23.9 billion in 2001. And that was at a time when all the world's economies were soft." (Holstein, "Canon Takes Aim at Xerox")

- "Mitarai is focused on profit, not market share or size for the sake of size." (Holstein, "Canon Takes Aim at Xerox")

McDonald's

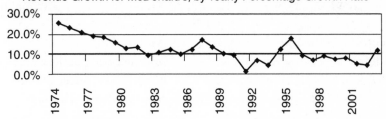

Revenue Growth for McDonald's, by Yearly Percentage Growth Rate

Note: 30 years of employee information was not available from McDonald's.

In 1948, Dick and Mac McDonald opened the first McDonald's in San Bernardino, California. In 1954, 52-year-old Ray Kroc visited their restaurant as a malt machine salesman and was inspired by their "fast-food" set up. He signed a franchise agreement with Dick and Mac, and a year later opened his first McDonald's in Des Plaines, Illinois. By 1957, Kroc had opened 14 McDonald's restaurants in Illinois, Indiana, and California. In 1961, Kroc bought out the McDonald brothers for $2.7 million.

In 1961, the Golden Arches became the company logo. In 1963, Ray Kroc served the billionth hamburger on the *Art Linkletter Show,* and Ronald McDonald debuted. In 1965, McDonald's went public and ran its first TV commercials. In 1967, the company opened its first restaurant outside the United States, in Canada. The next year it added the Big Mac to its menu and opened its 1,000th restaurant.

During the 1970s, McDonald's grew at a rate of 500 restaurants a year. The first Ronald McDonald House, a home-away-from-home for the families of seriously ill children undergoing treatment, opened in Philadelphia in 1974. And the first drive-through window appeared in 1975. Ray Kroc passed away in 1984. In 1990, the world watched as McDonald's opened its first restaurant in Moscow. In two years, the franchise moved into Beijing, China. It has been expanding throughout the world ever since.

"The company operates about 28,000 restaurants around the world. It's the nation's biggest buyer of beef, pork, and potatoes and the world's biggest owner of retail property. The company is one of the country's top toy distributors and its largest private operator of playgrounds. Ninety-six percent of American schoolchildren can identify Ronald McDonald. Roughly one of every eight workers in the United States has done time at the chain. The McDonald's brand is the most famous, and the most heavily promoted, on the planet. 'The Golden Arches,' Schlosser says, 'are now more widely recognized than the Christian cross.'" ("No Accounting for Mouthfeel," *New York Times*, January 1, 2000)

McDonald's Corporation is one of the rare companies with year-to-year growth for 30 years without acquisitions. Its brand recognition is unparalleled, and the company is constantly adjusting its image in order to please its customers and continue to be the best in its industry. McDonald's was #7 on the Franchise 500 for 2004 and #7 on *BusinessWeek*'s 2004 Global Brands Scoreboard.

- "The McDonald's Corporation is striving to revive its brand image with a big national campaign . . . The goal of the campaign, which carries the theme, 'Did somebody say McDonald's?' is to bring back warm, fuzzy feelings about [McDonald's]" ("The Media Business: Advertising; McDonald's Starts a Big Campaign to Revive Its Brand Image," *New York Times*, October 2, 1997)

- "McDonald's has seen U.S. sales rebound in the past year, bolstered by menu and operational improvements at existing restaurants in lieu of expansion. Sales in Europe, the company's second-largest market, are being invigorated by the launch of health-oriented meal-sized salads." ("McDonald's Profit Up 25 Percent," *New York Times*, July 22, 2004)

- "'This steady business momentum is what we planned to achieve when we launched our revitalization initiatives in early 2003,' Mr. Bell said, 'We will remain intensely focused on further building brand relevance with our customers around the world through operational excellence and leadership marketing.'" ("McDonald's Expects to Beat Wall Street's Quarterly Target," *Wall Street Journal*, July 14, 2004)

- "He [Ray Kroc] never tired of seeing another pair of Golden Arches go up, and he never felt the need to apologize for it, either. 'We provide food that customers love, day after day after day. People just want more of it,' Kroc said. As every salesman knows, you can't go wrong with giving people what they want." ("Ray Kroc: The Creator of the McWorld," *BusinessWeek* online, July 5, 2004)

Nokia

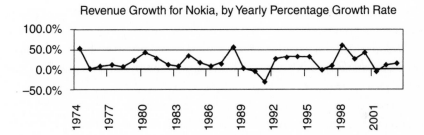

Revenue Growth for Nokia, by Yearly Percentage Growth Rate

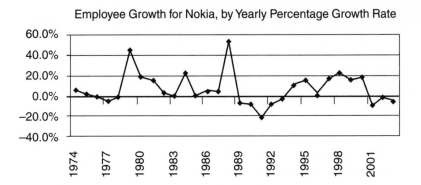

Employee Growth for Nokia, by Yearly Percentage Growth Rate

Nokia was founded in 1865, when Fredrik Idestam opened a mill to manufacture pulp and paper on the Nokia River in Finland. Nokia did well within Finland, but it did not become known to the rest of the world until it tried to become a regional conglomerate in the 1960s. It worked with a French computer firm called Machines Bull, for which Nokia researched radio transmission technology. With encouragement from the Finnish government, Nokia merged with Finnish Rubber Works and Finnish Cable Works in 1967 to form Nokia Corporation.

Because of the oil crisis in 1973, Nokia began shifting its focus to consumer and business electronics. Its foundational industries—paper, chemicals, electricity, and machinery—were modernized and expanded into robotics, fiber optics, and high-grade tissues. Through a number of other mergers and acquisitions over time, Nokia moved into the areas of telecommunications and information technology. In the 1990s, Nokia intensified its focus on telecommunications and sold its other units.

In 1993, Nokia began selling digital phones. It expected to sell 400,000; but in 1995, it shipped 20 million phones. In 1998, Nokia sold 40 million phones and became the world's number-one mobile phone company. After that, it began extending into the Internet industry, which became a strong side of their business.

Nokia is still the world's number-one maker of mobile phones. It was #8 on *BusinessWeek*'s 2004 Global Brands Scoreboard and received a Gold Award for Consumer Products in the 2004 Annual Design Awards. Nokia is focused on maintaining and building its brand name by concentrating on giving its customers the products and services that they want and by adjusting their efforts and actions toward that goal.

- "Nokia, the world's biggest maker of mobile phones, announced an effort . . . to win back customers and build up its crumbling share of the market." ("Nokia Aims New Models at the Midprice Market," *New York Times*, June 15, 2004)

- "Despite lower sales in the second quarter, Nokia managed to improve its overall margins from 11.7 percent a year ago to 13.7 percent last quarter, thanks to gains in divisions other than mobile phones. And net income climbed 14 percent, to $860 million. No other phone maker comes close on those two scores. Besides, Nokia spins off oodles of cash—$1.7 billion in the quarter—and has managed to hold onto nearly a third of the global handset market despite an aging model portfolio." ("Is Nokia Really So Bad Off?" *Business-Week* online, July 5, 2004)

Toyota

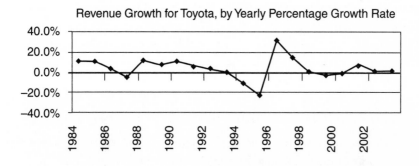

Revenue Growth for Toyota, by Yearly Percentage Growth Rate

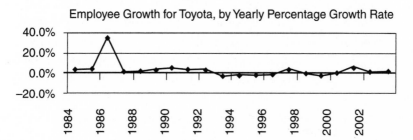

Employee Growth for Toyota, by Yearly Percentage Growth Rate

In 1926, Sakichi Toyoda founded Toyoda Automatic Loom Works. In 1930, he sold the rights to the loom he had invented and gave the money to his son, Kiichiro, to begin an automotive business. Kiichiro opened an auto shop in 1933; and when protectionist legislation improved prospects for Japanese automakers, Kiichiro split off the car department, went public, and changed its name to Toyota in 1937.

Toyota Motor Sales, USA, debuted in 1957 with the Toyopet Crown; but it was not high-powered enough for the U.S. market. They had better luck with the Corona in 1965 and also with the Corolla in 1968, which became the best selling car of all time. By 1970, Toyota was the world's fourth-largest carmaker. Toyota expanded rapidly in the United States.

During the oil crisis in the 1970s, there was a high demand for fuel-efficient cars, and Toyota was there to meet that need and increase its market share. In 1975, Toyota became the number-one U.S. auto importer; and in 1984, it began auto production in the United States. The Lexus line was launched in the United States in 1989; and in 1997, Toyota introduced the Prius.

Toyota is Japan's largest carmaker and the world's number-four carmaker by sales. It is the #1 high-growth value adder in Asia according to *Harvard Business Review*'s "Champions of Profitable Growth" and #8 on *Fortune*'s 2004 Global 500. It has created strong brand awareness and respect from customers over the years. It was #8 on *Fortune*'s 2004 Global Most Admired Companies and #9 on *BusinessWeek*'s 2004 Global Brands Scoreboard, breaking into the top 10 for the first time from #11 in 2003.

- "Part of the Japanese cool factor is the result of the new competition from China and Korea. Forced to compete with lower-cost products, Japanese designers have differentiated their goods by adding a bigger element of design and fashion. Toyota Motor Corp., for example, has had a big win in the U.S. with its Scion xB, a distinctly boxy wagon aimed at younger drivers that was originally a hit in Japan." ("Is Japanese Style Taking Over the World?" *BusinessWeek*, July 26, 2004)

- "Toyota has seen sales and profits soar because it offers buyers just about anything they want, from the smallest subcompact to the biggest road-hogging SUVs and pickups." ("How Honda Is Stalling in the U.S.," *BusinessWeek*, May 24, 2004)

- "The new forecasts highlight the continuing strength of Toyota, whose aggressive cost cutting has allowed it to keep prices reasonable, even as it equips its cars with the latest gadgetry—from navigation and safety systems to new fuel technologies. Toyota's sales goals put the company on track to surpass No. 2 automaker, Ford Motor Co. Toyota hopes to capture a 15 percent global market share by 2010, compared with 10 percent now. In 2010, it aims to sell about nine million vehicles." ("Toyota Pushes Up Its Global Targets for Sales, Output," *Wall Street Journal*, July 21, 2004)

- "[B]y the 1990s, it became apparent that there was something even more special about Toyota compared to other automakers in Japan.

It was not eye-popping car designs or performance—though the ride was smooth and the designs often very refined. It was the way Toyota engineered and manufactured the autos that lead to unbelievable consistency in the process and product. Toyota designed autos faster, with more reliability, yet at a competitive cost, even when paying the relatively high wages of Japanese workers. Equally impressive was that every time Toyota showed an apparent weakness and seemed vulnerable to the competition, Toyota miraculously fixed the problem and came back even stronger. Today Toyota is the third-largest auto manufacturer in the world, behind General Motors and Ford, with global vehicle sales of over six million per year in 170 countries." (*The Toyota Way*, McGraw-Hill, 2004)

- "Toyota invented 'lean production' (also known as the 'Toyota Production System' or 'TPS'), which has triggered a global transformation in virtually every industry to Toyota's manufacturing and supply chain philosophy and methods over the last decade." (*The Toyota Way*)

Wal-Mart

Revenue Growth for Wal-Mart Stores, Inc., by Yearly Percentage Growth Rate

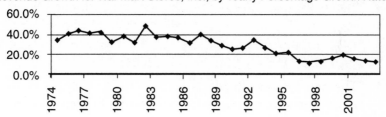

Employee Growth for Wal-Mart Stores, Inc., by Yearly Percentage Growth Rate

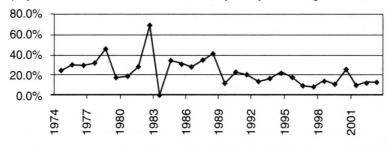

Sam Walton began his retail career as a management trainee at JCPenney. In 1945, he leased a Ben Franklin franchised dime store in Newport, Arkansas. In 1950, he relocated to Bentonville, Arkansas, and opened a Walton 5 & 10. By 1962, Walton owned 15 Ben Franklin stores. He suggested to the Ben Franklin management his idea of opening discount stores in small towns, but they rejected it. So he and his brother, James "Bud" Walton, opened the first Wal-Mart Discount City in 1962. In 1970, Wal-Mart Stores went public with $44 million in sales and 18 stores.

The aim was to avoid regional retailers by opening stores in small and midsized towns. In 1976, Wal-Mart sold its Ben Franklin stores, and by 1980, it had 276 Wal-Marts, with sales of $1.2 billion. In 1983, Wal-Mart opened SAM's Wholesale Club. In 1992, Sam Walton died; and a year later, Bud also passed away. Wal-Mart began to grow internationally in 1992 with an expansion into Mexico. It continued its international growth throughout the 1990s, and it seems as though that was just the beginning. Just in 2002, Wal-Mart opened 178 supercenters, 33 discount stores, 25 SAM's Club stores, and 107 international units in Brazil, Canada, China, Germany, South Korea, Mexico, Puerto Rico, and the United Kingdom.

It's hard to find a better example of a high-growth/high-impact company than Wal-Mart. Wal-Mart's growth over the past 30 years has been phenomenal. Not only has it had year-to-year growth for more than 30 straight years, but it is also the world's number-one retailer, with more than 4,800 stores. Although 75 percent of its stores are in the United States, Wal-Mart is expanding internationally. It is now the number-one retailer in Canada and Mexico; and it has already moved into Asia, South America, and Europe. It was #1 on both the Fortune 500 and *Fortune's* 2004 Global 500, the #2 U.S. high-growth value adder on *Harvard Business Review's* "Champions of Profitable Growth," and #1 on *Fortune's* 2004 Global Most Admired Companies.

Wal-Mart is such an engine of growth that it brings growth into any environment it enters. "But for hard-pressed urban neighborhoods, having a Wal-Mart is probably a good idea. People like the bargains—and the jobs. And with fewer small-town sites left, Wal-Mart's march into cities will only pick up. Ten years ago, it had only 13 stores in cities with more than 1 million people. Today it has 38, with more on the way." ("Who Says Wal-Mart Is Bad for Cities?" *BusinessWeek*, May 10, 2004)

THE REAL ESTATE INDUSTRY

Through researching and writing this book, we have been struck by the enormity of the real estate industry and by the effect it has and will have in all of our lives. The American Dream has always been home ownership. But that dream is not limited to Americans anymore. Home ownership is a dream that people share all over the world. As population and home ownership increase, we believe that the real estate industry is going to become an even larger part of our everyday lives. Soon the numbers that every family will have on file will be the babysitter, the doctor, and the local real estate agent.

Because this book has been focused on real estate, we found out some incredible facts about the real estate market. These stats will be interesting to an array of readers—those of you who just want to learn more about the industry, those of you who are thinking about joining the industry, those of you who are already in the business but want to learn more about the bigger picture of the industry, and even those who at any time in their lives will be buying or selling a house through a real estate agent. This industry will touch each of our lives, if it has not already.

RE/MAX Facts and Statistics

- RE/MAX is rapidly approaching two million transaction sides a year. (A transaction side is defined as either the selling or the buying of a house. For example, if an agent assisted in the selling of one house and the buying of another—or the selling and the buying of the same house—that would be considered two transaction sides.)
- RE/MAX has almost 100,000 agents worldwide, 75,000+ in the United States.
- The National Association of Realtors has one million members. RE/MAX is 7.5 percent of that. (Members can be any full-time workers in the industry, not just agents.)
- RE/MAX agents average 20 to 22 transaction sides per agent per year.
- On average, a non–RE/MAX agent averages 7 to 10 transaction sides a year.
- RE/MAX is approaching $360 billion to $400 billion in sales a year. (This stat is tricky because RE/MAX isn't selling CDs, clothing, or groceries like Wal-Mart; it is selling that amount of other people's property. Therefore, that number is not revenue of RE/MAX.)

RE/MAX Advertising Statistics

- In 2004, RE/MAX TV advertising generated 3.35 billion impressions (based on adults ages 25–54 gross rating points unequalized).
- The U.S. adult viewer will see RE/MAX commercials on average 29 times in 2004.
- In 2004, RE/MAX generated 56.8 million impressions on U.S. Hispanic TV (based on Hispanic adults ages 25–54 gross rating points unequalized).
- The U.S. Spanish-speaking adult viewer will see RE/MAX commercials on average 17 times in 2004.
- RE/MAX purchased more than 11,000 national TV spots for 2004.
- In comparison, in 2002, RE/MAX TV advertising generated 2.65 billion impressions, seen by the average U.S. adult viewer 22 times (increase of 50 percent).

- The average RE/MAX agent spends $10,000 per year in personal promotion and advertising. The law says that if you're an agent, you are required by the real estate commission to advertise your company along with any personal advertising. Therefore, all of RE/MAX agents' advertising has the RE/MAX name on it. With over 75,000 agents in the United States, that is $750 million being spent on RE/MAX advertising by its agents.

- A typical real estate agent spends 20 percent of what a RE/MAX agent does on advertising because he or she is usually not making enough deals to spend the same amount.

Home Sales Statistics from RE/MAX

- Existing new home sales in the United States in 2003 was 6.1 million.
- The estimate of existing new home sales in the United States for 2004 is 6.1 million to 6.3 million.
- The average U.S. house is selling for $180,000 (as of this printing).
- New home construction in the United States averages 1.25 million to 1.5 million units per year.
- Maslow's hierarchy of needs: Shelter is right behind oxygen and food. Everyone needs shelter. The American Dream is everywhere you go. It is not just the *American* Dream anymore. It is a dream for people all over the world to own a home.
- There are over 2 million people in the United States with real estate licenses. If 2.1 million have licenses, and there are 290 million people in the United States, 1 out of every 138 people is a real estate agent. But how many of those people are doing any business? Some are not really practicing; some are just not doing any business. That brings down all of the averages. It is true that 20 percent of the people are doing 80 percent of the business.
- The average home in the United States changes hands every five to seven years.
- The typical family moves six to eight times in their lives.
- One in seven Americans lives in California.
- 600,000 new people move to California every year.

*Statistics from a RE/MAX Press Release: "RE/MAX Firms Command REAL*Trends *500 Survey Again" (May 10, 2004)*

The 2004 REAL*Trends* 500 annual study of leading real estate firms has just been released, and RE/MAX operations lead all other franchises and combined independents again. Because of "ties," the list actually totals 567 firms, with 169 (29.8 percent) of them being RE/MAX firms. "Independents" (non-franchised firms) totaled 130 (22.9 percent) for second place in total firms, and Coldwell Banker was third with 109 (19.2 percent).

REAL*Trends* reported "a record number of firms attained $1 billion in total sales volume from closed residential sales in 2003" and lists 141 firms that achieved "The Billionaire's Club" status. Among them, 21.9 percent, or a total of 31, were RE/MAX operations.

This year's "Up-and-Comers"—those not making the REAL-*Trends* 500 but closing more than 500 transaction sides—also set a new record. Again, RE/MAX led this category with 119, or 36 percent, of the 330 total firms.

Statistics from the U.S. Census Bureau, Census 2000

- Total housing units = 115,904,641.
- Total owner occupied = 69,815,753 (66.2%).
- Housing units for sale = 1,204,318 (11.6%).
- 70 percent of house owners have a mortgage.
- 30 percent of house owners with a mortgage pay between $1,000 and $1,500 a month toward their mortgage.

Statistics from http://recenter.tamu.edu

"American's Aren't Moving Like They Used To"

- "It appears that we are moving less these days than we did 50 years ago. But the number of Americans moving long distances is on the rise. At least, that's the word from the U.S. Census Bureau. Between 2002 and 2003, 40 million Americans—some 14 percent of the population—moved. That's down sharply from the 20 percent who moved in 1948."

"Where Will the People Live?"

- "[T]he U.S. Census Bureau issued a projection that the population of the United States will double by the year 2100."

- "As we add another 300 million people to the present U.S. population, what do we expect life to be like?"—Richard P. Browne, University of Houston.

- "Browne asks what plans are being made to accommodate the 100 million new homes that will be required."

- "According to the Census Bureau, U.S. population density in 2100 would be 161.4 people per square mile."

- "The United Nations projects the world population will rise from the current 6 billion to about 9.4 billion in 2100."

"Housing Boom to Roll on for Years"

- "At the beginning of the twentieth century, less than half of all Americans owned their own homes. Today, low interest rates have pushed home-ownership rates to a record 68 percent, and that figure is still climbing. Experts say it will exceed 70 percent by 2013."

- "Ten years from now, experts say 24 million more home buyers will be enjoying their first homes. In the coming decade, America's families could need 125 million mortgage loans for home purchase or refinancing. That's some $27 trillion in mortgage originations."

- "At the end of [2003], America's homes had a whopping market value of $15.2 trillion, the most ever. That's one-third higher than it was just three years ago. At the same time, equity in American homes reached $8.4 trillion."

"Home, Sweet Multimillion-Dollar Home"

- "Ninety-seven percent of multimillionaires use a real estate agent."

Statistics from ALQ Real Estate Intelligence Report
(www.reintel.com/numbers.htm)

- There are about 290 million people in the United States and about 105 million households.

- There are about 72.1 million owner-occupied homes.

- About 68.4 percent of households are home owners. (In 1940, as the Depression was coming to an end, about 43.6 percent of Americans owned homes—the lowest rate in the twentieth century.)

- About 41 percent of home buyers are first-time home buyers.

- Existing home sales will decline by 5.1 percent in 2004 and fall by 3.6 percent in 2005 and be essentially unchanged in 2006 (very high by historical standards).

- New-home sales will fall by 7.2 percent in 2004 and fall by 3.3 percent in 2005, but remain unchanged in 2006.

Statistics from U.S. Census Bureau—"American Housing Survey for the United States: 2001"

- Number of householders who moved during past year from within the United States: 5,645,000.

- Median value of owner-occupied units—$123,886.

- Ratio of house value to current income—median: 2.4.

- Median purchase price—$68,899.

Statistics from the National Association of Realtors

"Real Estate Outlook, 2004"

Actual for 2004:

- Existing single-family house sales: 6,307,000 (up 3.4 percent from 2003).

- New single-family house sales: 1,155,000 (up 6.4 percent from 2003).

- Residential construction: $536 billion (up 6.2 percent from 2003).

- Median existing-home price: $181,500 (up 6.7 percent from 2003).
- Median new-home price: $209,600 (up 7.9 percent from 2003).

Prediction for 2005:

- Existing single-family house sales: 5,968,000 (down 5.4 percent from 2004).
- New single-family house sales: 1,033,000 (down 10.6 percent from 2004).
- Residential construction: $500 billion (down 7.2 percent from 2004).
- Median existing-home price: $188,800 (up 4 percent from 2004).
- Median new-home price: $219,500 (up 4.7 percent from 2004).

"The 2003 National Association of Realtors Profile of Real Estate Markets: USA" (October 2003)

- "[T]he number of households in the United States is forecasted to increase by 11.8 million between 2000 and 2010. This increase will be very similar to past trends of household formation by 1.1 million to 1.3 million per year. If the past trend holds, during the next 10 years, people in the 35-to-44 age group will fall by 2.7 million households. People in the 45-to-54 age range should increase by 3.8 million, and those in the 55-to-64 age group should increase by 6.5 million. The latter two age groups represent prime home-owning age groups."
- "During a 10-year period from 1993 to 2002, the home-ownership rate for the under-25 age group increased from 14.8 percent to 22.4 percent, or by 7.6 percentage points. The overall home-ownership rate for the comparable period increased from 66.1 percent to 67.8 percent."
- "The typical second-home owner is 61 years old, married, and has a household income of $76,900. Baby boomers are well represented in this group. With the aging population in the United States, second homes will continue to play a significant role in the U.S. housing market."
- "The typical home buyer is 40 years old with income between $60,000 and $70,000 and married. In 2003, 59 percent of home buy-

ers were married, which is a decrease from 68 percent in 2001. The decline reflects many younger cohorts entering the housing market because of the opportunities presented by low mortgage rates."

- "The typical home purchased was an existing single-family detached house located in the suburbs. Nearly four out of five home buyers purchased an existing single-family home, which is consistent with historical proportions."

- "The typical first-time home buyer in 2001 was 32 years old—14 years younger than the typical repeat buyer at 46 years old. Also, not surprising, first-time buyers are usually not as wealthy as repeat buyers, who are generally more experienced. In 2003, the median household income for first-time buyers was $54,800, which is substantially lower than the $74,600 earned by repeat buyers."

"Home Wealth Effect Survey"

- "Two-thirds of American households own their home. For three out of four of them, their homes represent a large portion of their wealth."

- Unrealized Gains—most homeowners have unrealized gains in the homes in which they live.

  - The typical homeowner has unrealized gains of $50,000.

  - Higher-income households have more equity in their home.

  - Households with incomes greater than $75,000 typically have a median of $100,000 in equity.

  - Households with incomes less than $40,000 typically have a median of $40,000 in equity

- Older Americans have more home equity.

  - Households aged 50 or older have a median equity of $80,000.

  - Households younger than 40 years old have a median equity of $35,000.

- "Sixteen percent of home owners who have unrealized capital gains in their property have changed their spending or saving behavior as a result."

- "Seventy-six percent of repeat home buyers used all of the capital gains from the sale of their previous home for the down payment on their current home."
- "Another 10 percent of households put some of the gains back into their new home."
- "Only 15 percent of repeat home buyers did *not* use the realized equity for the down payment on their current home."

"The 2001 National Association of Realtors Profile of Residential Real Estate Brokerages"

- While there is great diversity in the characteristics of today's real estate brokerages, recent survey results indicate that the typical residential real estate firm:
  - Is a single-office operation.
  - Has been in business for 10 years.
  - Has a sales force of four agents who are independent contractors.
  - Is not affiliated with a franchise and operates as a corporation.
  - Operates a web site and places the brokerage's listings on a number of web sites.
  - Generates at least 1 percent of its business from the Internet.
  - Has a policy that its sales force be accessible by e-mail.
- The diversity of real estate firms is most apparent by firm size:
  - 85 percent of residential brokerages have a single office, while 4 percent have four or more offices.
  - 67 percent of residential brokerages have a sales force of five or fewer agents; 3 percent have a sales force of 50 or more.
  - Large residential brokerages—those with at least 200 salespeople—have been in the real estate brokerage business for more than twice as long as small brokerages with 20 or fewer salespeople.
  - Two-thirds of large residential brokerages are engaged in mortgage lending, compared to 16 percent of smaller brokerages.
  - Two-thirds of large residential brokerages are affiliated with a franchise organization, whereas 10 percent of small residential brokerages are franchise operations.

"Real Estate Versus Financial Wealth in Consumption"

- "Housing has remained one of the strongest sectors of the economy, despite sagging economic growth, a weak job market, and rising uncertainty over geopolitical conditions. Home prices in many areas of the country continue to increase, offsetting some of the drop in household wealth resulting from the three-year decline in the stock market. Additionally, low mortgage-interest rates have provided households with an opportunity to reduce their housing costs or take cash out of their homes to sustain consumer spending and pay down debt."

- "While no one doubts the significant impact of housing on the economy, it is not always clear how these effects interact with other changes in economic conditions . . . the housing sector not only supports the economy during good times, but also provides offsetting benefits when financial markets deteriorate or the economy weakens. A healthy housing market not only directly benefits the real estate industry, but also conveys numerous benefits to the rest of the economy by acting as a stabilizing force during the ups and downs of the business cycle."

RECOMMENDED READING

Allen, David. *Getting Things Done: The Art of Stress-Free Productivity*. New York: Penguin USA, 2003.

ALQ Real Estate Intelligence Report (www.reintel.com/numbers.htm).

"America's Top 2000 Brands," *Brandweek* (www.brandweek.com), June 21, 2004.

Argyris, Chris. *On Organizational Learning*. Oxford, UK: Blackwell, 1992.

Argyris, Chris. *Overcoming Organizational Defenses*. Needham, MA: Allyn and Bacon, 1990.

Argyris, Chris, and David A. Schon. *Organizational Learning II*. Reading, MA: Addison-Wesley Longman, 1996.

Arndt, Michael. "Ray Kroc: The Creator of the McWorld," *BusinessWeek Online*, July 5, 2004.

Bennis, Warren. *On Becoming a Leader*. New York: Addison-Wesley Publishing Company, 1994.

BMW web site (www.bmwgroup.com).

Bossidy, Larry, Ram Charan, and Charles Burk. *Execution: The Dicipline of Getting Things Done*. New York: Crown Business, 2002.

"*Brandweek* Names Canon No. 1 in Customer Loyalty Award Survey for Office Copier Product Category," *Forbes*, July 23, 2004.

Branson, Richard. *Losing My Virginity: How I've Survived, Had Fun, and Made a Fortune Doing Business My Way*. New York: Three Rivers Press, 1998.

Canon web site (www.canon.com).

Charan, Ram. *Profitable Growth Is Everyone's Business: 10 Tools You Can Use Monday Morning*. New York: Crown, 2004.

Charan, Ram, and Noel M. Tichy. *Every Business Is a Growth Business: How Your Company Can Prosper Year after Year*. New York: Three Rivers Press, 1998.

Christiansen, Clayton, and Michael Raynor. *The Innovators Solution: Creating and Sustaining Successful Growth*. Cambridge, MA: Harvard Business School Press, 2003.

Clark, Dwayne. *Help Wanted: Recruiting, Hiring, and Retaining Exceptional Staff*. Privately printed, 2001.

Clifton, Rita, John Simmons, and Sameena Ahmad. *Brands and Branding (The Economist Series)*. New York: Bloomberg Press, 2004.

Cohen, David S. *The Talent Edge: A Behavioral Approach to Hiring, Developing, and Keeping Top Performers*. Toronto: John Wiley & Sons Canada, 2001.

Collins, Jim. *Good to Great*. New York: HarperCollins, 2001.

Collins, Jim, and Jerry I. Porras. *Built to Last: Successful Habits of Visionary Companies*. New York: HarperCollins, 1994.

Deal, Terrance E., and Allan A. Kennedy. *Corporate Cultures*. New York: Perseus Books, 1982.

Edmondson, Gail. "BMW: Crashing the Compact Market," *BusinessWeek*, June 28, 2004.

"Fastest-Growing Franchises 2000 Rankings," Entrepreneur.com.

"Fastest-Growing Franchises 2001 Rankings," Entrepreneur.com.

"Fastest-Growing Franchises 2003 Rankings," Entrepreneur.com.

Fisher, Roger, and Alan Sharp. *Getting It Done: How to Lead When You're Not in Charge*. New York: Harper Business, 1999.

"The 500 Largest Brokers in the U.S." *REALTrends 500*, May 2004.

"Franchise 500 2004 Rankings," Entrepreneur.com.

Gerstner, Louis V., Jr. *Who Says Elephants Can't Dance? Inside IBM's Historic Turnaround*. New York: HarperCollins, 2002.

Gobe, Marc, and Sergio Zyman. *Emotional Branding: The New Paradigm for Connecting Brands to People*. New York: Allworth Press, 2001.

Goldman, Abigail, and Nancy Cleeland. "An Empire Built on Bargains Remakes the Working World," *Los Angeles Times*, November 23, 2003: 5.

Haig, Matt. *Brand Failures: The Truth About the 100 Biggest Branding Mistakes of All Time*. London: Kogan Page, 2004.

Hammer, Michael, and James Champy. *Reengineering the Corporation: A Manifesto for Business Revolution*. New York: HarperCollins, 2001.

Harkins, Phil. *Powerful Conversations: How High-Impact Leaders Communicate*. New York: McGraw-Hill, 1999.

Harris, Jim, and Joan Brannick. *Finding and Keeping Great Employees*. New York: AMA Publications, 1999.

Hill, Napolean. *Think and Grow Rich*. New York: Random House, 1960.

Holstein, William J. "Canon Takes Aim at Xerox," *Fortune*, September 19, 2002: 3-4.

Hoovers Online (www.hoovers.com)

"Information Technology 100," *BusinessWeek*, June 21, 2004.

Jones, David S. "American's Aren't Moving Like They Used To," Real Estate Center (http://recenter.tamu.edu), news release no. 49, March 2004.

Jones, David S. "Home, Sweet Multimillion-Dollar Home," Real Estate Center (http://recenter.tamu.edu), news release no. 25, December 2003.

Jones, David S. "Housing Boom to Roll On for Years," Real Estate Center (http://recenter.tamu.edu), news release no. 66, June 2004.

Jones, David S. "Where Will the People Live?" Real Estate Center (http://recenter.tamu.edu), news release no. 64, June 2004.

Joyce, William, and Nitin Nohria. *What Really Works: The 4+2 Formula for Sustained Business Success*. New York: HarperCollins, 2003.

Kane, Courtney. "The Media Business: Advertising; McDonald's Starts a Big Campaign to Revive Its Brand Image," *New York Times*, October 2, 1997: D5.

Kaplan, Robert S., and David P. Norton. *The Balanced Scorecard: Translating Strategy into Action*. Cambridge, MA: Harvard Business School Press, 1996.

Keller, Kevin Lane. *Branding and Brand Equity*. Cambridge, MA: Marketing Science Institute, 2002.

Kotter, John. *Leading Change*. Cambridge, MA: Harvard Business School Press, 1996.

Laube, Jim. "Lessons from Ray Kroc," www.restaurantowner.com /public/89.cfm.

Lewis, James P. *Project Leadership*. New York: McGraw-Hill, 2003.

Liker, Jeffrey. *The Toyota Way*. New York: McGraw-Hill, 2004.

"McDonald's Expects to Beat Wall Street's Quarterly Target," *Wall Street Journal*, July 14, 2004.

"McDonald's Profit Up 25 Percent," *New York Times*, July 22, 2004.

McDonald's web site (www.mcdonalds.com).

McNatt, Robert. "Who Says Wal-Mart Is Bad for Cities?" *BusinessWeek*, May 10, 2004: 77.

Moffett, Sebastian. "Canon Manufacturing Strategy Pays Off with Strong Earnings," *Wall Street Journal*, January 30, 2004: 1.

National Association of Realtors. *Code of Ethics and Standards of Practice*. National Association of Realtors, Chicago, IL, Form No. 166-288 © 2004.

National Association of Realtors. "Real Estate Versus Financial Wealth in Consumption," by John D. Benjamin, Peter Chinloy, and G. Donald Jud. Report for the REALTORS® National Center for Real Estate Research. Used with permission. For more information, visit www .REALTOR.org/ncrer or call 1-800-874-6500.

National Association of Realtors. "Home Wealth Effect Survey," National Association of REALTORS®, www.REALTOR.org/research. Used with permission.

National Association of Realtors. "The 2001 National Association of REALTORS® Profile of Residential Real Estate Brokerages," © 2001 National Association of REALTORS®. Used with permission. For more information, visit www.REALTOR.org/research or call 1-800-874-6500.

National Association of Realtors. "The 2003 National Association of REALTORS® Profile of Real Estate Firms," © 2003 National Association of REALTORS. Used with permission. For more information, visit www.REALTOR.org/research or call 1-800-874-6500.

Nocera, Joseph. *A Piece of Action: How the Middle Class Joined the Money Class*. New York: Simon & Schuster, 1994.

Nokia web site (www.nokia.com).

Palmeri, Christopher, and Nanette Byrnes. "Is Japanese Style Taking Over the World?" *BusinessWeek*, July 26, 2004.

Parker, Ginny, and Norihiko Shirouzu. "Toyota Pushes Up Its Global Targets for Sales Output," *Wall Street Journal*, July 21, 2004.

Postrel, Virginia. "The Paradox of Prosperity," *New York Times*, July 15, 2004.

Quinn, James Brian. *Intelligent Enterprise: A Knowledge and Services Based Paradigm for Industry*. New York: Free Press, 1992.

RE/MAX web site (www.remax.com).

Reinhardt, Andy. "Is Nokia Really So Bad Off?" *BusinessWeek*, July 5, 2004.

Reis, Laura, and Al Reis. *The 22 Immutable Laws of Branding: How to Build a Product or Service into a World-Class Brand*. New York: HarperCollins, 2002.

Rossant, John. "Stars of Europe," *BusinessWeek* online, June 7, 2004.

Ryan, Jen. "Nokia Handset Portfolio to Improve after 3Q: Piper Jaffray," *Wall Street Journal*, July 26, 2004.

Schein, Edgar. *Organizational Culture and Leadership*. San Francisco: Jossey-Bass, 1992.

Senge, Peter M. *The Fifth Discipline*. New York: Currency Doubleday, 1990.

Stewart, G. Bennet, III. "Champions of Profitable Growth," *Harvard Business Review*, July–August 2004.

Still, Del J. *High Impact Hiring: How to Interview and Select Outstanding Employees*. Waco, TX: Management Development Systems, 1997.

Strider, Wayne. *Powerful Project Leadership*. Vienna, VA: Management Concepts, 2002.

Taylor, Alex III. "Toyota's Secret Weapon," *Fortune*, August 9, 2004.

Timmons, Heather. "Nokia Aims New Models at the Midprice Market," *New York Times*, June 15, 2004: W1.

Toyota web site (www.toyota.com).

Trademarked Linkage materials on recruiting and selection processes.

Treacy, Michael. *Double-Digit Growth: How Great Companies Achieve It— No Matter What*. New York: Penguin Group, 2003.

"2003 Global Brands Scoreboard," *BusinessWeek* (www.businessweek .com).

"2004 Global Brands Scoreboard," *BusinessWeek* (www.businessweek .com).

"The 2004 Global 500," Fortune.com (http://www.fortune.com/fortune /global500/subs/europe.html).

"2004 Global Most Admired Companies," Fortune.com.

U.S. Census Bureau (www.census.gov).

U.S. Department of Commerce (www.commerce.gov).

Walker, Rob. "No Accounting for Mouthfeel," *New York Times*, January 21, 2001, quoting Eric Schlosser in *Fast Food Nation: The Dark Side of the All-American Meal* (New York: Houghton Mifflin, 2001).

Wal-Mart web site (www.walmart.com).

"Web Exclusive: Masters of Organic Growth," Fortune.com.

Welch, David, and Ian Rowley. "How Honda Is Stalling in the U.S." *BusinessWeek*, May 24, 2004.

"What Is Strategy?" *Harvard Business Review*, November/December, 1996.

Wheeler, Alina. *Designing Brand Identity: A Complete Guide to Creating, Building, and Maintaining Strong Brands*. New York: John Wiley & Sons, 2003.

INDEX